MANAGING CHILDREN'S SERVICES IN THE PUBLIC LIBRARY

Third Edition

Adele M. Fasick and Leslie E. Holt

LIBRARIES

U N L I M I T E D

A Member of the Greenwood Publishing Group

Westport, Connecticut • London

Library of Congress Cataloging-in-Publication Data

Fasick, Adele M.
  Managing children's services in the public library / Adele M. Fasick
and Leslie E. Holt. — 3rd ed.
      p. cm.
  Includes bibliographical references and index.
  ISBN 978–1–59158–412–4 (alk. paper)
  1. Children's libraries—United States—Administration. 2. Public libraries—
United States—Administration. I. Holt, Leslie Edmonds. II. Title.
  Z718.2.U6F37 2008
  025.1'97625—dc22   2007032759

British Library Cataloguing in Publication Data is available.

Library of Congress Catalog Card Number: 2007032759
ISBN: 978–1–59158–412–4

First published in 2008

Libraries Unlimited, 88 Post Road West, Westport, CT 06881
A Member of the Greenwood Publishing Group, Inc.
www.lu.com

Printed in the United States of America

The paper used in this book complies with the
Permanent Paper Standard issued by the National
Information Standards Organization (Z39.48–1984).

10 9 8 7 6 5 4 3 2 1

Contents

List of Figures

Preface

As media converges and books, the Internet, DVDs, and podcasts offer much of the same content in varied formats, children's librarians have shifted the focus of their services. They have become guides and intermediaries between children and many varied forms of media. Libraries still develop print collections, but collections also include electronic formats, some are graphical rather than verbal, and many are ephemeral rather than lasting.

Many children access recreational media and information services from home or school or anywhere they are by cell phone or wireless connections, so the physical building of the library may not be the only or even the first point through which children connect to information. Rather, the children's department in the public library is part of a network of resources. For some children, the library provides the only entry point to electronic resources and books. Even if a child has computer access at home or a large collection of books, he or she will need to tap into both the library's larger collection and the more varied electronic access and expertise of library staff.

The child is at the center, and the library coordinates services to children through many different outlets both physical and virtual. The library also provides guidance in the use of information resources in many formats. Individual children will need library services tailored to meet their own situation. The successful children's librarian will understand that within the community there are a variety of needs in any group of children. As technology changes, as school curricula changes and as the community changes, children's use of the library will change.

Providing adequate public library services for children has always been a challenge and never more than now. Swiftly changing technology makes it possible for libraries to introduce children to a world of culture and information never before available, but technology also provides competition to books and traditional media, which also enlarge a child's understanding. Maintaining a balance between the new and the traditional is not easy. In this book we explore the ways librarians can manage their work, so that their collections and services give the maximum value to all the children of a community.

The book is organized in four sections. Section I deals with planning services for children in the context of a community. Section II breaks down the component parts of managing the department. It includes chapters on maintaining a productive work environment, recruiting and retaining staff, communicating with colleagues, annual reports, budgeting and fundraising, planning facilities, and keeping the department safe and secure. Section III focuses on managing services, including collection development, electronic resources, intellectual freedom, and reaching out to the community through programs and special events, working with other youth service organizations, and marketing children's services. Section IV, the final section, suggests ways in which children's librarians can participate in the larger professional community of librarians.

In preparing this book we have talked with many librarians, attended conferences and workshops, and consulted articles, books, and Web sites. We want to thank all of the libraries that allowed us to use their materials and the colleagues who generously shared their ideas.

Section I

Planning Services

1

The Library in Its Community

As media converges and books, the Internet, DVDs, and podcasts offer much of the same content in varied formats, libraries are shifting the focus of their service from offering collections of materials to being access points for many forms of entertainment and information. In the children's department, a child who borrows the latest Newbery Medal winner may follow up by posting a comment on the library blog, preparing a video book review for the library website or podcast, or perhaps by entering the library's MySpace site to discuss the book with friends.

Some typical children's department patrons:

- A two-year-old comes with her caregiver to a library story program. The booklist of stories will be available online for her parents to view at work and talk about with the child at home.
- A 12-year-old uses a home computer to check resources in the library's homework help center. Unable to locate the information, she wants about wildlife sanctuaries in South India, she has an online chat with the librarian, who helps her find a map and pictures.
- Three fourth-grade boys come to the library to participate in a gaming meet. The librarian arranges a schedule for them and others as they arrive. After playing, the boys add an entry to the library blog commenting on the games and suggesting others the library might purchase.
- A small group of fifth-graders in a local school exchange email with the public librarian to arrange a library visit. They are searching for books and pictures about the history of textile mills in their community.
- Two Chinese-speaking newcomers to the community come into the library to find dual-language books for themselves and a video with Chinese captions for their grandmother.

PLANNING SERVICES FOR TODAY'S CHILDREN

One important difference among the children served by a library is their age. In planning services, librarians must be sure they meet the needs of each age group, from toddlers to young teens. Both materials provided and interactions with them vary by age. Most libraries break their child patrons into groups.

Preschool Children

Preschool children may be infants brought to the children's department by parents or caregivers. Some libraries provide playpens where these babies can be left for a short time. Books of nursery games and rhymes for reading to babies as well as CDs and simple DVDs serve these youngest clients. Some libraries offer brief storyhours for babes in arms.

When children reach the toddler stage—when they begin to walk—the range of materials and services increases greatly. Toddlers require special materials—sturdy board books, music CDs, and appropriate DVDs, as well as toys. If programs are offered for the under-threes, provision must be made for a high ratio of adults to children. Often parents are required to attend and participate with their child. The difficulty of controlling the activities of toddlers means that direct supervision of each child must be available at all times.

By the time children reach the age of three or so, their needs and behavior are quite different from those of the toddlers. Children of this age can handle standard picture books, and a wide range of materials should be available to meet their varied and growing interests. In many libraries, some computers are designated for use by preschoolers and their caregivers. Three- and four-year-old children do not require as much adult supervision as toddlers. Programs for them can be held in larger groups and require less personnel time. Because preschoolers are interested in learning about almost everything, they are an appreciative audience for library programs. Many of the programs and services provided by traditional children's departments are aimed at preschool children and their needs. In designing facilities for children's departments, furniture suitable in size and design for preschoolers is important. Provision of a program room separate from the main department is often useful.

School-Age Children

Some school-age children (kindergarten to fifth or sixth grade) have a school library available as well as the public library. School-age children spend five to eight hours a day in school, so programming and special services aimed at this group are often more limited than those for preschool children. Many libraries provide special programs and reading clubs for school-age children during the summer months.

In most communities there is heavy use of the library by schoolchildren both for recreational and school-related materials. A large proportion of the materials in an average children's department are suitable for school-age children. Most of the reference services provided in the department will be for this age group, so the reference collection is usually slanted toward their needs. Because schoolchildren come to the library in the late afternoon, evenings, weekend, and holiday periods, they tend to make heavy demand during these times. Crowded conditions often occur when schoolchildren congregate in the library during school breaks. Many public libraries plan collections and programs specifically to provide homework help and actively work with local schools to coordinate library activities for students.

Transitional Users

Most children's departments are planned to serve children under the age of 12 or 13. Many children move quickly and happily into the adult department, but others find it difficult to make the adjustment. Children often need help to navigate the larger adult collection and may need the more personal help offered by staff in the children's room. Children whose reading skills are limited or whose native language is not English are more likely than others to have difficulty in making this transition. Parents also may expect older children to watch younger siblings and that keeps them in the children's department.

Children's departments in libraries without specialized young adult staff have a responsibility to provide bridging materials and services to help transitional users become independent users of adult services. A selection of teenage books, magazines, and other media is often necessary in a children's department.

Adults

Although adults are not the primary target audience for services offered by a children's department, many services are designed for adults. Adult users of a children's department include:

- adults choosing books for children
- homeschooling parents looking for materials and services
- teachers in both public and non-public schools
- daycare and youth workers in the community
- students of children's literature
- family literacy or English as a second language programs

The needs of adults are often different from those of the children. Literature students often ask for historical children's books that would not be kept in most children's collections; youth workers may want materials aimed very specifically at their programs; and parents sometimes request the inclusion or exclusion of materials expressing particular points of view. All of these requests must be considered and addressed.

Many libraries offer family programs and encourage parents and children to use the children's department together. Some libraries require children to be accompanied by parents or an adult when in the children's department. Use of the children's department by adults may necessitate the provision of adult-sized furniture or study carrels, and sometimes affects the overall noise and activity level considered acceptable. Some libraries provide rocking chairs or other comfortable furniture to encourage adults to read to children. Occasionally adults in the children's department may pose a threat to children. Security aspects of adults using the children's department are covered in chapter 9.

Differences Unrelated to Age

Besides age differences, there are other factors that affect the way children use libraries and their need for services. Each community has a different mix of elements that may affect library services, and an effective librarian considers them in planning.

Community Setting

Children in rural communities have different patterns of library use than those in large urban areas. Whether children can walk or bicycle to the library or are dependent on an adult to drive them will affect the scheduling of programs. The presence or absence of many other organizations serving youth will influence what libraries plan for their patrons. Variations in climate also affect the type of programs that can be offered, especially during winter months.

Ethnic Diversity

Children whose home language is not English may want materials and programming in other languages. Selecting and acquiring foreign language materials for children can be difficult and time-consuming. If the community includes several groups speaking different languages, the librarian may need to ask neighborhood groups for help in selecting materials. Providing services such as storyhours for different language groups is an even more complex task, and, unless library staff members have the necessary language skills, would require use of outside personnel.

Many communities serve African Americans, Asian Americans, or other racial minorities. These libraries will want to include materials by and about these minority cultures. The library may provide special cultural programs aimed at these groups; often this is done in cooperation with community groups.

Not all materials for non-English speakers will be in their home language. The library may collect materials that reflect the background and heritage of the various groups. Folktales and legends from particular cultures are important to increase children's sense of their heritage. Storyhours featuring English translations of stories from a particular cultural group may be a regular part of the program.

Homeschooled Children

Many libraries work with parent groups to provide programming and materials designed for families whose children are being homeschooled. Most communities have homeschooling parent groups who will work with the library in planning these.

Special Needs

Children with physical or mental differences have special needs that the library can serve. The needs of children with disabilities affect collection development, the layout of the department, and programming. These children must be considered when designing the overall program of a children's department.

The federal Americans with Disabilities Act (ADA) directs public institutions to provide facilities and services to children with a variety of disabilities. State and local governments often have specific regulations about how to design space and local advocacy groups often can provide guidelines for providing services.

Unattended Children

Library services should be provided not only to children who come to the library for a specific purpose, but also to those who habitually spend after-school hours there. These children, sometimes referred to as latchkey children or self-care children, are not primarily interested in the library's collection but in having something satisfying to do. The number and needs of these children will vary from one community to another and some of the challenges associated with their use of the library are discussed in chapter 9.

Other groups that may require particular services are transient children—those whose parents are migratory workers or who are on temporary assignments or contract work; children of the homeless living in shelters or elsewhere; and hospitalized and institutionalized children. The specific groups will vary from one community to another, but a library should assess the needs of all groups in the community when planning a program of services.

DEVELOPING SERVICES FOR THE COMMUNITY

Planning a departmental program to serve all groups and individuals is a difficult administrative task. There are three major components of the process:

- studying the community
- assessing the impact of services (see chapter 2)
- setting goals and objectives (see chapter 2)

Studying the community is the first step because library services are based on the needs of the community. Some of the background information librarians take into consideration are

population size and trends
education level
school issues/school library services
age levels
income
languages spoken at home

The government census provides the basic information about each community. Census figures are never completely up to date, but they give a baseline against which changes in the community can be measured.

The Annie E. Casey Foundation provides annual reports on children's demographics by state and county. Their publication, *Kids Count* (www.aecf.org/kidscount/), is available online and in printed form and provides data by state and for many cities and towns.

Under the federal mandate No Child Left Behind (www.nclb.gov), school districts are required to report information about students and about academic achievements by school. These reports may be online, published in the local paper or available from the state department education.

Community planning offices and school districts frequently have more recent figures than are available from the census bureau. School districts also report on schools' performances on state required tests, as well as, on other major educational programs that might impact needs for library service. State departments of education also report demographic and educational performance information for each school district in the state. Most school information is available online and updated regularly.

Library statistics on registration, circulation, and program attendance give additional information about library users in the community. In designing a departmental program, it is useful to break down library statistics by age level. If this is not done routinely, a sampling system can be used to obtain an approximation. (For specific details, see *Output Measures for Public Library Service to Children* [Walter 1992].)

Armed with statistical knowledge about the community, a librarian can make direct observations. Whether the librarian lives in the library's community or not, it is important to find ways to remain aware of what is happening in the community served. Reading the neighborhood weekly newspaper, and watching local television news gives insight into community interests. Telephone books and community directories list the number and type of schools, churches, recreational facilities, and community groups. A few hours spent driving and walking around the community and visiting local shopping outlets will provide information about the type of housing prevalent in various areas and the range and price levels of goods in stores. The number, ages, and activities of children visible in the community provide information about their interests and needs. Systematic observation can be as valuable as formal data to learn more about a community. Also talking with children, parents, and teachers to find out where children spend their time outside of school, what issues concern the community, and what's new or changing is an important way to keep up with community news.

TYPES OF SERVICES

Most libraries offer a basic menu of services for children, although the details and method of delivery varies from one community to another. While each type of service is distinct, they operate together to create the whole program of service to children.

Building Collections

Providing a collection of materials is a basic task of any library, although not all the materials may be in the library's physical site. A children's department collection includes fiction and nonfiction books, magazines, nonprint materials such as DVDs and CDs, and off-site electronic resources through databases and website.

Books are still the backbone of most children's collections and are divided into categories of some or all of the following:

- board books
- picture books
- books for beginning readers
- chapter books
- graphic novels
- nonfiction and textbooks
- foreign language books
- historical children's books
- child development books for adults

The development of information technology has expanded the definition of a collection. A children's department will typically try to combine the provision of on-site materials with that of access to off-site information. Collection development includes selecting databases, choosing link sites for the department's webpage, and deciding on the purchase of other electronic media.

Managing the children's collection involves setting priorities, selecting and purchasing materials based on library policies, and weeding worn or outdated materials.

Making the Collection Accessible

A collection of materials is of little value unless users can find items they want. The services for making resources accessible include cataloging and classification of materials, reference services to help individuals or groups find specific information for school or personal needs, and readers' advisory services to help individuals or groups find materials for recreation or education.

Online catalogs provide information about where and in what format materials are housed and make it possible to access or borrow materials from other libraries. Another access point is the library's webpage, from which children can search the catalog and the library's databases as well as recommended webpages.

Delivering Information Services

Answering children's questions is a basic part of a librarian's work. Questions include requests for specific books or other materials as well as for homework help or other information. These are the services that bring children and collections together and they may include

- recommending books or other materials;
- answering reference questions in the library or through telephones, email, online chats, instant messaging, or cell phones;
- teaching children how to use the catalog, databases, and Internet searching;
- helping parents, teachers, and caregivers to find materials for children.

Providing Educational and Recreational Programs

The familiar storyhours for toddlers, preschoolers, and older children are designed to develop literacy and encourage reading. Game days, summer reading clubs, art and craft programs, author visits, and the like are designed to give children cultural and recreational experiences that might not otherwise be available to them.

Some programs sponsored by libraries are not directly linked to library goals. These might include craft programs, dancing, filmmaking, gaming groups, and language classes. Often these programs use outside personnel as leaders, but the planning, registration, and publicity may be handled by the library. If this is so, they must be considered part of the children's department's overall plan of service.

Forming Partnerships

Some children's department offer programs and services outside the library building. Most common are visits to daycares and schools, but libraries also serve boys and girls clubs, camps, recreation centers, or other places that children gather. Outreach can include materials for circulation or programs. Some libraries participate in community fairs or school reading events, others host programs on public television.

The library may establish partnerships with organizations or agencies that serve children and families, such as schools or daycares. Partnership activities may include joint training of staff, homework alerts from teachers, or other regular communications. Partners can be health related with the partnership providing health information to families or library materials for hospital patients. Many local museums and libraries share exhibits and activities for children.

Marketing Services

Unless people know what the library has to offer, they will not take advantage of the collections and services. Parents of young children are eager to find resources for them, but many do not think of using the library. "Libraries are a beloved tradition in America, commanding respect, pride, and even a willingness to support the occasional bond issue. Yet, for an institution that has been around this long, the library has simply faded into the background for many in the general public" (Sass 2002). Librarians must work hard to ensure that their community is aware of all the materials and services the library offers.

Examples of library marketing:

- media releases to announce programs
- providing a new book column in local newspapers, including foreign language papers
- taping public service announcements for radio and television
- developing an attractive children's department website
- posting videos of library events on YouTube and other outlets
- producing an e-newsletter or a children's department blog

Specific methods will vary according to the community and will change with evolving technology, but the principle of informing people about library services is a constant. Public libraries are service organizations and the community should be informed about their collections and services.

REFERENCES AND ADDITIONAL READING

Brown, A. Reference Services for Children: Information Needs and Wants in the Public Library. *Australian Library Journal* 53: 261–274.

Cerny, Rosanne, Markey, Penny, and Williams, Amanda. 2006. Knowledge of Client Group. In *Outstanding Library Service to Children; Putting the Core Competencies to Work.* Chicago: American Library Association.

Sass, Rivkah K. 2002. Marketing the Worth of Your Library. *Library Journal.* http://www.libraryjournal.com/index.asp?layout=articlePrint&articleid=CA220888 (Accessed March 13, 2007).

UNESCO. 1994. *Public Library Manifesto.* The Hague: International Federation of Library Associations and Institutions.

Walter, Virginia. 1992. *Output Measures for Public Library Service to Children: A Manual of Standardized Procedures.* Chicago: American Library Association.

2

Strategic Planning and Outcome Evaluation

After a department has established the general outlines of its service program, steps are taken to implement that program in the most effective way. Traditional tools that managers find useful in monitoring progress are goal setting and outcome evaluation for specific aspects of the plan. The goals of a library and of a department grow out of the mission statement of the library. A mission statement sets forth in general terms the purpose of the institution. Examining the mission statement of your library and developing departmental goals that can be clearly related to it is a wise first step in planning. Goals and objectives are designed to make concrete the aspirations expressed in the mission statement.

Having a defined set of goals and objectives demonstrates to administrators and to the public that a department has a clear view of what it is trying to do and that it can measure the extent to which it achieves its aims. The time spent thinking about departmental goals and setting up a system to measure whether those goals are reached will make a department more effective in serving its public. In addition, using outcome evaluation will help librarians to demonstrate in a tangible way what it is that is being done and why it is useful. Systematic evaluation is increasingly necessary to support budget requests and continued administrative support.

DEFINITIONS

A MISSION STATEMENT synthesizes the purpose of the library in a sentence or short paragraph. This helps each department set priorities and establish goals and objectives, but it is the library board's responsibility to approve and review the mission statement. The purpose of a mission statement is to inform the community about the library's priorities in clear and easily understood terms. (Nelson 2001, 76)

GOALS are long-range, broad, general statements describing a desired condition toward which the library will work. Goals are the benefits the library community (or specifically children in your community) will receive because the library provides programs and services. (Nelson 2001, 79)

OBJECTIVES are short range and describe the results to be achieved in a specific time period. They are measurable, doable, time limited, and describe specific progress made toward a goal.

ACTIVITIES are strategies the library uses to achieve its goals and objectives.

OUTCOME EVALUATION is a systematic way to determine if a department has achieved its goals and what benefits are gained by the users of youth services.

OUTCOMES are specific benefits that occur to program participants or library users. Typically outcomes refer to a change in behavior, knowledge, skill, attitude, or status of library users. Objectives should describe desired outcomes.

INDICATORS are statements that describe how objectives will be measured and how to be successful in meeting objectives.

THE LIBRARY'S MISSION

Each public library has a history and tradition of service and most try to articulate its reason for existence by adopting a mission statement. This helps staff set priorities and establish goals and objectives for the library. Often administrative staff or consultants draft the mission statement, but it is the library board's responsibility to approve and review the mission statement.

EXAMPLES OF MISSION STATEMENTS

ST. LOUIS, MISSOURI

The St. Louis Public Library will provide learning resources and information services that support and improve individual, family, and community life.

To support this mission, the Library will organize and prudently manage its resources to:

- Ensure that the Library's resources are available to all
- Promote use of the Library
- Assist children and adults with life-long learning
- Promote literacy for all ages
- Assist individuals in finding jobs and educational opportunities
- Assist businesses with their development and growth
- Provide current information
- Provide recreational reading resources, media materials, and programs
- Promote public use of modern information technology

Adopted by the Board of Directors: January 31, 1994 (www.slpl.org; accessed 2006; 12–13)

COLUMBUS, OHIO

At Columbus Metropolitan Library (CML), our mission is "to promote reading and guide learning in the pursuit of information, knowledge, and wisdom." (www.cml.lib.oh./ebranch/about_cml/index.cfm; accessed April 4, 2007.)

HENNEPIN COUNTY LIBRARY

Hennepin County Library promotes full and equal access to information and ideas, the love of reading, the joy of learning, and engagement with the arts, sciences and humanities. (www. Hclib.org/pub/info/MissionVisionGoals.pdf; accessed April 4, 2007.)

Some libraries create missions statements to highlight major service roles and other use the mission statement as a primary tool for marketing the library. Obviously the mission statement can do both. To be effective a mission statement should have focus, identify who is served and how, motivate staff and donors, and be measurable (Wallace 2004, 4). The library's mission may only relate directly to the children's department in a few places, but it sets the tone for the department and the children's department's plan should always relate to the library's mission.

Many libraries have mission statements that are quite general and therefore can be interpreted in different ways. Nonetheless, the mandate is the statement that justifies expenditures on children's services and serves as the basic support for a librarian's program of services. It is usually wise to incorporate reference to the mission statement in departmental goal setting. Some children's departments create a departmental mission based on the mission of the larger library to use as a guide in planning, budgeting, and fundraising. A good mission statement is a source of guidance and inspiration, defines the unique contribution of your library (or the children's department), and is easy to say, read, and remember (Wallace 2004, 16).

ESTABLISHING CHILDREN'S DEPARTMENT GOALS

The process of establishing, attaining, and evaluating goals and objectives is a continuous one. Goals are set for longer terms than are objectives, but even goals must be examined periodically to see whether they are still appropriate. Goals grow out of the mandate of the library and in many libraries they are intended to remain unchanged for three to five years. Objectives are set for shorter periods of time, usually one or two years; at the end of that time, the success or failure in meeting the objective can be measured. Objectives should grow naturally from the goals of an organization and each objective should relate to a specific library goal. In looking at the goals, the objectives should be seen to flow logically from the goals; it should also be possible from looking at the objectives to see how these work to carry out the direction of the goals. Activities describe what library staff will do to achieve objectives and they too should have a clear, specific, measurable link to stated objectives and goals.

Goals and objectives should state the desired outcome clearly enough so library staff can measure and report how successful the library has been in meeting them. Goals and objectives should also include desired outcomes in terms of the library's users. For example, a goal that a library "provide reading material for all members of the community" might be better stated as "circulation will increase because readers will find what they want at the library." With a more specific objective, for example, that " use of the beginning reader section of the department will increase because young children and their families and caregivers will find materials that help children learning to read." Activities might include purchase of more beginning readers, new signage, more bibliographies, and booktalking beginning readers to kindergarten classrooms. Goals and objectives should describe the effect on library users of library services, not merely the existence of library services. Figure 2.1 shows this relationship in graphic form.

Because of the difference in their level of specificity, goals may be established either by the library as a whole, or by individual departments. Objectives are almost always set at the departmental level. Departments may cooperate on a project. In this case each department would have similar objectives. The library may have a coordinated library-wide goal (upgrade of computer technology

Figure 2.1
Goals and objectives for service.

GOAL

To create and strengthen reading habits in children from an early age.

OBJECTIVE

Provide story hour programs to 25 percent of the day care centers in the community by the end of 2008.

ACTIVITIES

Use community directories to establish a list of local day care centers. Contact the director of each center to set up appointment.	Send one staff member to ALSC preconference workshop on programming for toddlers.

or webpage, improved service to immigrants, or a tax campaign, etc.), so some children's services departmental objectives would be set to meet the library's specific initiative.

Once objectives have been determined, specific activities flow naturally from them. The cost of these activities becomes easier to justify because the activities flow clearly from overall departmental goals. In the example given in figure 2.1, it is easy to see that the money requested for increased collection development is done with a specific purpose in mind, rather than a vague notion that more books in the collection is a good idea.

STATING GOALS AND OBJECTIVES

Goals

Goals are usually stated in general terms so that they will remain valid for several years and cover a variety of circumstances. For this reason the goals of many public library children's department sound similar. The goals listed below are adapted from the UNESCO Manifesto on Public Libraries (1994):

* to create and strengthen reading habits in children from an early age;
* to support both individual and self-conducted education as well as formal education at all levels;
* to provide opportunities for personal creative development;
* to stimulate the imagination and creativity of children and young people;
* to promote awareness of cultural heritage, appreciation of the arts, scientific achievements, and innovations;
* to facilitate the development of information and computer literacy skills;
* to support literacy activities and programs for all age groups, and initiate such activities if necessary.

Goals are overall aims of a department. They set the general direction in which service is heading and are good ways to start designing programs of service. Sometimes they have to be broken down into sub-goals before it's possible to set objectives. An overall goal of a children's department might be stated thus: "To select a variety of media that satisfies the informational, recreational, and intellectual needs of a diverse community of children."

Goal statements are almost always wholesome statements, that is, statements with which no one would disagree. The advantage of writing them out is that the process makes librarians think about what they are doing or should be doing. Goals by themselves are not powerful management tools. "To provide equal access to library service for all children" sounds fine, but it does not indicate what specific actions should be taken aside from opening the doors in the morning. Objectives state what goals mean in terms of operation.

Objectives, Activities, and Indicators

Objectives are statements that focus work on some specific aspect of a goal. Each goal could have several appropriate objectives. Objectives give specific, measurable, and time-oriented indications of how well a department is moving toward the attainment of goals by meeting the stated needs of those served or describing what benefits or outcomes library users will attain.

Activities describe or list specific activities that the children's department will do to achieve the objectives. The activities should relate directly to the objective and be as specific as possible. Rather than "improve the collection" or "offer programs," activities statements might state "purchase 20 percent more beginning reading titles before summer" or "provide 10 new programs for kindergarteners."

Indicators are statements that describe how objectives will be measured. It is the specificity of objectives and the fact that they are measurable that make them useful. Goals can be nonspecific because they only point the direction in which the library is moving. Many goals will never be completely achieved. Objectives and activities statements, on the other hand, spell out what the department intends to do and how staff members expect to do it, and indicators define how staff members will know whether or not they have achieved their aims. At the end of the time period it is easy to see whether or not the objectives have been met.

Hallmarks of Useful Objectives, Activities Statements, and Indicators

An objective should describe an intended outcome for the user rather than a procedure done by library staff. Activity statements specify *what* the department is doing (the input), objectives specify *why* it is being done—what the impact to the user or community will be. The objective "to provide sufficient personnel so that a librarian is at the reference desk after school hours" is not as useful as, "Increase children's knowledge and improve their ability to successfully complete homework assignments by providing correct answers to their reference questions." An activity might be "hire one more professional children's librarian to provide reference service during non-school hours." The indicator would state "children will always be served by a reference librarian in the children's department and library staff will answer children's questions correctly at least 80 percent of the time." The first example states what you are going to do but does not necessarily indicate an outcome. Having someone on the reference desk reading library journals and glaring at every kid who comes near might reach the first objective but would not improve your reference service greatly. When writing objectives you should be sure the intended outcome is obvious to other people and not just to you and that the standard of success stated in the indicator is possible to obtain and is a true measure of the objective.

A children's department planning includes three things:

- what is to be accomplished (objective)
- what specific activities will be done to accomplish the objective (activity statement)
- how success will be measured (indicator)

Objectives should have a time frame. They should indicate what you expect to accomplish by a certain date so that you can check on how well you are doing. For example, an objective might be, "50 percent of library visitors will use wireless Internet access in each branch by the end of 2008." Sometimes objectives are broken down into stages: "80 percent of elementary school teachers will know how to use the library's website by the end of the 2008 school year, and 80 percent of middle school teachers will be able to access the library's website by the end of the 2009 school year."

Most departmental objectives are designed for periods of from one to three years. Very few challenging objectives can be met in less than one year, and very few plans can be made for more than three years. Short term objectives for specific programs or projects are often useful supplements to the overall departmental objectives.

Setting Objectives

To devise realistic objectives, encourage input from all levels of staff in the department. The first step is to call a staff meeting to discuss the project. The department head reminds the staff of the departmental goals and talks about the reasons for setting objectives. Every staff member is encouraged to suggest areas in which objectives would be useful and what the objectives might be. It is also a good idea to seek input from library users or interested community groups (teachers, scout leaders, preschool caregivers, etc.) through formal surveys and focus groups or less formally though conversation with children and adults. Input can be invited on the library website. Asking users about their needs and priorities can help focus objectives on the real needs of the community served. The next step is the formation of a committee to prepare written objectives. If the staff is small, the department head may work alone to draw up a draft of the objectives.

Objectives should be clear, specific, and realistic. While some librarians feel that there are aspects of service that cannot be quantified, objectives should, at the least, indicate how those things that are not quantifiable are to be judged: the enthusiasm at storyhours, greater response from teachers, and so forth. Objectives should be attainable but challenging. They must strike a balance between an over-enthusiastic "consult with all teachers about their assignments" and statements that require no change of service—"answer reference questions." The purpose of setting objectives is to move you toward meeting goals. There is no point in setting them unless something is achieved by meeting them.

Staff members who will be responsible for meeting the objectives need to accept them as reasonable. If staff members believe objectives are plans sent down by administrators who do not understand the day-to-day operations of the department, they may not implement them eagerly. For this reason, even though an individual or a small committee may be responsible for drafting objectives, they should be discussed and revised by all members of the department both professional and non-professional.

If staff members have not worked with formalized objectives before, they may see them as a threat. To avoid this, the department head may encourage the staff to set limited and easily met objectives the first time around. If the employees see that objectives can benefit them by providing a means of documenting their achievements, they may be ready to set more challenging objectives on the next round.

First-time users of objectives may go to the other extreme and set unrealistically ambitious objectives. One way to avoid this is to measure on a short-term, usually monthly, basis how well the objectives are being met. If objectives are too ambitious, it will become apparent in a month or two. The objectives can then be modified to be more reasonable in time for the formal assessment at the end of the year.

Working with Objectives

Objectives can enhance the effectiveness of a department only if the staff remains aware of them. Some departments use visual reminders, such as notices on the staff bulletin board, to remind people about departmental activities that meet objectives. These can take various forms, for example:

- We need to develop a list of suitable science websites. How many have you discovered this month?
- We want to have five class visits per week. So far this month we have had only four.

As with all notices placed on bulletin boards, these must be changed frequently or people will cease to notice them, much less read them. It helps too if bright colors and entertaining graphics are used to draw attention to the message. Brief reminders can also be used as tag lines on staff email or crawl lines on a staff section of a website. This technique should not be overdone or the messages will become an intrusion and annoyance.

At staff meetings and, more informally, in conversations, department heads can mention objectives. This should never be done in a threatening way, but as a good-natured reminder of the department's objectives. Monthly reports should include progress made toward meeting objectives.

Although objectives are formal statements designed to be formally evaluated, there must be some flexibility in their use. Occasionally an unexpected disaster such as a fire will cancel out all of the previously planned objectives. Even lesser events such as a succession of staff illnesses, or resignations, changes in the library administration, or community problems caused by a plant closure or agricultural crisis may require modification of a department's objectives.

When it becomes clear that some objectives are going to be unreachable, a staff meeting and discussion can lead to modifications to make the objective realistic. Naturally, these changes should not occur every year or else the setting of objectives becomes meaningless. Like all management tools, however, objectives must be modifiable in the light of actual events.

The department head should assess objectives on an ongoing basis throughout the year. If it is clear that objectives are not being met, it is better to make adjustments early rather than to announce at the end of the year that there has been a disastrous failure. Oftentimes objectives need to be modified if that can be done without a great deal of effort. At other times, it may be best to forget about a particular objective and to work on the underlying problems that the failure to meet it may reveal. If objectives are being met, it is useful to let the staff know how well they are doing. The bulletin board, website, and staff meetings can be used to announce the successes in meeting objectives on a monthly or quarterly basis.

EVALUATING ACHIEVEMENT

Formal assessment of how well objectives are being met is usually done on a yearly basis, although the timeframe for the objective may be longer than that. As mentioned earlier, most objectives are set for a period of one to three years. An assessment at least once a year is needed to ensure that the department does not get too far off track in meeting its planned goals. The annual assessment is a formal one, with the results given to all staff members so they can see how well—or how badly—the department is doing. Most annual assessments become part of the library's annual report that is given to the library board and made available to the public.

The method of evaluation should be set at the same time the objective is adopted. Some evaluation measurements stated in the indicator or activity statements are obvious: for collection development, the number of books purchased in a particular area; for programming, the number of programs or the attendance; for staff development, the courses or workshops attended. Other objectives such as those concerned with the number of reference questions successfully answered or the amount of reading guidance given may require specific sampling and counting techniques. Because outcomes state changes for library users, it is important to gather information from users. This is often done by using surveys, interviews, or focus groups to get input directly from adults and children who use the department.

Statistical Evaluation

If special, non-routine, measurements are needed, provision should be made for these at the time the objectives are set and be stated as indicators of success. A good guide to ways of measuring the amount of services used is the American Library Association's *Output Measures for Public Library Service to Children: A Manual of Standardized Procedures* (Walter 1992). If specific periods are set aside during the year for the measure of services, the task need not be onerous. These output measures might include:

- Library use measures (visitation)
- Materials use measures (circulation and in-house use)
- Materials availability measures (children's needs are met successfully)
- Computer use (computer session in-house, hits on kids webpage, user satisfaction)
- Information services measures (reference)
- Programming measures (attendance, satisfaction)
- Community relations (school and day care contacts, other community contacts)

Using some or all of these measures can help the library to decide whether objectives are being met. The decision as to which measures to use in evaluation is made at the time the objectives are set.

Outcome Evaluation

To judge whether the department has had a positive impact on library users some information in addition to statistical measures described above should be collected. While attendance at programs or use of the library's collection is a strong statement of the library's function it does not tell the specific impact of use for users or the community. So in addition to gathering data on how much the library is used, information on how using the library has helped people should also be collected.

Outcome measures provide a systematic way to find out whether services are meeting or exceeding the objectives set for them.

- what works best for the people who use your services
- how to change programs and services as your community changes
- how to best use the resources you have and get the resources you need to provide library service to children

In addition to increasing the knowledge of youth services staff, outcome evaluation (OE) provides the following:

- OE helps staff work smart by providing a system to measure success and specific information to use to adapt or change programs and services.
- OE strengthens library planning and budget allocation.
- OE allows library staff to understand and describe the impact of its program and services on its users. OE enables communication amongst youth services staff and between library departments, including administration. OE enhances communication with the community, donors, and program partners.
- OE provides accountability for public agencies including libraries. OE is required by the federal government and will be increasingly required by agencies using state and local funds. OE may be required by private donors as well. (Dresang 2006)

An example of outcome evaluation is shown in figure 2.2.

Techniques used to measure impact include systematic observation, interviews, surveys, or focus groups with specific user groups. While these techniques are fairly new to libraries, other service agencies including United Way, the Girl Scouts, and many community health organizations have adopted these techniques and might provide training locally for library staff new to using them. As in the example above outcome evaluation need not be complicated. Observing how many children are successful in a task and noting the results, adding these many observations together, and using the results to improve the program is possible to do with some planning and the commitment to including the users in the evaluation. Asking children what they learned or enjoyed during a program can also give good information about how a particular program helped (or did not help) meet a particular objective.

Figure 2.2
Outcome evaluation example.

	Definitions: • Intended impact	Examples: • Students will have basic Internet skills
Indicator	• Observable and measurable behaviors and conditions	• The 125 students will be trained to bring up an Internet search engine, enter a topic in the search function, and find one example of the information being sought within 15 minutes
Data Source	•ˈ Sources of information about conditions being measured	• Searching exercise, trainer observation
Applied to	• The specific group within an audience to be measured (all or a subset)	• Howard County 7th–8th graders who complete the workshop
Data Interval	• When data will be collected	• At end of workshop
Target (Goal)	• The amount of impact desired	• 85% of approximately 125 participants

Source: IMLS, 2003. Accessed April 4, 2007, from www.imls.gov/applications/basics.shtm.

USING THE RESULTS OF EVALUATION

Whatever method is used to evaluate how well a department is meeting its objectives, it is important to remember that the method should be decided upon when the objectives are first set. If this is not done, the department may find itself unable to decide whether or not its objectives are met.

When objectives are successfully met, staff members can congratulate themselves on a job well done and are frequently eager to move on to setting new objectives for another year. The failure to meet objectives is much more difficult to deal with. If a department has set itself the objective of contacting 50 percent of the teachers in their jurisdiction, but manages to reach only 25 percent, the staff may feel demoralized and discouraged. The task of the department head in this situation is to help the staff analyze the reason for failure and move toward either reaching the objective or setting one that is more realistic.

It is important that no one member of the staff be made to feel responsible for failure to meet a departmental objective. If there is a problem with one member of the department, that should be discussed privately with the individual. Setting and attaining of department objectives are group processes. After the measurements have been taken to see whether or to what extent objectives are met, a staff meeting should be called. The degree to which each objective is met will be announced and the reasons for success or failure discussed. Some of the causes of failure in certain situations are

- Objectives are unrealistic when compared with the practice of most public libraries. An example would be to attempt to reach an objective of having 90 percent of the children in a community borrow at least one book.
- Objectives are unrealistic in terms of the personnel available: for example, to have at least 10 class visits per week in a library with only two staff members.
- Conditions have changed making the objective unreachable: for example, the assistant librarian has left and not been replaced so the head of the children's department has been carrying out two library jobs for six months.
- Budget has not been sufficient to meet the objective; for example, an attempt to buy 500 Chinese language books has revealed that these books are more expensive than had been expected, so only 400 books were actually bought.
- Personnel has not been able to manage change: for example, an attempt to train a staff member to sign storyhours has failed because the staff member was unable to become proficient enough in signing within the time allocated.

Frequently the cause of the failure to meet an objective indicates the steps that need to be taken to ensure success next time. Occasionally the department head may feel that failure is due to the inadequacy or lack of interest of a particular staff member. In that case, the staff evaluation interview ought to focus on the objective involved. Setting and measuring objectives can, in fact, become a useful staff evaluation tool.

The most important point to remember in dealing with the failure to meet objectives is to focus on the reason for the failure and find a way to succeed. Failure should not lead to discouragement but to a renewed commitment to setting better objectives that can and will be met by the department.

In addition to evaluating success, often evaluation provides unanticipated results and information that can help the department become more effective. A department may find other groups of people that could be served (in addition to working with school librarians, reading teachers might help kids know more about the public library) or identify issues for users (kids can use computers with skill, but have trouble using the library's computer sign up system). With the information collected to evaluate success or failure to meet objects plus other information collected in the evaluation can be used as the basis for setting the next round of objectives.

REFERENCES AND ADDITIONAL READING

Dresang, Eliza T., Gross, Melissa, and Holt, Leslie Edmonds. 2006. *Dynamic Youth Services through Outcome-Based Planning and Evaluation.* Chicago: American Library Association.

Durrance, Joan, and Fisher, Karen. 2005. *How Libraries and Librarians Help People: A Guide to Developing User-Centered Outcomes.* Chicago: American Library Association.

Nelson, Sandra. 2001. *The New Planning for Results: A Streamlined Approach.* Chicago: American Library Association.

New Directives, New Directions 2003. (www.imls.gov/applications/basics.shtm) Institute of Museum and Library Service.

Rubin, Rhea Joyce. 2006. *Demonstrating Results: Using Outcome Measurement in Your Library.* Chicago: American Library Association.

Search for Schools, Colleges and Libraries: (www.nces.ed.gov) National Center for Educational Statistics-NCES and Library Statistics Cooperative Program. (www.nclis.gov/survey.html) National Commission on Libraries and Information Science-NCLIS.

Wallace, Linda K. 2004. *Libraries, Mission and Marketing: Writing Mission Statements That Work.* Chicago: American Library Association.

Walter, Virginia. 1992. *Output Measures for Public Library Service to Children: A Manual of Standardized Procedures.* Chicago: American Library Association.

Section II

Managing the Department

3

Creating a Productive Work Environment

An effective children's librarian needs skills beyond those required for storytelling or puppetry. Although management techniques are not the most visible work skills children's librarians bring to their jobs, they are essential for running a productive department. Management is the process of getting things done. Libraries today are trying to achieve their goals with fewer resources and less personnel than were available in past years, so using resources effectively is more important than ever. A successful manager inspires people to work toward library goals and monitors the department to ensure these goals are achieved and shown to be achieved. Unless a department is well managed its personnel and other resources will not deliver the best possible library service.

SUPERVISING A DEPARTMENT

A library department head is a first-line supervisor—someone who transmits policy on a day-to-day basis to employees. Whether working in a small library or a large library system, a department supervisor communicates in two directions—to administrators and to employees. Like a node in a network the supervisor receives information from a variety of sources and routes it to those who need it. Some of these relationships are shown in figure 3.1.

The more effectively the supervisor communicates, the better the information flows. This can translate into a superior working environment for staff and enhanced services for patrons.

Besides transmitting information, the supervisor must decide what to do with it. Information informs policy decisions and effective decision making turns policy into practice and programs.

Many of the techniques for supervision in libraries are similar to those in other management situations, but libraries also have management issues specific to them.

Figure 3.1
Links to and from children's department.

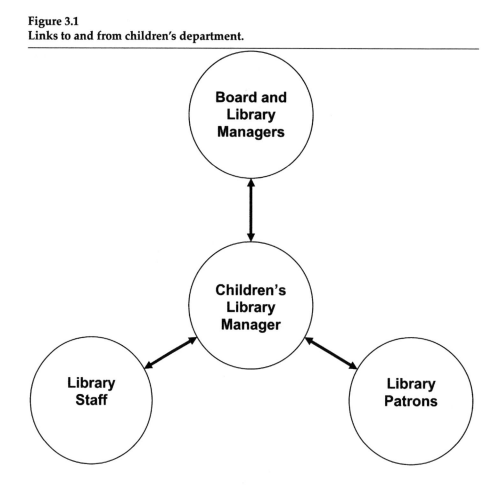

Size of Unit

Most children's departments are small units by business standards. A department head typically supervises fewer than a dozen people, often only two or three. This means that relationships within the department tend to be close and personal. The department head does not deal with employees known only by a personnel number but with individuals who are well known to everyone in the department. This may make it easier for a supervisor to allocate tasks individually and take advantage of each person's strengths, but it may also make it difficult for the supervisor to maintain the distance necessary for objective performance appraisals. Close personal relations may tempt a supervisor to discuss administrative decisions or problems inappropriately. This can easily turn into gossip and undermine the supervisor's effectiveness. Finally, close personal relations may allow an individual to manipulate the supervisor into allowing an unequal distribution of the departmental workload.

Another complication in some children's departments is the relative stability of clerical and professional staff. In many library systems, clerical staff remain in one branch for many years and build up seniority. Librarians more often move between branches or library systems. Young professionals often find themselves working with clerical assistants who are considerably older than they are and have many years of experience in the department. The skills learned through professional education are not always as evident as the clerical staff's intimate knowledge of the branch collection and the local community. The supervisor has to gain the confidence of all staff members and persuade them to follow administrative leadership. Anyone moving into a situation like this should be careful to show respect for the clerical staff's knowledge. At the same time, the young professional must not downplay the broader base of skills learned through professional education and association with the wider library world. Both professional and clerical staff play vital roles in developing effective library service.

Measuring Results

Library departments also differ from businesses because they dispense service on a nonprofit basis. Measuring the productivity of an employee or of a department is difficult when there is no tangible product. A supervisor's success cannot be measured by the number of products produced. The increased skill of staff members in answering reference questions or selecting books is extremely difficult to quantify. A supervisor's success in creating a productive work environment may be revealed only slowly through an increase in the use of services and an anecdotal record of users' perceptions. The lack of immediate, measurable results can be discouraging in the short term, but eventually a well-run department should be seen as more productive.

PERSONNEL SUPERVISED

The personnel supervised by a department head may include librarians, library assistants, clerical staff, pages, and others, such as maintenance or security staff and volunteers. Each level of staff requires a somewhat different type of supervision.

Professional Staff

Supervision of professional staff is usually collegial. Typically the interactions between supervisor and staff include:

- frequent informal communication in person, by email, and telephone
- regular meetings
- discussion of problems
- decisions made by consensus

In supervising librarians, one goal is to help them develop skills necessary to take positions as department heads in other branches or libraries. Sharing background information about policies and decisions helps librarians understand the *why* as well as the *how* of administration. It also enables them to follow the spirit as well as the letter of institutional goals.

Library Assistants and Clerical Staff

Support staff members need to know some of the background and reasons for library policies. Their major need for information, however, is to help them do their daily jobs, not to participate in administration. (This is not necessarily true of nonprofessional staff who may become candidates for professional education.) For the many library assistants who expect to remain as nonprofessional staff, learning technique and procedures take precedence over discussing general policies. That said, no library employee should blindly follow rules without thinking about them. Many clerical tasks—registering new borrowers, for example—are governed by specific procedures. An individual will handle these more efficiently if he or she understands the reasons for them. Some supervisors think they will save time by teaching procedures without explaining why things are done in a certain way, but mistakes are more frequent when someone tries to carry out a rigid set of rules without understanding their purpose and recognizing when they should be modified.

Pages and Shelvers

In many libraries, pages are high school students in their first job. Some are unused to the demands for punctuality and for continuous work during their shifts. Some pages do not understand they are expected to show up for work whenever they are scheduled and that unexplained absences are unacceptable. While direct supervision of pages is often the responsibility of a senior clerical staff person, the department head is responsible for setting policy and for maintaining overall supervision. Pages often are not interested in the inner workings of the library or overall library policy, although some may be. Supervisors should always recognize their important contribution to the efficient operation of the department. All library staff should treat pages as respected members of the team.

Maintenance and Cleaning Staff

The library's central administration usually supervises maintenance staff. The department head typically makes requests for specific tasks—changing a light bulb or moving a bookcase—through established procedures. Most libraries also have procedures for complaints about maintenance. Problems with maintenance staff often result from misunderstandings about who is responsible for specific tasks. A department head must find out which tasks are considered routine maintenance; which are acceptable special or emergency tasks; and which department personnel are expected to handle themselves. These categories can vary widely from one library to another. Like other employees, maintenance staff generally work best in a department where their work and expertise are respected and acknowledged. Even such a simple thing as addressing individuals by name helps promote cordial relationships.

Tips for Dealing with All Staff Members

Some of the issues that cause resentment in a department seem trivial ones:

- *Using first names with other staff members.* Pages are usually called by their first names, but sometimes they are expected to address other staff members more formally. This distinction is acceptable in some communities but resented in others. Policy should be the same in all departments of the library. The trend is for first names to be used among all staff members. Many libraries let staff choose their own form of address to accommodate cultural and age differences.
- *Dress codes.* Many libraries have a written dress code for all employees. Requirements that have no direct bearing on job performance should be avoided. Pages can generally shelve books just as well in flip-flops as in hi-tops. If other staff members or patrons object to a page's clothes and style, a general staff discussion may lead to an acceptable compromise on standards. Most people accept decisions in which they participate more willingly than regulations handed down from the administrator.
- *Taking breaks.* Scheduling break time can be an annoyance when some staff members feel they are getting the least desirable times. A supervisor often finds the staff are satisfied if they work out a schedule on their own rather than having the supervisor suggest one. A supervisor should only step in if intractable differences appear.
- *Using personal technologies.* Cell phones and personal music players have become issues in many libraries. Staff members, including pages, should have clear direction on if and when these items may be used at work. Input from staff members on guidelines for use will help to make decisions acceptable.

MAKING DECISIONS

One of a manager's most important tasks is making decisions. Few things harm an organization more than a manager who defers or evades decisions. A decisive manager has a better chance of running an efficient department. Everyone wants to make correct decisions, but most choices are between better and worse rather than right or wrong; usually any decision is better than vacillation. If a choice must be made whether the storyhour should be for three- to five-year-old children or for four- and five-year-old children, either decision would enable the library program to move forward. Not making a choice might result in delaying the program, annoying parents who must call back later to register a child, or killing the enthusiasm of the librarians who are eager to plan the program. Any of these results is more detrimental than making the so-called wrong choice. Figure 3.2 gives an example of how a decision table can show the choices to be made.

Moving toward a Decision

The person who makes a decision gains power; on the other hand, he or she may also be blamed or reprimanded if the decision has unpleasant consequences. Supervisors should not evade decisions because of the possibility of making the wrong one. To become a leader in the library, a children's librarian must

Figure 3.2
Example of decision table.

Who makes the decision?	Type of decision	Implementation	Input required
Library board	Major policy decisions Financial decisions	May request input from library staff or the public. Decisions are binding	Input is advisory. Final decision made by board
Chief administrative officer	Operational decisions affecting the entire library General library policies	May request input from library staff or delegate decisions to department heads	Input is often advisory with final decision made by administrator. Some managers accept collegial decisions based on majority of staff opinions
Department head	Policy and operational decisions affecting one department	Usually requests input from library staff and sometimes from patrons	Depending on the decision, input may be advisory or may determine the decision

demonstrate a readiness to become a decision-maker by being willing to make decisions, to stand by them, and of course by making successful decisions.

The library director might ask a children's department supervisor to arrange a larger library project such as an anniversary or holiday celebration or exhibit. These assignments give a librarian a chance to demonstrate leadership within the entire library community. It is important to understand the extent to which decision-making has been delegated. The librarian should clarify exactly what kind of input is desired. Is the department head being asked to give informational input into a decision, make a recommendation, or make the decision and act on it?

Decisions within a Department

When a decision must be made, the first task of a department manager is to decide what type of decision it is. Decisions may be joint decisions, individual decisions, or executive decisions.

Joint Decisions

Some decisions should be made by the entire group or by a subgroup or committee. To start the decision-making process, the manager explains to the staff whether they are being asked merely for information and suggestions or whether the group will make the decision. Group decisions are most appropriate when the entire group must accept the decision and the time limit for making it is fairly long. In a children's department, a group might decide how to allocate work to minimize the disruption caused by major repairs to the building. Each individual is likely to know best how the repairs will affect a particular job. Allowing each staff member to suggest ways for coping with inconvenience will minimize general resentment. The manager will not appear to be the person who handed down decisions that cause inconvenience.

Individual Decisions

Decisions that affect the work of an individual but not the overall running of the department are best made by the individual. The time at which each staff member takes a coffee break or lunch break is not crucial as long as the department is adequately staffed at all times. The same is often true of vacation scheduling or the sequence in which tasks are done. The manager can often leave such decisions to the individuals involved. This allows the staff members to control aspects of their work that may be important to them, which in turn will make them feel better about their jobs. Giving an individual some control over his or her job, however minor the decision, encourages people to think about why they do something one way rather than another. Elaborate rules are often unnecessary in small working departments. Flexibility encourages people to take ownership of a job and to develop a sense of responsibility for handling it.

Executive Decisions

Not all decisions can be made by individual staff members or by a committee. The department head should be prepared to make many of the major decisions. When a decision must be made, there are specific steps a manager can take to make the decision effectively.

Steps toward a Good Decision

- Review the available information—this includes documentation and input from people involved. List all the possible choices. If there is documentation, read it. If you need to ask people about their plans or ideas, do so with an open mind.
- Evaluate the advantages and disadvantages of each choice. Consider what the staff wants, what the department has traditionally done, and how the CEO or outsiders might evaluate the results. Are there political implications to one solution or another?
- Set a time frame. Is it important to make the decision immediately or is there time for discussion? If possible, allow time for deliberation. The greater the change, the more money or staff time involved, the more time should be spent making the decision. Although delay can sometimes allow the impetus to slip away, a leader should not be pressured into making a premature decision.
- Consider possible negative consequences of the decision. Think about the attitudes and values of people who will be affected. Does the decision fit in with the way things are normally done in the organization? Consider whether an unusual opportunity will slip away if not taken. Ask yourself whether a decision is being delayed because of a desire for perfection.

One helpful tool is the decision table. For example, figure 3.3 shows what a decision table might look like, if a children's department has the goal of improving the style and value of its homepage.

Figure 3.3
Individual decision table.

Strategy	How will it help?	Expense	Negative impacts
Hire a website designer on contract	Produce an eye-catching site	Very expensive—need grant or major shift of resources	Difficult to maintain high quality without additional staff
Use library technology dept.	Webpage will be similar to other library pages	Expense medium; some dept. budget funds allocated to tech dept.	Work may be delayed or interrupted for needs of other depts
Find volunteer from the community	Save money and give volunteer useful experience	Expense low except for staff time supervising project	No guarantee of work quality; may not be completed
Use dept. staff	Page will reflect needs of dept. and staff wishes	Expense hidden in costs of staff time, but may be high	Work quality may not be professional level; takes time away from other activities

A chart of this kind will not make the decision, but it should help. To be useful, the information about each choice has to be as complete and accurate as possible. The table lays out all the possibilities and identifies the advantages and disadvantages of each choice. Using it should help decision makers to make the most appropriate choice for a particular situation.

The initial choice might be modified or changed in time. One component of decision-making is monitoring results so appropriate modifications can be made.

Sometimes a department head may make a decision carefully and reasonably but nonetheless realize after a while that it was the wrong decision. A manager must know when to reverse a decision, but should try to avoid appearing to vacillate. If a decision must be changed, the manager should consider the alternatives calmly and try to decide the next move before discussing the change widely. In announcing the reversal of a decision, the department head should explain as clearly as possible the reasons for the change and should try to avoid apologizing too much or dwelling on the fact that a mistake was made. All managers make mistakes. An important aspect of leadership is to be able to acknowledge a mistake and move on quickly to remedy the situation.

COMMUNICATION WITHIN THE DEPARTMENT

Effective supervision depends on good two-way communication within the department, with the emphasis on two-way. The manager not only gives information about library policies, procedures, and plans, but also listens to staff members' comments, ideas, and complaints. *The real message is not the one the speaker sends, but the one the listener hears.* Several pitfalls can interfere with the effectiveness of a message.

Clarity

Almost all speakers believe they are sending a clear message and blame the listener for any failure to understand, but it is the speaker's responsibility to guard against misunderstanding. Some common problems with clarity are outlined as follows.

Overestimating Background Knowledge

A supervisor may forget that a staff member does not have all of the necessary information necessary for understanding. "You'd better check the condition of our Chinese language titles because we may have extra funding available at the end of the budget year" is not a useful directive for a new librarian. To do the job, the new librarian needs to know when the budget year ends and whether to check only books or include serials and videos. To be clear, the department head should briefly discuss the timing of the budget and the possibility of extra money. It is also important to have written criteria for evaluating materials and a definition of the materials to include. This information is more effective in written than in oral form because it is probably too detailed to remember easily.

Using Jargon

Librarians use many words and phrases that have a special meaning in the library and are often incomprehensible to outsiders. These words should be avoided or explained. A supervisor who asks a new page to straighten up the chapter books or to remove books from the OPAC tables may get a look of blank incomprehension. Simply asking, "Do you understand?" may be ineffective because an employee may not wish to reveal ignorance. Asking "Is that clear?" puts the emphasis on the clarity of the statement rather than on the capacity of the listener. Sometimes a lack of understanding is shown by facial expression or body language. Repeat the message in different words or expand the statement and give more information. Asking the listener to repeat the message can help, but only if the listener rewords the original message; people can parrot words without understanding them.

Long-windedness

Some managers fail to communicate because they do not give enough information; others bury the message in a glut of extraneous information. When giving directions, it is usually best to omit alternatives that have not been chosen. For example, if a manager says

I want you to move the children's videos. They are too close to the reference desk. I had thought of putting them under the window in the picture book corner but they shouldn't be in the direct sunlight, and the little children might damage them anyway, so it would be best to put them in the space between the easy readers and the parents' collection. Anyone who is old enough to borrow them can easily find them there and whoever is on the reference desk will be able to keep an eye on them.

The person who is to do the moving may have difficulty sorting out what is to be done. Background information should be given only when it is useful; otherwise it is merely confusing.

Organization

Good organization can help to make even complicated messages more understandable. One organization scheme is to follow the rule of three:

- tell people what you are going to say,
- say it,
- tell them what you have said.

In practice, this might lead to an organization like this:

- The manager says, "Today I want to explain the plans for our summer reading blog."
- Then the manager describes the software and outlines the goals for the activity.
- The manager follows up, saying, "Now that you know the general outline of our plans, we can discuss the implementation in our branch. Does anyone have a suggestion as to how this will work here?"

This kind of organization does not stifle discussion but channels it in useful directions. Staff members understand the overall structure and do not waste time trying to plan from scratch. Although impractical ideas and plans may still be suggested, the group as a whole will have some guidelines as to what is feasible. Once people understand the context, the group should be able to select useful ideas.

A similar type of organization works when training a new employee. For example, the statement, "Today I will explain how our overdue system works," would be followed by an explanation and concluded with the statement, "That's the general outline of our procedures. Helen Chung will be able to answer specific questions that come up. Are the overall procedures clear now?" It takes practice to learn how much detail should be included in an explanation. Organizing the message will help make it clear no matter how brief or detailed the specifics are.

Barriers to Communication

A supervisor's attitude can become a barrier to effective communication. Attitudes that set up walls between people include:

The "That's impossible" reaction. If a new staff member suggests that picture books should be interfiled with the fiction collection, the first reaction may be to say, "That wouldn't work." This not only kills this suggestion, but also reduces the chance of getting other ideas in the future. Any idea brought forward should receive courteous attention. Even if the idea is rejected, the response should affirm the validity of making suggestions.

A joking or flippant response. If a librarian jokes about pages' or colleagues' suggestions, communication is likely to be cut off. It takes time for a new staff member to understand when a supervisor is joking. It is best to avoid jokes about serious matters until a good working relationship has developed. Heavy-handed humor, practical jokes, and sarcasm should always be avoided. Needless to say, jokes that make fun of ethnic, racial, disabled, age, or gender groups must never be used.

The "Hurry up, I'm busy" attitude. A staff member should never be brushed off when trying to present an idea. If you are working on something that must be finished, arrange a time to listen, or ask for the suggestion in writing. Every staff member deserves a chance to be heard.

The "I've been here a long time and I know all the answers" attitude. Some supervisors cut off discussion by saying "We tried that 10 years ago and it didn't work," or something similar. Judging what will work in the future by what has been successful in the past is dangerous. Times change, and libraries and their clientele change too.

FORMAT OF COMMUNICATION

Managers spend much of their time communicating with staff and patrons. Within the department, most communicating is done by talking, sending email, or writing memos. Each of these channels has advantages for some purposes.

Face-to-Face Communication

The greatest advantage of face-to-face communication is that it gives an opportunity for immediate feedback. The manager hears what the listener has to say and can observe his or her body language and facial expressions. To use face-to-face communication to best advantage, a manager should spend as much time listening as talking. Concentrating on the message given rather than on the one being received is a waste of time. The listener's reaction to a message and feedback on it is what makes the interaction useful.

Some useful techniques to encourage interaction:

- Look at the individuals or group. Make eye contact with an individual. With a group, look around and include each individual.
- Notice signs of disagreement or boredom and acknowledge them. For example, "You seem to disagree. Am I wrong in saying we have a vandalism problem?" or "Have you heard all this before? Why don't we move on to discuss solutions instead of talking about the problem."
- Allow the listeners to move the discussion along when they are ready. There is no real communication when an individual or group listens to someone without having an opportunity to respond.
- Listen closely and pay attention to what the other person says. Even if it seems trivial, the manager owes the staff member the courtesy of listening.
- Ask questions to clarify points of disagreement or gaps in information.

Written Communication

Face-to-face communication is not always the most appropriate choice; written communication has the advantage of precision and permanence. For an important issue, both oral and written communication may be needed. The preliminary oral discussion allows for the free flow of ideas and suggestions or the airing of complaints. The written follow-up enables each participant to read and remember what was discussed and what decisions were made.

Written communications are often most appropriate in these situations:

- announcing changes in library policy—new borrowing regulations, for example
- clarifying or changing library procedures
- establishing library closure dates or holiday hours
- reminding staff of deadlines
- calling attention to special events
- providing notes about a staff meeting or individual discussion

As a rule, any important staff information should be given in both oral and written form. The more detailed the information, the more important it is to have it in writing.

The principles of clarity and organization that hold for oral communication apply equally to writing. Brevity is desirable, most staff members scan memos quickly; very few read more than a page. When some staff members need additional background information, the memo should suggest who to ask or where to look it. Jargon and clichés should be avoided. The message should be stated succinctly, usually in a style similar to spoken language. Do not write

All personnel are requested to pay strict attention to the regulations about allowing food in the public areas of the library. An increase in the incidence of insect pests has been noted by the maintenance staff. This has required more frequent use of pesticides and has increased the workload for maintenance people. Children and their parents should be advised of the existence of our policy and told that infringement will result in the loss of library privileges.

A more effective message would be

Please remember that no food is allowed in the public areas of the library. Roaches have been seen in the children's room during the past month. If you see children or parents eating or carrying food into the library, ask them to take the food outside and eat it there. Children who persist in bringing food to the library will be denied entry.

Email Messages

The number of emails facing a librarian every morning when she turns on the computer seems to increase daily. Messages from staff and from the public as well as ads, professional association announcements, and spam clutter everyone's mailbox. Even though many people complain about the number of emails they have to deal with, these messages have become indispensable in running a library. Handling email effectively keeps the department running more smoothly.

Investigate all the options in your email system. Most services provide filters that send messages into folders according to their urgency. You could put messages from within your library into one folder, messages from associations in another, personal messages in still another. (Often it is useful to use an entirely separate account such as an Internet based Yahoo, Google, or Hotmail address for family members and friends. Then you can deal with it separately on your lunch hour or another convenient time.) Most mailing lists offer the option of checking messages on the web site rather than having them delivered to your inbox.

Many email providers allow you to have more than one address for an account. If you are active in an association, you could use a different email address for messages relating to that work and save your main address for messages directly related to your job.

If your library allows parents to register their children for library programs by email, set up a separate mailing address, so that all the registration chores can be handled separately from other tasks.

Like any other communication, email messages should be clear and concise. There are specific techniques that make email easier to read and understand.

- Make the subject heading clear and useful. If a message is particularly important, add URGENT to the subject line, but be careful of overdoing this. If a message does not require a response, add FYI (for your information) to the subject line to indicate this.
- Delete old subject headings. A string of messages and replies with the same old subject heading is confusing.
- Never write a one-word message. Saying "yes" or "agreed" without quoting the previous document forces the recipient to waste time checking back.
- Write short paragraphs. Most people do not like to read long blocks of text online.
- When including a web link, write out the whole address including http:// so the recipient can link directly to the site. It is convenient to put a web link on a separate line.
- Using ALL CAPS to call attention to a particular section of a message is often considered rude. If you use this technique, do so sparingly.
- Avoid the use of graphic emoticons except in messages to people you know well. They can appear unprofessional and some email programs do not accept them.
- Use a spell checker to avoid careless mistakes and typos.
- Add a signature to your emails. Generally, a professional signature should include your name and title, the name of the library, and often a link to the library website.
- When replying to an email message, choose the "reply" option if only the writer of the message needs the information you are sending, and "reply all" if the information would be useful to everyone who received the original message.
- Copy your message to the people who would receive copies of a written memo on the subject. This may include the administrator, individual staff members, or a professional colleague.

Telephone Communication

Telephones are not often used within a department except when a staff members calls in to report an absence or lateness. Every telephone messages should be carefully recorded by whichever staff member receives it. When a message is left, it is important to indicate what kind of follow-up is expected.

Sometimes a telephone call involves an absence regulated by the employment agreement, such as a certain number of days allowed for a death in the family. In such cases the supervisor should send the staff member a letter clarifying the length of time allowed for the absence. This should be done in a humane way to indicate that the supervisor sympathizes with the staff member's loss, but it is important that the individual understands the library's expectations. Misunderstandings frequently arise when such information is only given orally or when the supervisor assumes that an individual is aware of the appropriate policy.

REFERENCES AND ADDITIONAL READING

Brophy, Peter, and Coulling, Kate. 1996. *Quality Management for Information and Library Managers.* Brookfield, VT: Aslib Gower.

Carson, Paula Phillips, Carson, Kerry David, and Phillips, Joyce Schouest. 1995. *The Library Manager's Deskbook: 102 Expert Solutions to 101 Common Dilemmas.* Chicago: American Library Association.

Cole, Kris. 2002. *The Complete Idiot's Guide to Clear Communication.* New York: Penguin.

Crittendon, Robert. 2002. *The New Manager's Starter Kit; Essential Tools for Doing the Job Right.* New York: American Management Association.

Giesecke, Joan, ed. 1997. *Practical Help for New Supervisors.* Chicago: American Library Association.

Heller, Robert. 1998. *Making Decisions.* Essential Managers. New York: DK Publishing.

———. 1998. *Motivating People.* Essential Managers. New York: DK Publishing

Kratz, Abby, and Flannery, Melinda. 1997. Communication Skills. In *Practical Help for New Supervisors,* ed. Joan Giesecke, 43–57. Chicago: American Library Association.

McCallister, Myrna J., and Patterson, Thomas H. 1997. Conducting Effective Meetings. In *Practical Help for New Supervisors,* ed. Joan Giesecke, 58–74. Chicago: American Library Association.

Panszczyk, Linda A. 2004. *HR How-to—Intergenerational Issues: Everything You Need to Know about Dealing with Employees of All Generations in the Workplace.* Chicago: CCH Knowledge Point.

Staerkel, Kathleen, Fellows, Mary, and Nespeca, Sue McCleaf eds. 1995. *Youth Services Librarians as Managers: A How-to Guide from Budgeting to Personnel.* Chicago: American Library Association.

4

Recruiting and Retaining Staff

Children using library services today may be at home, in the library, on a cell phone, or accessing a wireless network in a coffee shop. No matter where they are or how they contact the library, they deserve proactive staff members who understand their needs and are enthusiastic about serving them. Libraries spend more than half of their budgets on staff salaries because the staff is the key element in providing services.

SOURCES FOR STAFF

All staff members play an important role in providing services in a children's department, but it is the professional staff who set the tone and direction of services. Most public libraries recruit their professional staff from library schools that offer an American Library Association accredited program. In recruiting staff, libraries compete with corporations, government departments, schools, and other organizations that recognize the value of a degree in library and information studies

The work of a children's librarian is not highly visible in the media or in the day-to-day life of most people, so not many young people seek it as a career goal. One way of increasing the pool of applicants is for librarians to publicize the importance and interest of the work. Some libraries have had success in working with schools to present talks at career days and to provide information for guidance counselors. Going into high schools and colleges to publicize information about what children's librarians do can help recruit a diverse group of young people into the profession.

The message to take to young people is the challenge and rewards of working with children in a library setting. As one children's coordinator writes, "work as a youth services librarian offers a career with the potential for creativity, variety, and independence" (Salvadore 1995, 75).

Candidates for recruitment into the field may be found among the pages and clerical workers in the library as well as among patrons. A part-time library job during high school or college years is often the impetus that leads to a library career. Department heads should notice signs of interest among pages and clerical workers and find time to discuss the possibility of going on to professional library work. Occasionally the parent of a child patron will decide he or she wants to become a librarian.

PROCESS OF HIRING

After a position becomes open, due to the library board's approval of a new position or to a staff member's resignation, the department will work with the chief librarian and the library's personnel officer to find the most appropriate person for the job. In almost all library systems, job openings are posted first within the system and often within the municipality. If there is no suitable candidate within the system, an advertisement is placed in library journals, electronic job services, and professional mailing lists. Additional recruitment may be done at professional conferences or library schools.

Any advertisement for a position must meet government standards for fairness and follow the format approved by the municipality. It should be specific enough to encourage qualified applicants and discourage those without sufficient education or experience. A few words about the community and the library may arouse interest among applicants.

SAMPLE AD FOR CHILDREN'S LIBRARIAN

YOUTH LIBRARIAN. Become part of a winning team in an active library system serving a five county region in scenic Idaho. Wild River Public Library is seeking an energetic individual who will bring imagination and creativity to all aspects of service including programming, outreach, and collection development. Requirements include an MLS from an accredited library school, a current driver's license, and the willingness to work some evenings and weekends. The Wild River Public Library is an equal opportunity employer. Starting salary range $32,500–$38,500 plus competitive benefits. Visit www.wildriverpl.org. Send resume to Jane Doe, Black Wild River Public Library, 200 Grizzly Road, Wild River, ID. Emailed resumes can be sent to janedoe@wrpl.org

---

The ads published in recent issues of *American Libraries* or on electronic mailing lists may suggest ideas for wording and for details to include.

Interviewing

In large library systems, preliminary screening of job applicants is usually done by the Human Resources Department. In smaller libraries, the chief librarian and the head of the children's department may go over each application. Whatever the procedure, it is important for the person in charge of children's services be closely involved in selecting new children's librarians. Experience in children's services is the best background for understanding the demands of the job and the suitability of individual candidates.

Most libraries like to interview five or six candidates for each open position. If there are many out-of-town candidates, some of the interviewing may be done by telephone, but personal interviews are preferable. Often a library conference offers an opportunity to conduct interviews with several candidates.

In preparing to interview a candidate, a librarian should

- Carefully review the application
- Check references
- Prepare questions to allow the candidate to demonstrate knowledge and skills
- Create an up-to-date packet of information about the library and the community
- Establish procedures and decide which staff members will help with the interview

In some library systems the human resources officer conducts a preliminary interview and passes on the most promising candidates to the head of the children's department and finally to the chief librarian. Other libraries prefer a more informal group meeting with three or four librarians present. Whatever the method, the purpose is to find the best individual for a particular position. The interview is also the opportunity to convince the strongest candidate to take the position when it is offered.

The interview should always be held in a private, welcoming atmosphere, either an office or a meeting room. Water should be provided for the candidate and often tea, coffee, or a soft drink is offered. This allows the interviewers to establish a pleasant friendly tone. A few minutes of small talk can help to ease the way into the more formal interview.

Both the interviewers and the candidate use the interview as an opportunity to learn more about each other and to assess how well they might work together. When interviewing several candidates for a job, it is useful to ask the same question of each candidate so comparisons can be made. At the same time, each candidate should be allowed to talk freely and to express ideas, so each interview may move in a slightly different direction.

Before deciding on the questions to ask the candidate, interviewers must think about the qualifications needed. The job application supplies information about formal qualifications such as undergraduate and professional degrees and past experience in libraries. The interview should focus on the personal characteristics and attitudes of each applicant. If a new librarian is to work in a small branch library without direct supervision, decision-making skills and initiative are important. If the new librarian will be working with several diverse language and cultural groups, then language skills and cultural sensitivity should be assessed.

The interviewer will want to open the conversation by briefly describing the job and the objectives of the interview. The candidate has already read a job description, but it is helpful to start off by reviewing the job description because the applicant may have questions. Be sure you have a thorough understanding of what the job involves, especially if the candidate is a recent library school graduate. You don't want to exaggerate the difficulty of the job, but to give a fair estimate of the pace and rigor of the work and the amount of support available from other staff. If there have been behavior problems with children in the branch, for example, you want to find a candidate who will view that as a challenge rather than an overwhelming problem.

The next step after telling the candidate about the position, is to ask questions. Open-ended questions are often best because they give a candidate a chance to reveal how they think and how they would react to the job. Try to avoid yes or no questions. Instead of asking "Have you worked with preschool children before?" you might phrase it, "Tell me about your experience working with preschoolers." Also, avoid questions that put words in the candidate's mouth. Don't say, "You have helped to set up a website before, haven't you?" but rather "What experience have you had working with websites?"

Observe the way candidates answer questions and their body language. Both can tell you a great deal about a candidate's attitude and confidence.

Typical questions asked in an interview might include

- Why do you want to be a children's librarian?
- What part of the job do you look forward to the most?
- What has been your experience with public libraries as a library user?
- What age group of children are you most comfortable with? The least comfortable?
- How would you handle a situation in which a parent complained that a book was inappropriate for children and should be removed from the library?

All questions in a job interview must ask for information relevant to the position. Asking personal questions is not acceptable. All questions must conform to the guidelines issued by the Equal Employment Opportunity Commission. Examples of questions that are prohibited include the following:

- How old are you?
- Are you healthy?
- Do you smoke?
- Are you married?
- Do you have children?
- Do you have any plans to become pregnant?
- What are your childcare arrangements?
- What is the occupation of your spouse?
- What kind of discharge did you receive from the military?
- Have you had any major illnesses in the past five years?
- Have you ever been treated for drug addiction or alcoholism?

In general, all non-job-related questions are prohibited, although some specific questions about physical abilities are acceptable.

- Can you meet the attendance requirements of this job?
- Can you perform the functions of this job with or without reasonable accommodation?
- Can you describe or demonstrate how you would perform these functions? (Russell 1997, 1)

Keep careful notes during each interview so comparisons between the candidates can be made. The same questions should be asked of each candidate, although follow-up questions may vary. Try to maintain a neutral attitude throughout the interview and do not indicate to the candidate what their chances are. After allowing a few days for consideration, all the people involved in interviewing the candidates should discuss each interview. If the group does not agree on which candidate was the strongest, you may need a second interview. Eventually a decision must be made and the successful candidate offered the job. As soon as the position is accepted, other candidates should be thanked for their applications and told the position has been filled.

Orientation of New Staff

For permanent, full-time employees, the department head usually conducts the introduction to the department. If another person is designated to do this, the department head should meet and welcome the new employee as soon as possible. Part-time employees, especially pages, are often introduced to the library by the member of the clerical staff who supervises their work. The department head should meet and welcome each new page personally.

Orientation to the physical environment of the library is important because libraries are complex organizations. Every employee needs to know the location of various departments and services, all entrances and exits, staff lounges and facilities, and the location of other branches in the system. A floor plan of the library often helps to orient new employees. Within the department, new employees need to know the location of various sections—the reference, picture book, and program areas—as well as computers and photocopiers, meeting rooms, public access washrooms, staff lounge and lockers, and public telephones. It is easy for a person who has worked in one building for several years to forget to mention some of these facilities. A checklist can help to avoid this and serves as a reminder of information to be covered during the tour.

Introducing a new employee to people working in the department, as well as relevant people outside the department, is as important as giving the tour of the building. Whoever is conducting the tour should be sure to introduce each person who works in the department and should make notes to ensure that the people who are off duty will be introduced as soon as possible. A welcoming and personal introduction to the department, as opposed to being thrust into a new situation without knowing co-workers, can make a crucial difference in shaping the newcomer's attitude.

In some departments, it is customary to have a coffee hour or staff meeting to introduce new professional staff. This occasion gives both new and old staff members an opportunity to talk casually and to fix identities firmly in mind. It also gives the department head a chance to explain the new person's role and set the tone for a smooth and pleasant transition.

Social customs such as contributing to a coffee fund, taking turns bringing refreshments, or having an annual staff potluck supper should be explained at this time. Details about who is responsible for making coffee in the morning and where employees are expected to park may not seem important, but they make a difference in establishing friendly working relationships.

The time involved in teaching a new employee the procedures to be mastered varies with the position. A new page may be expected to shelve and check materials in and out with an hour or two of training, while a new librarian will spend many weeks learning different aspects of the job. Whatever the level of training, the department head should make sure it is effective. Simple procedures should be clearly described and demonstrated. The new employee should watch someone perform the task and then practice. Few people can remember oral instructions for long, so a written description of the procedure should be available for future reference.

STAFF RETENTION

Library jobs are complex and demanding and loss of a staff member causes difficulties throughout the department. A library manager should work hard to make sure all staff members find their jobs challenging and satisfying, so they will be less likely to look for other employment and more likely to provide excellent services. The value of a library to its patrons depends on the quality and dedication of its staff. Library managers should never take staff members for granted but should consider thoughtfully the best ways to help them develop skills and professionalism.

Ongoing Staff Training

Libraries frequently introduce new practices and modify old ones, so staff training must be continuous. Conferences and workshops offer training, especially for professional staff, and an effective administrator encourages staff members to attend such meetings because they not only learn specific skills but have a chance to discuss new ideas with colleagues. Meeting colleagues from other libraries or other professions often leads to an exchange of ideas, which can broaden the scope of a library's work. There is a danger that a staff member will choose to attend workshops in only one area—storytelling or puppetry, for example—and will resist suggestions that a course in website design might be more valuable. Most library departments need staff members who are proficient in a variety of skills, and one of the tasks of the department head is to encourage a broad-based continuing education program.

Large library systems sometimes provide staff training for children's librarians within the system. This program may be directed by a youth services coordinator, or each branch may take a turn planning a workshop. Depending on the budget, these workshops may be directed by outside experts or allow local library staff to exchange ideas. In either case, getting together to share ideas about programming or services generally benefits the staff and should be encouraged on a regular basis. The stimulation of new ideas can enliven a department's services and prevent staff burnout.

No matter how extensive the opportunities for continuing education outside the department, some staff training within the department is necessary. The introduction of new technology frequently requires formal staff training. When a library is planning a major change, such as a installing a new computer system, careful thought should be given to staff training. The usual practice is to have outside experts instruct a small group of library staff members. Those staff members train other staff members until eventually everyone can handle the new technology. All staff members must have the opportunity not only for instruction but also for sufficient practice to become comfortable with the system. The department head may require all employees to use new equipment because employees who do not practice at least twice a week tend to lose skills. After the skills have been mastered, most staff members will incorporate use of the new technology into their normal work practices.

Introducing even minor changes, starting a staff blog in the children's department, for example, requires carefully planned staff training. Each individual should be given ample time to practice until he or she feels comfortable. Staff members show various degrees of interest in new technology, but few people are actively hostile to it. All staff members who might be called upon to help patrons with computers must become comfortable in dealing with them. When one or two staff members are allowed to become the resident experts and monopolize the computer facilities, service usually suffers. Because computers are standard equipment in most children's departments, the department head should expect all appropriate staff members to be able to use them, give instruction on them, and know when a service call must be made.

Not all staff training involves technology. Changing community demographics may call for continuing education sessions about working with different cultural groups, people with disabilities, or the aging. Legislative changes may mandate training in copyright regulations or Internet policy. Social conditions may make it necessary to teach staff members better security measures. Some library administrators make all decisions about how to deliver staff training, others leave the decision to the discretion of the department head. The department head should always try to remain aware of the issue and be ready to give suggestions or provide training when necessary. Figure 4.1 gives a breakdown of the components that should be included in this kind of training presentation.

Although testing is rarely an acceptable way to check what the staff has learned, a survey evaluating training sessions might be helpful in assessing how well the training program works . Short questions and answers in the staff newsletter, bulletin board, or online, especially questions phrased in a humorous way, can remind staff of what they heard at a workshop. Although administrators often initiate ideas for staff training, asking staff members to suggest topics can lead to more active learning. Managers are sometimes unaware of staff members' areas of concern.

Effective Meetings

Almost all employees complain about having to attend meetings, but they feel short-changed if they are not informed about library developments. A good manager tries to organize meetings that are informative, effective, and achieve the goals of the organization. Meetings can accomplish many different objectives.

- share information
- solve problems
- eliminate time-consuming repetition in individual sessions
- generate ideas

Figure 4.1
Elements of educational presentation.

Introduction	Be sure the staff understands the scope of the topic: what will be included and what is excluded. Sometimes a video, Power Point, or other media presentation can introduce a topic and arouse interest.
Motivation	It is important that staff members believe the training is necessary, and the topic important. An authoritative outside speaker is often more persuasive than the department head or another staff member.
Explanation	Experts from inside or outside the library can present detailed information. Sometimes a panel of experts can present different facets of the topic. When possible, information should be given in more than one format: print, visual, audio, for example. Interactive sessions with opportunities for questions and discussion engage people more than passive presentations. If the training includes suggested actions, such as the way to react to a hostile intruder, role playing makes the learning more realistic and memorable than straight presentation.
Reinforcement	Print materials help people remember what they have heard and seen. The library website or a departmental blog is a good way to facilitate ongoing staff discussion and provide reference materials. Most effective training includes several types of reinforcement.

- gain cooperation
- promote team spirit and consensus
- lessen impact of rumors
- assign responsibilities and initiate action
- provide training in new techniques and provide staff development activities (McCallister and Patterson 1997, 59)

Effective meetings are usually carefully planned. The first question a manager should ask is whether a meeting is the best way to accomplish the objective wanted. If the primary goal is to inform staff about a change in procedures or personnel, sending a memo or email message may be more effective than calling a meeting. Meetings are generally good at generating discussion and raising questions, so if the purpose is to introduce a policy decision that might be controversial or appear threatening to some staff, a meeting is probably the best way to introduce the subject.

A written agenda for staff meetings helps individuals know what to expect and how to prepare. The agenda should go to participants several days before the scheduled meeting and should include the date, time, and place of the meeting, and the items to be discussed. Set a limit on the time allocated for each item. Often it is useful to specify the type of meeting—decision making, planning, reporting. Send out background material with the agenda as well as suggestions about papers or information to be brought to the meeting. If there will be guests, it is courteous to let staff know their names and the reason for their presence.

Organizational cultures vary in the degree of formality of meetings. In some libraries, participants sit comfortably in a circle of chairs and coffee and cookies are provided. In others, the setting is a formal board room and water is the only refreshment. A manager should balance between maintaining an aloof style that might be intimidating and having the meeting degenerate into a cozy but ineffective social event. Staff members appreciate amenities, but they also want a well-organized and efficient meeting that doesn't waste time.

Even though the agenda and information has been sent out ahead of time, it makes sense to bring extra copies to the meeting. Arrange for a recorder to keep minutes. Generally action minutes, recording decisions rather than the group discussion, are sufficient for regular meetings. If controversial items of particular importance are discussed, it may be preferable to tape a portion of the meeting for future reference rather than try to capture the discussion in written minutes.

Guidelines for effective meetings:

- start on time
- invite new items for the agenda when meeting starts
- appoint a recorder
- ensure each participant a chance to speak without intimidation
- stick to the agenda
- summarize decisions and action plans when meeting is concluded
- distribute minutes within 24 hours
- save a file copy of minutes

Rewarding Staff Achievement

Financial benefits to library staff are controlled by city administrators or the library board who make the salary decisions for all employees. Unlike many managers in profit-making organizations, the library manager may have little control over how library salaries are allocated. This is particularly true in a unionized library, but generally applies to all public libraries.

Managers in public sector organizations should be aware of the ways in which non-monetary rewards can be used to recognize employee achievement. Libraries benefit when employees are happy in their jobs

Among the non-monetary rewards that have been used one of the most popular is flexible scheduling of work. Flextime allows employees the freedom to plan work schedules that fit their life patterns. Because the library is a public service organization, this freedom is limited by the need to have the library staffed during busy hours of the day and days of the week. Even working within these constraints, however, a manager can often find a way to allow employees some voice in their scheduling. Ordinarily allowing flextime would be a decision made for the entire library rather than one department, but it is an important enough issue for a manager to advocate on behalf of all staff.

Another way to increase employees' job satisfaction is to provide opportunities for career development. Some forms this can take are

- job rotation to broaden competencies
- sending staff to training courses or workshops
- supporting participation in professional associations
- inviting suggestions
- encouraging collaborative problem solving
- honoring job commitment

Celebrations of achievement through public recognition of particularly outstanding service or a project completed makes employees to feel appreciated. "Achievement is its own reward—but it is never enough. Achievers also want recognition. Even a simple 'thank you' is an important, underused reward that costs nothing" (Heller 1998, 61). Writing a note to an employee who has done an outstanding job is welcome, so is recognition in a meeting or newsletter. The only danger of this kind of recognition is that some employees may decide the manager has a few favorite employees who are valued more highly than others. When a department head recognizes achievement, he or she must be sure all individuals have an equal chance to be honored. A star system where some employees are highly visible and others work in obscurity can foster an unhappy and discontented work environment.

A manager should recognize the benefits of rewarding staff achievement, but be aware of the danger of playing favorites. A balanced approach should allow each employee's strengths to be recognized and encourage greater job commitment.

Handling Potential Conflict Situations

Most managers like to believe that relationships within the department are friendly and supportive; they are shocked and unprepared when a conflict erupts. Unfortunately, no matter how well managed the department, disagreements between staff members or between a staff member and the department head occur. A department head should never react as though disagreements were a personal attack or a reflection upon individual management styles. Instead, the conflict should be treated objectively as a normal part of life within any institutional setting.

Conflict about Work Habits

Most library departments are small enough for all of the employees to fall under the direct supervision of the department head. Sometimes a second level of management oversees clerical assistants and pages. The small size allows direct relationships and frequent opportunities for face-to-face meetings. The department head wants to be friendly and approachable, but this congeniality may occasionally conflict with the need to maintain an efficient workflow.

Because of the small size of work groups, library workers often have greater flexibility than workers in factories or large offices. For example, a new staff member who tells the department head that she has instructed her eight-year-old son to call her every afternoon as soon as he arrives home from school, may be encouraged to receive this call. If one day the department head notices three patrons are waiting for the attention of this staff member, who is on her cell phone giving detailed instructions about which play clothes to wear, the supervisor is likely to feel that library service is suffering. What is the most effective form of intervention?

The supervisor may solve the immediate problem by offering to help the patrons, and the call will probably end quickly. However, more direct discussion is also needed. The supervisor should speak to the staff member privately to ensure that the situation does not occur again.

The supervisor must first find out exactly what happened. If there was a crisis at home and the call had to be extended, the incident might be overlooked. Anyone can occasionally have an emergency that disrupts library service. It is more likely, however, that the calls have become longer or more frequent because either the employee or the son enjoys them. If the child has fallen into the habit of calling three or four times during the afternoon to ask about one thing or another, the employee's workload will suffer.

The supervisor must set limits on the calls and see that the limits are adhered to. A warning may be sufficient to remind the employee of other obligations and reduce the number and length of calls. The supervisor must unobtrusively observe whether the librarian is spending an unacceptable amount of time on the telephone. It might be desirable for the child to call another library employee, with whom he will not be tempted to talk for long, to say he has arrived home safely. If the child needs to talk with his mother for a longer time, the employee might be encouraged to schedule her break, or even her lunch hour, when the child returns home. Then, the longer conversations can be conducted in the staff lounge.

Most libraries limit the use of library phones to library business. Staff members can use cell phones, email, or instant messaging for contacting family members. Because the use of cell phones in a library is distracting for patrons and staff alike, they should be used for personal calls only in staff lounges during break periods.

Most employees recognize that the library has a right to maintain working efficiency. They accept limitations on their behavior as long as they believe that the entire staff is being treated in the same way. In fact, a manager who does not require appropriate work habits is not likely to be respected as well as one who enforces reasonable and fair regulations. The department head should have close, friendly relationships with staff but owes it to the library to maintain effective library service.

Whether the problem is librarians shopping online instead of helping patrons, pages exchanging instant messages while working, or circulation clerks making inappropriate comments about children's book choices, the principles are the same. The supervisor should first ask questions to find out what is going on and whether the incident is a unique occurrence or a habitual pattern. Then the supervisor should interview the employee privately. The supervisor should always treat the employee with respect and try to understand the reasons for the problem behavior. Whatever steps are taken to resolve the issue should be based on changing the behavior, not on punishing the individual. The supervisor should explain why the behavior is a problem and describe appropriate behavior. Finally, it is up to the supervisor to suggest a solution. Usually it is better to suggest a different behavior rather than prohibiting problem activities. A clerk who makes disparaging comments about the books children choose might be advised to give each child a book list and suggest that they might enjoy those books.

A summary of the discussion should be recorded in writing for the staff member's personnel file. After choosing a solution, the supervisor must observe whether the undesirable activities cease. If the behavior occurs again, the supervisor should have another meeting with the staff member and follow up by sending the individual a written description of the agreed solution. The supervisor must keep a complete written record of problem behavior because it may eventually lead to dismissal. To terminate employment there must be a complete written record of the unsatisfactory performance and of all of the ways in which the supervisor worked with the individual to try to resolve the problem.

Dealing with Grievances

Most libraries have standard procedures to be followed when an employee files a complaint concerning a management decision. A department head should be familiar with the steps to take when a formal complaint, or grievance, is filed. These procedures are often determined by state regulations and may vary from one jurisdiction to another. If the library staff are members of a labor union, the union contract will govern grievance procedures. Whether determined by legal regulations or union rules, the steps are specific and should be carefully followed. Even when the complaint is not formally filed as a grievance, it should be handled in a way that is compatible with legal requirements.

The supervisor must take every complaint seriously and listen to what the employee says. Careful listening is a sign of respect for any employee. Occasionally a supervisor reacts to a complaint as if it were an idle comment. For example, a clerical staff member tells the department head that his vacation has been scheduled for August when he wanted it in early July. If the supervisor says something like "Oh, well the beach is better in August. Your tan will last longer," the employee's unhappiness and sense of grievance will grow. The supervisor's friendship with staff members should not interfere with the role of manager and the responsibility for mediating between the library administration and the staff.

After allowing the staff member to explain the grievance, the supervisor may need to ask other staff members about the facts of the case. Were the vacations schedules drawn up without working out overlapping requests? Did the circulation clerk fail to tell the pages they could go on their breaks? Has one librarian been assigned to work every Saturday for a month? Was a new circulation assistant scolded in front of library patrons? Supervisors must determine the accuracy of the charges before making any decision. Often, complaints are caused by misunderstandings that disappear when the facts are made clear.

If one employee treats another badly, the department head should try to rectify the situation and make sure it does not happen again. If someone did not receive the required break time, nothing can undo that action, but an apology and perhaps some extra break time will help to make up for the mistake. The supervisor's most important task is to correct the person who made the mistake and firmly impress upon him or her that it should not happen again. This means the supervisor should have a private interview with the individual, explain why the action was inappropriate, and request a change in behavior. A written account of this interview should be placed in the offender's personnel file so it will be available if something similar happens later.

A supervisor should try to find out how similar grievances have been handled in the past. A new supervisor can do this by looking at personnel records or talking with a human resources officer or with the chief librarian. Making a sharp break with tradition is usually unwise. Staff members expect the library's response to be consistent with past practice.

To sum up the steps to be taken when an employee makes a complaint:

1. Listen carefully to the employee's explanation of what happened.
2. Check the facts with library records and other staff members.
3. Find out who was responsible for the offending action.
4. Examine how previous grievances of the same type have been handled.
5. Speak privately to the employee who made the mistake and state clearly that the incorrect behavior must not happen again.
6. Offer an apology to the person who complained.
7. File a written record of the incident.
8. Check at appropriate times to ensure the offensive behavior does not happen again.

Preventing grievances is far better than trying to handle them when they arise. A supervisor should be sensitive to the mood of the department—not only among the librarians but also among the clerical staff and pages. Is there bickering, snide comments, or a set of cliques? These often indicate divisions among staff members that may cause problems later. If the library is undergoing changes—a large growth in community population or substantial building renovations—the added tension fosters an increase in complaints.

When these conditions exist, the department head should make an effort to develop a good spirit in the department. The department head should request additional staff members or budget increases if the workload is growing. If the staff believes the department head is trying to improve working conditions, they are likely to feel happier about their jobs. A manager who is seen to be working fairly and consistently to increase the library's effectiveness and who treats staff members with respect usually has fewer problems with grievances than one who appears remote and uninterested in or unaware of staff problems.

PERFORMANCE APPRAISAL

Evaluating a staff member's work is an important part of being a supervisor, although the task of performance appraisal is one many managers dislike. Evaluating another person's work requires objectivity as well as sensitivity to the strengths and weaknesses of each employee. Tact is especially important in evaluating a colleague with whom you work closely on a day-to-day basis.

Preparing to write a performance evaluation starts with keeping a personnel folder up-to-date and complete throughout the year. When a patron tells you that so-and-so found just the right materials for her child's homework project, or when you observe a page being particularly helpful to a child searching for a book, make a note and add it to the personnel file. Complaints or failures such as tardiness or mistakes should, of course, also be recorded. This file gives you the basis for an evaluation.

Usually the evaluation process starts with a request to each employee to write a statement about the year's goals, projects, and events. The employee should evaluate his or her own performance and record achievements on the job and in professional activities.

Most libraries have standard forms for performance evaluations. A typical example:

PERFORMANCE REVIEW

Name:
Position Title:
Department:
Review Completed By:
Date:
1. Responsibilities
2. Areas Where Performance Standards Are Being Met
3. Areas Where Improvement Is Required
4. How Are Improvements Going To Be Made?
5. Employee's Comments
Employee's signature_____ Date
Supervisor's signature_____ Date

The responsibilities listed are based on the employee's job description. An employee should not be faulted for not taking on responsibilities beyond those listed in the job description. This is why a well-written job description is so important. On the other hand, if an employee goes beyond the standards required by the job, while at the same time meeting all of the stated requirements, this achievement should be commended.

The most important part of the performance appraisal is the one-to-one interview with each staff member. This may be quite informal, especially for a long-time employee whose appraisals are consistently good, but it should not be omitted. The interview gives an opportunity to step back from daily work and consider what is being done on a yearly basis. This may lead to a discussion of new projects, or changes in routine. The supervisor may learn about new ideas and professional plans of an employee, which do not come up in the ordinary course of work.

For a new employee, or for one whose performance has not met expectations, the interview is crucial. If there is any chance that an employee might be laid off or not achieve tenure, every step of performance appraisal must be fully documented. Documentation of the failure in the form of written complaints, records of tardiness or absence, statistics on programs conducted or books selected in comparison with other employees should be available. After some discussion of possible reasons for the inadequate performance, the supervisor and employee should agree on steps to be taken to improve the rating for the following year. This agreement must be in writing and signed by both parties.

Although confronting staff members about negative performance is a difficult task for most supervisors, it is an important function of management and must be done throughout the year, not just during the annual performance appraisal. Tolerating inadequate job performance by one employee is unfair to other staff members who usually have to take over more than their share of duties. This causes resentment and lowers general staff morale. A supervisor should react promptly and carefully to performance failures.

In most libraries, a first or second minor offense such as being late for a shift, or failing to attend a required meeting calls for an oral reprimand. If the offense is repeated, the supervisor should send a memo to the person describing the behavior and stating that the offenses must stop. A written report should also be sent to administration officials. (A serious offense, for example, using abusive language toward a patron or staff member requires immediate written reprimand with a copy to higher administrators.) If the behavior does not change, the individual should receive a strongly worded reminder laying out the further disciplinary action that will be taken if the offenses continue. An example of a series of memos demonstrating this sequence is given in Orlando (1995, 130–131).

Like other important personnel records, memos concerning unsatisfactory performance should be printed out dated and signed by both the supervisor and the employee. Electronic documents may not be acceptable in formal procedures if the individual contests any of the actions taken. Copies should remain permanently in the individual's file.

Performance appraisal may not be as pleasant as other aspects of a manager's job, but it is an important part of maintaining a well-run department. A supervisor who is known as a fair and objective evaluator is likely to win the respect of both employees and administrators

REFERENCES AND ADDITIONAL READING

Adkins, Denice, and Hussey, Lisa K. 2005. Unintentional Recruiting for Diversity [July/August 2005]. *Public Libraries* 44: 229–233.

Bell, Arthur H., and Smith, Doyle M. 2004. *Winning with Difficult People: Barron's Business Success Guides*. Hauppauge, NY: Barron's.

Crittendon, Robert. 2002. *The New Manager's Starter Kit: Essential Tools for Doing the Job Right*. New York: American Management Association.

Giesecke, Joan ed. 1997. *Practical Help for New Supervisors*. Chicago: American Library Association.

Heller, Robert. 1998. *Motivating People: Essential Managers*. New York: DK Publishing.

McCallister, Myrna J., and Patterson, Thomas H. 1997. Conducting Effective Meetings. In *Practical Help for New Supervisors*, ed. Joan Giesecke, 58–74. Chicago: American Library Association.

Orlando, Marie C. 1995. Staff Evaluation. In *Youth Services Librarians as Managers: A How-to Guide from Budgeting to Personnel,* eds. Kathleen Staerkel, Mary Fellows, and Sue McCleaf Nespeca, 115–133. Chicago: American Library Association.

Padilla, Irene M., and Patterson, Thomas H. 1997. Rewarding Employees Nonmonetarily. In *Practical Help for New Supervisors,* ed. Joan Giesecke, 35–44. Chicago: American Library Association

Panszczyk, Linda A. 2004. *HR How-to—Intergenerational Issues: Everything You Need to Know about Dealing with Employees of All Generations in the Workplace.* Chicago: CCH Knowledge Point.

Russell, Thyra K. 1997. Interviewing. In *Practical Help for New Supervisors,* ed. Joan Giesecke, 6–14. Chicago: American Library Association.

Salvadore, Maria B. 1995. Recruiting and Retaining Youth Services Librarians. In *Youth Services Librarians as Managers; A How-to Guide from Budgeting to Personnel,* eds. Kathleen Staerkel, Mary Fellows and Sue McCleaf Nespeca, 74–82. Chicago: American Library Association.

Staerkel, Kathleen, Fellows, Mary, and Nespeca, Sue McCleaf eds. 1995. *Youth Services Librarians as Managers: A How-to Guide from Budgeting to Personnel.* Chicago: American Library Association.

Wendover, Robert W. 2002. *Smart Hiring: The Complete Guide to Finding and Hiring the Best Employees.* Naperville, IL: Sourcebooks, Inc.

5

Communication and Leadership

Public libraries are frequently asked to demonstrate their value to the taxpayers they serve. Chief administrators represent the institution to governing bodies and must justify every aspect of the library. Department heads are responsible for keeping administrators and other staff members aware of the programs and services of the children's services department.

Libraries are complex organizations divided into a number of departments, each of which has a different function. Some of these departments form an operating chain; for example, the acquisitions and technical services departments receive orders for materials from the public service departments, acquire and prepare the materials, and deliver them to the ordering department, which provides public access to them. This keeps the acquisitions department aware of materials in the public service departments. Other departments may have little interaction with one another. Adult services, especially in large libraries, may operate quite independently of the children's department and may be unaware of changes in either materials or services. This isolation is dangerous for both departments because the public views the library as a unified service.

Larger libraries may have a number of departments on which the children's department relies to give quality service. There may be a marketing department that will help publicize children's programs. There may be a custodial and maintenance department that needs to keep the children's department clean and in working order. And there may be a computer/electronic resources group that is responsible for hardware, software, and the library's website. In smaller libraries there may be individuals who perform these functions who do not report to the head of the children's department. It is as important to communicate effectively with these colleagues as it is with the other public service departments.

BUILDING AWARENESS WITHIN THE LIBRARY

Adult and children's services are complementary and individuals will at various times draw on both departments. Most library users are introduced to the library through the children's department. If they enjoy the experience, children often become users of adult services. The patron's transition between departments should be smooth and easy; this happens when the departments work closely together.

When budgets are allocated, the importance of children's services should be apparent to administrators and other people in the system. Some children's librarians believe that if they work hard and provide good programs and materials, the rest of the library staff will notice their achievements without prompting. Unfortunately, people are so busy with their own work that they can easily miss what is happening in other departments. In a large library the children's department must publicize their work to avoid having staff members in other departments view the children's department as providing essentially the same materials and services it did 5 or 10 years ago.

Because of the specialized work and the physical isolation of some children's departments, people who work there may be unfamiliar to staff members in other departments. The head of children's services should encourage staff members to attend social events, staff and committee meetings, and other all-library activities.

Youth services personnel should get to know other staff members and tell them about what is going on in the children's department. They can develop informal contacts with staff in other departments and by participating in general library work. Children's staff should volunteer for committees and show an interest in the activities of all library departments.

Service on library committees is an important way for staff members to work together on issues that affect the entire library. Children's librarians who demonstrate expertise in technology or reference service and who offer sound suggestions about solving library problems earn the respect of colleagues. Their organizational abilities and clever ideas can be demonstrated in committee work. When the library staff comes to know children's librarians as bright, well-rounded professionals, they are more likely to respect the work of the children's department.

Children's librarians must do more than remind other staff members of who they are and of what is going on in the children's department. They must also convince others of the value of the work. It is important to avoid the cuteness trap—being seen as a nice person who has a fun job working with cute little children, making cute little puppets, and reading picture books. If staff members from the children's department sit in the staff lounge discussing the number of paper pumpkins they made that morning, other staff members may believe the work of the department is trivial. Every department has its share of non-professional work, but the reasons for the work are professional. Instead of talking about trifles, librarians should mention some of the program's goals—the knowledge of shapes and colors children gain from handling the pumpkins, for example. Obviously, a coffee break or lunch hour is not the time for giving a lecture on child development, but it is wise to be aware of the stereotypes that may be reinforced by talking only about the details rather than the rationale of the programs.

Librarians in small libraries may not face the image problems that occur in large systems. Nonetheless, many of the general principles of professional communication hold true in small and informal contexts, especially if there is a change of personnel.

EFFECTIVE INFORMAL COMMUNICATION

Informal communication goes on constantly among colleagues in the work place. Much informal communication is face-to-face, but telephone conversations, memos, and email play a role. To make the communication as effective as possible choose the channel your listener prefers—stopping by the office for a chat, telephoning, writing a memo, sending an email. The channel you choose should suit your listener and your purpose, not your own preference.

Face-to-Face Communication

Advantages

- immediate feedback on message
- speaker can modify the message if listener indicates a problem
- allows two-way communication
- speaker can invite immediate comments and questions

Disadvantages

- listener may not listen carefully or take message seriously
- listener may argue
- unexpected response may throw the speaker off balance
- speaker may be tempted to reply hastily and inappropriately to a comment

In talking with an administrator, a department head should think about the style of presentation. Sometimes an administrator is a man and the children's librarian is a woman, and this may increase communication problems. Research on the way men and women express themselves at work suggests that many women undermine their authority in their speech. Women more often than men speak indirectly (Tannen 1994). An example of speaking indirectly is saying, "I think it would be a good idea for us to hire a library clerk to replace the library technician who is leaving," instead of saying, "I've decided that we can save money by replacing our library technician with a clerk and assigning some of the technician's work to our professional staff."

Frequently women make themselves sound even more tentative by ending a statement with a rising voice as if asking a question: "A series of storyhours in the playground this summer might attract new users to the library[?]." Tannen believes women speak this way because they are trained to seek approval rather than to announce decisions. The result is that the female manager appears to be indecisive and asking for direction rather than making a statement. A department head should speak in a businesslike way, neither apologetic nor aggressive.

Telephone Calls

Telephone communication shares many of the advantages of face-to-face communication because feedback is immediate, questions can be raised and explanations given immediately; however, one big difference is that it is impossible to see the listener's body language. The speaker has to develop sensitivity to small clues such as silences and clearing of the throat. Chief librarians and other administrators usually have secretaries to screen their calls but many librarians do not; for the latter a call may interrupt an important task or duty. When you call, ask if you are calling at a convenient time. It is better to call back when the individual can give your message full attention than to talk to a person who is distracted by other duties. When someone calls you at an inconvenient time, ask if you can return the call later. Communication suffers when either person is trying to cope with more than one thing simultaneously. If you promise to return a call, you should do so as soon as possible. Playing telephone tag is annoying and can sabotage communication. Some people may find it worthwhile to set aside a certain time for telephone calls—the first hour in the morning, before the department is busy, for example—so calls can be taken or returned without distraction.

Because telephone calls are often sandwiched between other activities, they may be easily forgotten. When you receive a call it is usually wise to make notes about the caller, the date, the subject, and any action to be taken. These notes will remind you of promises and agreements. When an important agreement is reached on the telephone, follow it up with an email or memo formalizing and recording the decision.

Electronic Mail

Email messages are a major communication format in most libraries. They take the place of all but the most formal memo and can be sent quickly to individuals or groups within the system or elsewhere.

Advantages

- take little effort and are easy to send
- usually arrive more quickly at recipients' mailbox than other formats
- can be printed to provide a record of the message
- can be erased if message is ephemeral
- do not interrupt other people but can be read at the receiver's convenience

Disadvantages

- some people do not check their inboxes frequently
- may be lost in number of spam messages received
- unless a receipt notification is requested, the sender does not know whether message has been received
- technical problems can delay receipt of message

Using email effectively

1. Do not send unnecessary or trivial messages.
2. Make the subject heading clear and useful. If a message is particularly important, add URGENT to the subject line, but be careful of overdoing this. If a message does not require a response, add FYI (for your information) to the subject line.

3. Delete outdated subject headings. A string of messages with the same old subject heading is confusing.
4. Never write a one-word message. Saying "yes" or "agreed" without quoting the previous document forces the recipient to waste time checking back.
5. Write short paragraphs. Most people do not like to read long blocks of text online.
6. When including a weblink, write out the entire address so the recipient can link directly to the site. It is convenient to put a weblink on a separate line.
7. Using ALL CAPS to call attention to a particular section of a message is often considered rude, so use it sparingly.
8. Avoid the use of graphic emoticons except in messages to people you know well. They can appear unprofessional and some email programs do not accept them.
9. Use a spell checker to avoid careless mistakes and typos.
10. Add a signature to your emails. Generally, a professional signature should include your name and title, the name of the library, and a link to the library website.
11. When replying to an email message, choose the "reply" option if only the writer of the message needs the information you are sending, and "reply all" if the information would be useful to everyone who received the original message.
12. Copy your message to the people who would receive copies of a written memo on the subject: an administrator, individual staff members, or a professional colleague.
13. Keep a record of any important message sent or received electronically by archiving it.

Fax machines are a quick and relatively inexpensive way of sending memos, letters, or other documents. Because fax documents are printed before being sent, the sender has a record of the message. Or print documents can be scanned, sent electronically, and saved as a computer file. Some formal documents are not official in a faxed version, so the original document may need to be sent by mail.

MORE FORMAL COMMUNICATION

Memos

One of the most frequently used forms of communication in any organization is the memo, a form that can range from quite informal to formal depending on the subject and format. Most administrators find memos an efficient way of keeping in touch with what is going on in various departments. A department head will usually keep the chief librarian informed by memo of activities within the department, issues that may grow into problems, suggestions for changes in library procedures, and requests for increased budget or other services. Most memos are now sent as email attachments, but they are often printed out to provide a permanent record.

Occasions for sending memos

1. Record decision made at a meeting or in a telephone call
2. Document an issue that may become a problem within the department
3. Suggest a change in policy or procedures
4. Remind people of a meeting or event
5. Protest an action taken by a supervisor or other personnel
6. Announce the schedule for holidays or other events

7. Transmit information about changes in the library system
8. Ask questions or get permission for an action.

Memos are used in following up on whether decisions are implemented, problems solved, and plans followed. They are also used in writing annual reports. For this reason, a department head should try to ensure that important departmental issues are documented in memos. Memos are generally filed by subject matter, so each memo should be devoted to a single issue. Otherwise, the less important issue may be lost or ignored.

When memos serve as documentation for decisions, they become formal communications. Whenever a memo dealing with an important issue is sent, a copy should be kept in the department files for verification. This is particularly important if the memo deals with a request for action. If, for example, an agreement has been reached that an additional computers will be installed in the children's room, it is important to record the date of the agreement. If the action is not taken within a reasonable period of time, the department head can follow up with a reminder as shown in the sequence of memos in figure 5.1.

A memo that deals with a personnel problem is filed in the individual's personnel file. These memos serve as important reminders to supervisors preparing performance assessments and are invaluable if disciplinary measures are needed. Memos of commendation are also important for writing performance assessments and for writing recommendations for employees who are leaving the library.

Although it is important to keep files of memos, the files should be weeded frequently. Memos, whether paper or electronic, that refer to specific events or ephemeral matters should be discarded at regular intervals. Memos can also be used as legal or procedural documents. Many libraries have records management rules that should be followed when memos are to be discarded.

Forms

Many libraries have forms designed to report events or situations including challenges to materials (see chapter 12), equipment problems, missing materials, and so forth. These forms should be carefully completed and sent to the appropriate office with a copy filed in the department. Details that may not seem important at the time can often be necessary if an incident becomes a problem. If a form seems to be overly complicated or unnecessary, a suggestion for changes might be raised after several experiences using the form.

Letters

Letters are written between departments in a library system to document changes in status such as promotions, increases in salary, formal reprimands or commendations, and resignations. Because letters give the title and position of the writer and recipient, they are preferable to memos whenever the document may need to be made available outside of the library system.

Reports

Another common type of formal communication is the written report. Many of the principles of writing any report are the same as those for annual reports,

Figure 5.1
Sequence of memos.

TO: Rosa Moraga, Chief Librarian

FROM: Darcy Shapiro, Children's Department

DATE: April 12, 2008

The entire staff of the children's department are excited that our request for two new computers in our Homeschooler's corner of the library have been approved. The large screen monitors will enable parents and children to work together and make full use of our databases. We are looking forward to having this section upgraded for the opening of school in September.

TO: Rosa Moraga, Chief Librarian

FROM: Darcy Shapiro, Children's Department

DATE: July 24, 2008

As noted in my memo of April 12, we are looking forward to having our new Homeschooler's corner ready for use by the opening of school this fall. The new computers have not yet arrived. I called R.W. Simmons Library Supply Company several times but have not received a satisfactory explanation for the delay.

TO: Rosa Moraga, Chief Librarian

FROM: Darcy Shapiro, Children's Department

DATE: Aug. 20, 2008

Thank you for contacting R. W. Simmons Company on our behalf. The new computers finally arrived and were installed yesterday. I hope that you will be able to attend the coffee hour on Sept. 23 at 4:00 pm, which will mark the official opening of the refurbished Homeschooler's corner. Mary L. Wabinski, President of the Homeschool Association of North Dakota, will be the guest of honor.

---

which are discussed in chapter 6. Occasions for preparing a formal report might be

- describing success of an ongoing programs
- requesting a new program or type of service
- outlining departmental needs in a building renovation or new building
- advocating the purchase of a new media format
- presenting information about demographic or other community changes
- reporting recurring problems in the department
- justifying request for additional personnel

Reports should be well-organized, clear, complete, and persuasive. Frequently the writer of a report must assimilate a great deal of background information before preparing even a short report. However, time should not be wasted in reading everything available on the issue. Most people find it useful to start by preparing an outline of the points to be covered. A number of books and software programs can help those who find it difficult to construct an outline.

Many reports are written as Power Point presentations. The slides may serve as a visual outline to follow when making an oral presentation, or as headings in a written report. Because graphics and tables can be incorporated into Power Point presentations, they give information in varied formats to appeal to different audiences. They can also be mounted on a website.

Reports should cover all of the important points in a concise style. Library boards and administrators do not want to read dense pages of prose to find the facts necessary for decision-making. Most reports start with an executive summary (written after the report is completed) that includes the most important factors to be considered and the action recommended. The report itself should contain these sections:

1. a brief introduction giving the reason for the report
2. an explanation of the factors to be considered
3. facts, figures, and narrative to support the argument put forth
4. suggestions for action implementation
5. appendices giving sources of information, documentation, and amplification of issues

Reports should be as presented as professionally as possible. Desktop publishing programs provide different typefaces and a variety of graphics that strengthen the impact of the report. Although the content is the most important factor, a clear, crisp presentation conveys the impression that the author is a competent professional who has probably been as careful in assembling the facts as in presenting them. Alternative formats for presentation should be considered. Some library board members might prefer a report to be available as an audio or video file to listen to on an iPod or view on a computer or TV screen.

COOPERATING WITH OTHER DEPARTMENTS

While most official communication takes place between the administrator and the department, it is also important to communicate frequently and effectively with other departments in the library. Face-to-face conversation is the most common means of communication, and in a small library this may be all that is needed. Occasionally, however, people are lulled into a sense of security because they talk informally with members of other departments every day. Unless work-related topics are discussed, however, other librarians may not know much about what is going on in individual departments. Information about a department's events and projects should be sent to other departments, noted on the library mailing list, and posted on well-read bulletin boards.

Department and branch heads should be copied on information emails sent to administrators. Librarians can also use staff meetings to talk briefly about projects and issues within departments and distribute printed information. Librarians in children's departments should be sensitive to the flow of power within the library system and make an effort to tap communication channels to decision makers on both an informal and formal level. If department heads eat lunch or have coffee breaks together, the head of the children's department should try to be included. It is not always easy at the beginning for the newest and often the youngest member of the management team to be accepted by others with more experience, but the effort is worthwhile.

In any busy library, staff members work hard at their individual jobs and have little time to observe what others are doing. One of the tasks of a department head is to make it easy for others in the library to remain aware of what is going on in their department. Good communication techniques keep pathways open to administrators and staff members throughout the library system.

SYSTEMWIDE COORDINATORS OF CHILDREN'S SERVICES

The traditional task of a children's services coordinator is to coordinate activities throughout a library system. The early leaders of children's services such as Anne Carroll Moore at the New York Public Library and Lillian H. Smith at the Toronto Public Library selected the children's staff, set policy for book selection, conducted in-service training, and acted as spokesperson for children's services throughout the system. The position, while subordinate to that of the chief librarian, was almost a parallel one, because children's services were often left almost entirely in the hands of the children's coordinator. Because children's services were generally seen as successful, they did not often require or receive intense scrutiny by the chief administrator.

As library budgets grew smaller during the second half of the twentieth century, the number of coordinators of large public libraries decreased. Some systems failed to fill the positions when a coordinator retired, others moved the children's coordinator to another position (Rollock 1988, 54–55). The coordinator's role has been redefined in many library systems as new management patterns have emerged.

Coordinator as Executive Officer

Children's coordinators who act as executive officers are responsible for maintaining high-quality children's services and for representing these services both inside and outside the library system. Under this system, the coordinator's office makes decisions about policy and hiring, and handles relations with state or provincial library departments. The work usually includes writing funding proposals, responding to legislative initiatives, and lobbying. The coordinator also represents children's services to schools and other community groups, attending meetings, and initiating individual contact with leaders.

Coordinator as Adviser

Many large library systems have moved control away from a central administration and given more power to branches as a way to make library branches more responsive to local community needs. This usually means that branch heads exercise greater control over collections and services in their branch than in more centralized systems. Allowing a system coordinator to determine the children's collection and programming policies tied the branches to decisions that might not serve their unique situation. In this model, the coordinator is less of an administrator and more of an adviser to children's librarians. Children's coordinators recommend, but individual departments make the final decisions subject to the approval of branch heads.

This change shows up clearly on administrative charts, but it also has an observable impact on the work of librarians. In one large library, for example, the reorganization meant that branches could buy materials that were not on the coordinator's selection list. Librarians hired for children's positions were interviewed by representatives of the personnel office and the branch librarian but not by the coordinator. Systemwide book selection meetings were abandoned as were most staff-training events. Children's services in various areas of the city began to differ considerably from each other depending on the philosophy of the staff within the particular branch.

TASKS OF A CHILDREN'S COORDINATOR

Personnel

Personnel decisions set the tone for library services, so they require thoughtful planning. An important part of a coordinator's work is helping branch staff write job descriptions. Job descriptions serve many purposes:

1. clarifies what the employee is expected to accomplish
2. gives the basis of agreement between supervisor and employee as to what activities are expected
3. provides clear written list of skills required
4. helps to recruit appropriate applicants
5. indicates how a specific job fits in with the overall work of the library
6. justifies disciplinary actions and provides legal backing for termination of employment
7. specifies points on which to base performance evaluation

A job description should include the position title, the department in which the job is located, the position of the person to whom the employee reports, a statement of the duties of the position (often including the percentage of time allocated to each), the equipment used to perform the job, physical demands of the job, and the supervisory requirements of the position. The date of the job analysis that led to the description should also be included. An example of a job description for a children's librarian is given in figure 5.2.

Developing Policies

In a large library system, the children's coordinator is responsible for seeing that appropriate selection and collection development policies are available and maintained in every branch (see chapter 10). Specific guidelines will vary from one branch to another, but the coordinator should ensure that the rationale for these differences is clear and that they fit within the mandate of the system. If the library does not have a written selection policy, the coordinator should assign its preparation a top priority. If a selection policy is already in place, the coordinator makes sure it is reexamined and updated periodically. The mechanism for this may vary from one library to another, but most systems appoint a committee to solicit suggestions and to pass on whatever suggestions seem appropriate. The coordinator normally chairs this committee and sees that its decisions are implemented.

Librarians often write selection policies in general terms that must be interpreted for specific occasions. The coordinator should maintain a record of

Figure 5.2
Example of job description.

Wessex County Public Library

Title: Children's Specialist

Supervisor's Title: Children's Service Manager

GENERAL SUMMARY

Under general direction, works from established policies and procedures, and participates in setting early childhood program objectives. Provides comprehensive library services to the library system, patrons and community agencies specializing in early childhood.

ESSENTIAL JOB FUNCTIONS

1. **A.** Complies with work scheduling and attendance requirements according to reasonable policy and practices. Staffing for branch and regional libraries requires rotational scheduling, which includes evening and weekend (Saturday and Sunday) hours.

1. **B.** Consistently presents Wessex County Public Library and its services in a positive manner and adheres to customer service guidelines and procedures as established by the Library.

1. **C.** Complies with the established rules of operation, procedures, and policies when using library computers, peripheral hardware, and software. Individual passwords and any other confidential information regarding library records shall be kept confidential.

2. Promotes project LEAP, literacy and library resources to community, parent and educational groups.

3. Creates and updates project LEAP story-time kits.

4. Provides information and training regarding developmentally appropriate materials and programming targeting early childhood.

5. Evaluates materials for children birth to age five, and makes recommendations for purchase.

(continued)

Figure 5.2 *(continued)*

6. Plans and provides additional training in the form of workshops and in-service training for staff, care providers and parents to augment their knowledge of early childhood literature and programming.

7. Supports literacy development through the publication of a quarterly newsletter, and creation of bibliographies and other informational materials.

8. Provides collection development guidance for children's services staff, adult staff, parents and care providers.

9. Shares resources and information with other libraries, educational organizations and social service agencies.

10. Supervises development of Project LEAP mailing list, mailings, statistical reports and files.

11. Works with other Children's Services staff in the creation of new programs, projects and materials.

The intent of this position description is to provide a representative summary of the major duties and responsibilities performed by incumbents of this job. Incumbents may be requested to perform job-related tasks other than those specifically presented in this description.

JOB REQUIREMENTS

Knowledge, Skills, and Abilities

1. Comprehensive knowledge of early childhood development theory, practice and programming.

2. Knowledge of children's literature, audiovisual and other resources for children, and programming.

3. Strong organizational skills.

4. Ability to develop and implement programming appropriate for target groups associated with children birth to age twelve.

5. Writing skills necessary to create bibliographies, newsletters, and reviews.

6. Strong communication, interpersonal and oral presentation skills for creating and presenting developmental programming to various groups.

7. Knowledge of standard word processing and database programs.

Summary Minimum Education & Experience Required

1. Master's degree in Library Science and undergraduate work specializing in early childhood development.

2. Two to four years of experience in a library setting.

(continued)

Figure 5.2 *(continued)*

OTHER TESTING / LICENSES REQUIRED

1. License
   Requires a valid State Driver's license and own vehicle preferred, for visiting branches and area functions.

2. A criminal background check is required.

PHYSICAL DEMANDS AND WORKING CONDITIONS

1. Job is physically comfortable.

2. May require moderate physical effort such as stooping, bending, lifting boxes weighing approximately 30 pounds.

---

interpretations accepted by the chief administrator or the library board. Some of these interpretations may be integrated into the policy at its next revision; others may remain as part of the record of administrative decisions.

Other important policies are those governing Internet access and the use of filters on computers available to children, policies on gifts received, and the use of fines for overdue materials. These policies are governed by the library board, but the children's coordinator is responsible for helping children's librarians understand the rules and apply them in each branch. The coordinator usually makes recommendations on all policies that affect children's services.

Setting Procedures

A children's coordinator in many library systems coordinates materials selection procedures and acquisition. There are three common models of materials selection:

- Systemwide selection meetings—staff members evaluate materials sent by publishers or jobbers. The coordinator prepares and circulates a list of all materials available for inspection. Reviews from journals or that are written by a staff member may be circulated. Oral reviews can also be given.
- Regional or state examination centers—coordinator or a rotating committee of librarians examine materials. Lists of recommended materials are circulated to every branch.
- Reviews and recommended lists—in smaller systems, much selection is done on the basis of reviews. The coordinator examines, or assigns others to examine, relevant journals and catalogs, and compiles a list of suggested titles.

Each children's department can select materials from the lists compiled by any of these methods. In some systems, each branch is given considerable freedom to select materials not on the list; in others the coordinator must approve these off-list choices.

Once the materials are selected, they must be acquired. (Details of this process are discussed in chapter 10.) In most library systems the acquisitions process is centralized. A children's coordinator is responsible for making suggestions about how the acquisition process might better meet the needs of children's departments.

Handling Complaints

In addition to being responsible for materials selection, the children's coordinator often has to handle complaints made by children, parents, or other adults. Most complaints originate at a branch library and sometimes the children's librarian and the branch administrator can settle the matter satisfactorily. A children's librarian should send information about a complaint to the coordinator, even if the problem was resolved quickly. Similar complaints often show up in several different branches and it is useful for the library to see the pattern. A coordinator needs to be aware of complaints in order to stay in touch with community feeling about library materials.

When a complaint is not settled satisfactorily at the branch level, the coordinator should be involved in handling the issue. While the chief administrator and library board have the final responsibility, the children's coordinator can collect the documentation necessary to defend the item. Wide background knowledge about children's materials is very helpful in dealing with complaints about specific items.

Guidelines for handling censorship attempts are an important part of library management (see chapter 12). The children's coordinator should ensure that effective guidelines are in place and that all children's services staff are aware of them. Preparing for complaints and learning procedures for handling them are an important part of ongoing staff development. The coordinator's role will be much easier if each step of the procedure is competently carried out.

Programming

In some library systems, the children's coordinator sets programming policy for all children's departments. These policies may include:

- target groups to be served (by age or other category)
- general objectives of programming
- level of personnel involved in programming
- approximate amount of staff time spent on programming

After these policies are accepted, the coordinator helps children's department personnel to develop programs that fit within the policy guidelines.

One advantage of centralized programming is that publicity and program materials can be efficiently shared by all branches. More money can be spent on designing and producing a professional looking product if it serves all branches. A coordinated listing of programs covering all branches can also be mounted on the library's website and sent to community organizations.

Some coordinators prefer to work with a committee of children's librarians to coordinate programming. The goals and objectives of programming may vary from one branch to another, as will target groups and possibly the personnel involved. The coordinator works with each branch to help the staff to achieve the branch objectives. In this model, the role of the coordinator is supportive rather than directive.

Library systems within a state or region frequently coordinate programming for summer reading programs. The savings that result from centralized production of publicity and other materials make it possible to achieve high visibility across a wider community. Because the summer reading program is often the most widely publicized children's program in the library, the individual or committee that plans themes and implementation must spend considerable time on the project. A successful summer program often involves the cooperation of schools, businesses, and other community agencies, so it offers good public relations opportunities as well as providing valuable reading experiences for the children. Many coordinators regard planning the annual summer reading program as a major part of their overall responsibility for publicizing the role of the children's department

When outside groups or individuals are brought in to present programs, the coordinator is usually the person responsible for managing the details of inviting, scheduling, and handling the visit. Some library systems regularly arrange a special program, puppet show, magician, or theater group for holidays. Other opportunities for outside programming present themselves when an author or illustrator visits the region. A coordinator should take advantage of geographic proximity to plan events that will raise the library's profile as well as provide effective programming.

Budgeting

A coordinator's responsibility in the budgeting process may include determining budgets for the children's department of each branch, or it may mean advising branch managers on budget decisions. The coordinator's task is to present the needs of children's services reasonably and persuasively in the context of the overall system budget. (See chapter 7.)

After the overall budget allocations are made, the coordinator works with the branch heads and the children's departments to determine how the budget will be spent at the branch level. Needs and services vary from one branch to another. It is the coordinator's task to try to ensure that the children's department receives an equitable share of the branch budget. The children's coordinator can help branch staff make the most effective presentation about their funding needs to branch heads.

Some systems do not include the coordinator in basic budget decisions. Instead, the coordinator's role is limited to advising children's librarians on budget decisions. Some coordinators find that busy children's librarians do not always take an appropriate interest in budget matters. It is easy for the staff of a children's department to become so overwhelmed by their regular busy workload that they do not spend time on budget decisions. A wise coordinator knows that setting budgets is more important than most other tasks and the time spent on budgeting will strengthen the department.

Maintaining Communications

One of a coordinator's most important tasks is maintaining good communication among the children's librarians in the system. Electronic mailing lists allow both formal and informal communication among all members of the group. The coordinator can send out notices of meetings or deadlines, or lists of materials under consideration. Any member of the group can post questions from patrons that have been puzzling a branch, or mention an upcoming program or event. If only a few of the children's librarians attend a conference or workshop, they can post their notes for the entire group.

Some libraries have created blogs or wikis to facilitate communication between librarians. These can also work well, but one individual has to take responsibility for seeing that new information is posted often enough to keep people interested in viewing the blog or wiki page. Responsibility for this can be rotated among different branches, but the coordinator will want to monitor the site frequently to be sure it is being viewed and that librarians are participating in discussion. Librarians are very busy and may resent having to spend time on the blog if they do not consider it valuable. Communication is a two-way street and coordinators must take into account the preferences of individuals in the group and which communication channels they prefer.

WORKING WITHOUT A COORDINATOR

Most small library systems and some medium sized ones do not have children's coordinators. In many libraries with one or more branches, the head of the children's department in the main library is responsible for the tasks a coordinator would normally handle. These tasks include

- coordinating programming and materials selection
- representing children's services to the library board or other groups
- participating in personnel hiring
- arranging professional development opportunities

While the system remains small, it may manage very well without a coordinator, but there are disadvantages. The head of any children's department is tied to branch responsibilities much of the time and is not free to move around the community, to meet with educational or business groups, and to visit schools and other institutions. It is difficult to achieve a high profile for library children's services unless there is a coordinator who can spend time outside of the library.

Some systems have a committee of children's librarians to carry out tasks that would otherwise be handled by a coordinator. In a small system, each branch usually has a representative on the committee, while in a larger system the branches may rotate membership. A committee of six to eight individuals is probably the largest that can be effective. The committee may be chaired by the senior member or the chair may rotate among members. At regular meetings, usually held monthly, the committee decides on program plans, discusses problems, and agrees on systemwide publicity. Subcommittees of one or two members carry out specific tasks between meetings. Although a committee structure presents some problems in administration, this system can work well when colleagues cooperate and respect one another's professional views. It is certainly preferable to making no attempt at coordinating children's services throughout a library system.

REFERENCES AND ADDITIONAL READING

Cole, Kris. 2002. *The Complete Idiot's Guide to Clear Communication.* New York: Penguin.

Feehan, Patricia. 1994. Take Me to Your Ladder: The Issue of Plateauing in Children's Services Positions. *Library Administration and Management* 8: 200–203.

Giesecke, Joan ed. 1997. *Practical Help for New Supervisors.* Chicago: American Library Association.

Heller, Robert. 1998. *Motivating People: Essential Managers.* New York: DK Publishing.

Kratz, Abby, and Flannery, Melinda. 1997. Communication Skills. In *Practical Help for New Supervisors,* ed. Joan Giesecke, 43–57. Chicago: American Library Association.

Panszczyk, Linda A. 2004. *HR How-to—Intergenerational Issues: Everything You Need to Know about Dealing with Employees of All Generations in the Workplace.* Chicago: CCH Knowledge Point.

Rollock, Barbara. 1988. *Public Library Services for Children.* Hamden, CT: Library Professional Publications.

Shipley, David, and Schwalbe, Will. 2007. *Send: The Essential Guide to Email for Office and Home.* New York: Alfred A. Knopf.

Staerkel, Kathleen, Fellows, Mary, and Nespeca, Sue McCleaf eds. 1995. *Youth Services Librarians as Managers: A How-to Guide from Budgeting to Personnel.* Chicago: American Library Association.

Tannen, Deborah. 1994. *Talking from 9 to 5: How Women's and Men's Conversational Styles Affect Who Gets Heard, Who Gets Credit, and What Gets Done at Work.* New York: William Morrow and Company.

6

Annual Children's Department Reports

Library annual reports have changed format over the years. Instead of the of black-bound annual reports lining the shelf of twentieth century libraries, today's reports are likely to be colorful, electronically stored files. Changes in format reflect changes in the way people send information, but the information sent is much the same as it always was. In 1913, Lillian H. Smith wrote one of the earliest children's services reports:

Children to the number of 9,180 have been present at the 180 story hours held regularly at the branches during the year with the exception of the months of June, July, August and September. These figures do not include the informal story hours, which are carried on at the request of the children when the heaviest part of the day is over. At three branches a division of the story groups was made, the younger children coming Saturday morning to the ever-popular fairy tales, legends, and nature stories, while the older children at a different hour find equal enjoyment in the achievements of heroes and historic events as recounted by the Children's librarian. (Toronto Public Library 1913, 12)

Ninety years later, Park Ridge Library is reporting their year electronically, as shown in figure 6.1.

No matter what the format, annual reports being prepared today will serve future historians as sources of information about public libraries at the beginning of the twenty-first century. In the interests of maintaining an accurate account of what happens in a library on a year-to-year basis, librarians should recognize the importance of preparing careful annual reports.

Annual reports are management tools, so decisions about who is responsible for authorship and format are important. There are several options (see figure 6.2 for more information).

Figure 6.1
Example of annual report.

❖ Annual Report

CHILDREN'S SERVICES DEPARTMENT

FISCAL YEAR 2005/2006

- To assist children, parents, teachers and other adults in utilizing the Children's Services Department and its resources and to encourage the love of reading by providing access to books and programs that children will enjoy.

COLLECTIONS

- Added 8,925 new books to the Children's Services Department in all areas of the collection. This resulted in a total print collection for the Department of 81,289 items.
- Added 1,186 audio-visual items in a variety of formats. This resulted in a total audio-visual collection of 8,571 items.
- Weeded 12,094 books and 765 audio-visual items from the collection in order to maintain a collection that fits in the current shelving.
- Circulated 306, 539 items at an average rate of 25,544 per month. This is on the average 415 more items per month than during the previous fiscal year.
- The changing needs of the community have continued to be met by the purchase of an increasing number of books on CD, DVDs, and hanging bags with CDs and books for emerging readers.

Source: http://www.parkridgelibrary.org/arcd.html

Whatever the overall plan, the children's services department should try to have as much influence as possible on the type and amount of information submitted and on the content and design of the report.

SHAPING ANNUAL REPORTS

The length and format of annual reports vary from one jurisdiction to another. Some localities have legal requirements as to the form and content; others leave these decisions to the library administration. Legal requirements must be observed, but often these requirements are minimum standards and additional information can be included. A variety of styles may be used:

- brief, general statistical and factual material
- statistical tables plus anecdotal reports of special events and services

- statistics presented graphically with the addition of illustrations and text
- brief online reports with links to more detailed statistical and factual information

Figure 6.2
Methods of preparing annual report.

Report Author	Method	Relevant Factors
CEO of Library PR Department	Departments submit data in prescribed format; report is drafted by individual	Unified presentation for the public; activities of departments may not stand out
Staff Committee	Departments submit data and have a representative on committee; input from several individuals determines content and format	Time-consuming to work through a committee; each department can emphasize specific departmental concerns
Individual Department	Each department prepares a document, deciding on format and content	Departments can prepare report suitable for their audience; lack of uniformity may cause confusion in overall message

Reports of other libraries in your area or available online can suggest ideas about effective ways to present information.

Audiences for Annual Report

The format of the annual report can vary from a sober, official looking compilation of data to a professionally designed piece of graphic art that resembles an advertising brochure. Many libraries produce the report in more than one format: a formal report for the library board, a shorter version for the public, and an online report for the library's website. The audience for each version of the report determines the format. The library board wants a full report including all the appropriate statistics and facts. They usually expect a well-designed presentation of information, but most of them are willing to contend with large arrays of figures. Most members of the general public, on the other hand, will not read anything but a brief annual report with statistical information given in graphs and charts. Readers on the library website will expect brief text, many illustrations, possibly including short videos, and links to more detailed information. Preparing material that is useful and accessible to all groups and also serves the purposes of the historical record is a challenging task. The time and effort spent in planning and preparing for the compilation of the annual report can pay dividends in the form of increased public visibility and good publicity for the services provided by the library.

Preparing the Report

Preparation for an annual report goes on all year long. Statistics about acquisitions and circulation are compiled automatically by the library's computer system, but sometimes they are not generated in the form most useful for the children's department. Talk to the systems person in your library about getting reports that separate children's materials and circulation from adult statistics. Think about the most useful way to present your information and make sure the library system will give you the data you need (for a detailed list of important data, see figure 6.3).

In large departments, a committee is often formed to write the report. Committee members may include all of the professional staff or only two or three department members. Writing a report by committee usually means assigning various sections of the report to different individuals, circulating the drafts for comments and suggestions, and seeking group approval for the final report. This can be time-consuming, but involving several staff members in the department's yearly work can lead to a more complete and balanced report than one generated by one individual.

In small departments, the department head usually assumes responsibility for writing the annual report. It is a good idea to ask other department members for ideas and suggestions. The backbone of the report may consist of prescribed statistics and factual material, but often you can include additional information to give a fuller sense of the department's activities and accomplishments. If possible, circulate a draft copy of the report inviting suggestions for changes and improvements. No one knows more about the department than its staff; their input can make the difference between an effective report and one that is merely technically correct.

Figure 6.3
Information collected for annual report.

Event	Information Collected	Additional Items
Programs Offered	Date Attendance Presenter Subject Evaluation	Pictures Publicity pieces News reports of event
Staff Added	Brief biographical information Role in department	Picture Interviews if available
Staff Leaving	Brief biographical information Appreciation of services	Picture
Renovations	Description of changes Impact on services Report of opening celebration	Before and after pictures Interviews with patrons
New Services	Description of change Expected impact	Pictures if possible Interviews with patrons
Gifts and Donations	Description of gifts Purpose or expected outcome	Pictures of donors Press coverage

Writing the Report

Annual reports should have a theme. One effective report posted on a library website starts with title page (see figure 6.4).

More specific information comes later, but follows the same theme of expanded hours and services.

Your report should not be merely a collection of facts and figures. You should analyze the material, decide what the information says, and organize your facts so the reader can understand your message. Few people care about or understand rows of figures unless they are presented in a meaningful way.

What is the message that your report is trying to convey?

* "This has been a great year capped by the opening of our new branch library."
* "We have worked with a limited budget this year, but our fundraising efforts have been successful and we expect next year to be better."
* "Our library is recognized as a strong force for good in the community."

Figure 6.4
Example of title page.

Contents

Volusia County

Public Library
Annual Report
2005

Extended
hours
Expanded
services

"I have always imagined that Paradise will be a kind of library."

Source: http://www.vcpl.lib.fl.us/annualreport/2005/

- "Moving to the new building caused turmoil, but our services are still effective."
- "Exciting innovations have strengthened our traditional services."

Once you clarify the basic message the pieces will fall into place as you arrange them in a logical and cohesive order.

Some basic items should be included in every annual report:

- major achievements
- highlights of the year
- changes, including new materials, new staff, and new programs
- problems (Your frankness about these depends on the uses to which the report is put.)
- plans

Audiences for Departmental Report

Administration: The chief administrator needs to know what is happening in the department through formal reports as well as informal communication. Staff members in other departments also need to know what is going on in the children's department. The larger the library the more formal communication is needed.

Staff (the children's department staff, including clerical staff and pages): As a rule every member of the staff has an impact on services, so it is useful for everyone to know how well the department is doing.

Funding bodies: The library board wants to know what is happening in each department. Granting agencies will be interested in seeing an annual report whenever a grant request is made.

Outside groups: The whole community, but especially parents, teachers, and the children themselves, are part of the department's public. Anecdotes that highlight services and clarify the meaning of the statistics get your message across and linger in people's minds. The anecdotes should be short and each one should make a point. These anecdotes are often used by local newspapers or other media in stories about the library's annual report.

GRAPHICS

When gathering information for the annual report, ask yourself whether any of the appropriate information can be presented in graphic form. Graphs and pictorial presentations have much more impact than tables of numbers. Information presented graphically will stick in people's minds and make your point more emphatically than facts buried in tables or in paragraphs of text.

Tables and Graphs

Comparisons show up well in graphs. For example, if you are increasing the number of programs offered in the department, and more children are attending them, you can easily construct a graph to show the growth (see figure 6.5).

A line graph can show the changing patterns of usage of reference or other services. This format is especially useful in showing trends over an extended period of time (see figure 6.6).

Figure 6.5
Growth in children's programs.

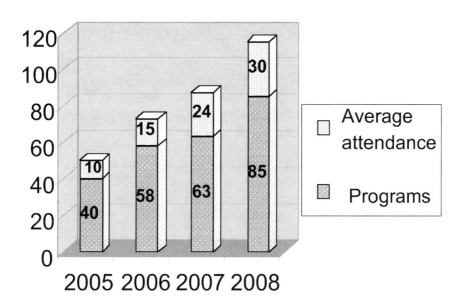

Pie charts are useful for comparing groups of patrons, types of materials, or size of different collections (see figure 6.7).

It is easy to experiment with different formats of graphs and charts to show the information you want to include. Minor differences in format make a real difference in how easily people can understand the data you present. Ask for other people's opinion so you find the format that appeals to most people, especially those who are not as familiar with the library as the staff is.

Figure 6.6
Changing patterns of reference service.

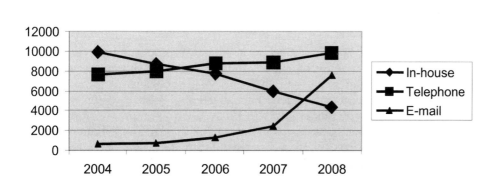

Figure 6.7
Languages spoken by children at home.

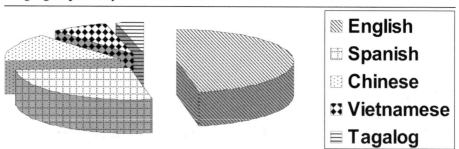

Another way to present material simply and clearly is to describe a person or activity in terms of average statistics. An average patron may be described as follows:

> In West Riverton, the average child with a library card:
>
> visits the library 27 times a year
> uses the library website 23 times a year
> attends 6 programs a year
> borrows 46 books a year

This method can be used to construct an average program, or the average day of a staff member

> In Northpoint Harbor, the typical children's librarian:
>
> recommends 22 books a day
> talks with 3 parents and 30 children a day
> helps 7 patrons to use computer resources
> updates the children's department blog twice a day

The ways in which to use a profile are limited only by imagination.

Pictures

When looking at a report, most people look at pictures first and then turn to the text. Pictures set the tone for the report, so they should be chosen carefully. Pictures of events at the library, especially highly visual ones such as puppet shows or storytelling, attract many readers. Plan ahead and get permission from parents for using photos of their children in a report. If a program is covered in the press, the library can ask permission to reprint that photograph in both print and electronic versions of reports. Be sure to include a wide variety of children, boys and girls, different ages and ethnic groups, and children with disabilities. Almost every library has at least one staff member who enjoys photography and is willing to take pictures of events and physical changes in the library. Digital formats are best because these can be inserted into either print or electronic formats.

TAILORING REPORTS TO DIFFERENT GROUPS

The department head will want to distribute evaluative information to several groups, each of which requires a different approach. The author of a report must decide how much and what kind of information is appropriate for each audience (see figure 6.8).

Figure 6.8
Audiences for annual reports.

Audience	Format	Distribution
Children's Department Staff	Complete report	Staff meeting to discuss implications of report
Chief Administrator	Complete report	Department chief meets with CEO to discuss report
Library Board	Complete report	Department head reports at board meeting, or CEO presents information
Outside Groups	Brief report in print and electronic version on library website	Media releases to local newspapers and other media outlets

Oral Reports

The annual report is only the beginning of the reporting process. Sometimes the most effective presentation is an oral report. These oral presentations are a challenge, but they are also opportunities to let people know about the work of the children's department. It is worth taking some time to ensure an effective presentation.

The most common way of organizing a report is to prepare a PowerPoint presentation. People who attend frequent meetings and conferences often complain about overuse of this method, but no appropriate substitute has yet been found. Used with skill, a PowerPoint can be an effective way to give people information in a memorable form.

- Keep text brief on each slide.
- Use font size that can be seen by entire audience.
- Do not use complicated graphics—keep them simple.
- Vary slide format using text and graphics.
- When listing items, place the general statement first followed by examples.
- Change slide about every 90 seconds.
- Include meaningful title on each slide (e.g., avoid using vague titles, such as "introduction" or "more points").

How do you organize your presentation? One authority recommends using 5 percent of the time for introduction, 75 to 80 percent for the body of information, 5 percent for conclusion, and 10 to 15 percent for questions at the end (Rosenberg 2005, 228).

People have very short attention spans, especially when listening to someone else talking. A report of the year's work in a children's department should not take more than 5 or 10 minutes, or people's attention will wander. If you have a great many appealing pictures of children's programs, show them as a slide show while you speak. There is no need to comment on each one.

Oral presentations supplement the written report. Do not try to include in your oral report all of the information in the written report. Concentrate on the highlights—outstanding successes or problems, or plans for the future. People remember less information from an oral presentation than a written one, so limit the number of points to no more than 10.

Move through your presentation at a brisk pace and then invite questions. Many people enjoy asking questions and you can give additional information in answer to questions rather than trying to include it all in the presentation.

Reporting to the Public

Some libraries, especially larger ones, have a public relations staff to prepare information for distribution to the community. Most public relations staff welcome suggestions from departments as to events or information to publicize. The release of an annual report may spur newspapers or other media to contact the library and ask for additional information about services. This is more likely to happen if the report is well designed and well presented, and offers concrete information that can be built into media stories.

In dealing with the public, there are several points to remember.

Catch People's Attention

Information from the library enters a vast sea of information from the media. Choose highlights from library service and present them in a dramatic way. If the department's priorities include innovative services not associated with traditional libraries, be sure to emphasize them.

Avoid Clichés

Have a concise version of your annual report available in the children's department for parents to pick up when they come in for programs or materials. Send copies to local schools to let teachers know what services and materials are available. Make a strenuous, ongoing effort to break through the clichés and present an honest picture of the serious work being done by the children's department.

Use Several Different Channels

Make the library report available in many different ways.

- Post text of annual report on the library website.
- Prepare a short podcast of highlights from the report.

- Link a short video of highlights on library website.
- Prepare bookmarks listing significant achievements.
- Make public service announcements for local radio and television stations.
- Send highlights from annual report to electronic mailing lists.

The release of the annual report is an occasion for calling attention to the library's services. Many daycare centers, parent-teacher associations, church groups, and parenting groups like to have librarians talk to them about the resources and services of the children's department. With careful planning you can use your annual report not only to publicize your services, but also to improve them through increased community support.

REFERENCES AND ADDITIONAL READING

Ali, Moi. 2001. *Marketing Effectively: Essential Managers.* New York: Dorling Kindersley Ltd.

Banks, Paula. 1995. News Releases, Photo Releases, Public Service Announcements. In *Part-Time Public Relations with Full-Time Results,* ed. Rashelle Karp, 1–9. Chicago: American Library Association.

Karp, Rashelle S. ed. 1995. *Part-Time Public Relations with Full-Time Results: A PR Primer for Libraries.* Chicago: American Library Association.

Rosenberg, Barry J. 2005. *Spring into Technical Writing for Engineers and Scientists:* Spring into Series. New York: Addison-Wesley.

Sass, Rivkah K. 2002. Marketing the Worth of Your Library. *Library Journal.* http://www.libraryjournal.com/index.asp?layout=articlePrint&articleid=CA220888

Toronto Public Library. 1913. *Annual Report.* Toronto: Toronto Public Library.

7

Budgeting, Finance, and Fundraising

Managing the children's department money is an important task. If budgets, accounting for the money as it is spent, and fundraising are done well, children's librarians will get the most out of the resources available. Sloppy handling of money or inattention to budgets or an unwillingness to fundraise will ultimately shortchange the children and families served because fewer programs and services will be supported. The other issue is that it is important—and required—that those handling public money or contributed money are accountable for how these funds are used.

THE BUDGET PROCESS

In most libraries the board is has the responsibility of accepting a balanced annual budget and approving expenditures against the budget during the year. In the United States, public libraries get the majority of their funds from local property tax directly or as a part of city or county government. Libraries also may get funds from the state or provincial libraries, fees, grants, and donations. Most libraries have an annual audit of the expenditures at the end of the year. This audit is provided by an outside firm and usually involves checking that the library has paid its bills, spent money as the board had planned, and used acceptable accounting practices. Independent library districts and libraries that are funded as part of city or county government are regulated by law.

While the board is ultimately responsible for the budget, the library director and administrative staff prepare the budget, manage funds during the year, and organize and carry out fundraising activities. The timetable for budget preparation, who participates in creating the budget and how funds are designated, varies from library to library, but at some point the manager of the children's department will be asked to submit a request for funds for the department. In some libraries, children's services are represented by the head of the public services department, which includes both adult and youth services. In other libraries, the branch heads take part in the budget-planning process, and they make decisions about the budget for children's services within their branches. The manager of the children's department may be asked only for input about spending for the current and following year.

Constructing a budget requires a great deal of time and effort, but, if carefully prepared, a budget is an important means of organizing library services. As organizational instruments, budgets help librarians determine priorities and achieve goals and objectives. According to Prentice (1996, 20), "Budgeting and planning are, or should be, parallel activities. The budget should be seen as a plan with dollar figures attached." A department's budget indicates the resources that will be needed to meet the department's goals and objectives. No matter how ambitious the proposed objectives are, they will become realities only if they are funded.

Libraries generally have two major types of budgets: the operating budget and the capital budget. Capital budgets deal with one-time expenditures, such as building a new library or making major renovations, upgrading computers or a new phone/telecommunications system. A manager at the departmental level deals most often with operating budgets—the allocation of funds for the ongoing activities of the department, though most managers can ask for furniture and equipment that are infrequent costs as part of the annual budget request.

Preparing Budgets

Because the budget is such an important document, the individuals involved in its preparation have the power to make influential decisions. In small libraries, the library director will likely work with staff to make the budget and present it to the board. In larger libraries the budget may be prepared by a committee of administrators. A department head should seize the opportunity to have as much input into these decisions as possible. A department that is represented on the budget committee will be more autonomous than one that simply accepts the budget handed down by a branch or department head.

Even if the head of the children's department is not part of the group developing the budget, he or she can prepare a budget proposal to present to them. According to one experienced librarian, "do not sit back like a victim who has no control and must simply take what is given" (Deerr 1995, 16). One way to increase the chance of being appointed to the budget committee is to be aware of the processes and knowledgeable about departmental needs. At the very least, anything connected with preparing budget reports or requests should be top priority for the department head.

It is important to prepare a convincing case for suggesting budgetary changes. Almost all new budgets are presented within the framework of previous budgets, so the parameters of the current requests are set by the extent to which they change from past budgets. A proposal to double a department's budget because someone suddenly realized how much could be done with more money is likely to be rejected. Instead, budgetary changes should be realistic increments of the current budget. The department head must support each suggestion or request by carefully documenting the need for the increase. If the library system is operating under a flat budget, this will mean cutting back on some programs when new ones are added. If there are loses of revenue, departments may need to set priorities and reduce the budget request.

A budget grows out of the department's strategic planning; meeting the department's goals and objectives justifies budget requests. A manager should be able to defend budget requests on the basis of meeting the objectives set and approved by the administration. This holds true regardless of what budgeting system the library uses.

Budgets can be prepared in various formats. Many states and provinces mandate which budget format public libraries must use. In other jurisdictions, the local municipality selects the budget format to be used by all departments, including the public library. For use within the library, however, budgets may be reformatted, and more detailed breakdowns may be added to enable administrators to track trends and changes.

The line-item budget is the most traditional and commonly used type of budget. Most people are familiar with line-item budgets because they are often used for personal budgets. Because it is simple, a line-item budget can be prepared by an inexperienced person, based on the past year's budget. In a line-item budget, amounts are listed for each item of expense (see figure 7.1).

These figures should be clearly related to programs or services but are based on the expenditures of previous years or on information about what other libraries spend. This type of budget makes it easy to see how the money is spent, whether the budget has been met, or whether spending is over or under the projected figures. A line-item budget also makes it easy to project how much

Figure 7.1
Sample line-item budget.

Juvenile Collections	$115,000
Books	$85,000
Periodicals	$5,000
Electronic Products	$25,000
Salaries	$190,000
Full-time	$175,000
Part-time	$15,000
Benefits (25% of salary line)	$48,750
Programs	$20,000
Summer Reading Club	$10,000
Supplies	$1,000
Marketing	$4,000
Performer Fees	$5,000

funding is needed for the coming year, based on inflation. Also, it is as easy to cut a line-item budget as it is to add to it.

As well as completing the line items in the budget, the children's department head should provide a budget justification that explains both the details of how the budget with be subdivided and how the budget will meet the department's goals. Librarians have also started to include what outcomes are expected. For example, the book budget might be divided into fiction and nonfiction and further divided by picture books, readers, chapter books, and YA novels. Each category would have a dollar amount assigned it.

An example of a budget narrative might be, "the children's department will add approximately 575 new books to the collection this year. These will replace and update old books and add the best of newly published items. Because the curriculum has changed in the public school, new science and nature books will be purchased for young readers, to meet the anticipated demand for this type of book. The outcome for children using the department will be they will find a better selection of books that will attract them to reading and meet their school homework needs."

The actual format of the budget and the budget justification will be set by the library director and board. Following this format will make managing the budget easier. Knowing how budgets are usually divided, if there a special budget lines that can be used, but are not regular in every year and how much increase or decrease is expected in revenues for the specific year will help the children's department manager get the most money possible for the department. It may be possible or expected for department heads to work together to create a draft budget, so creating the budget may take several months. It usually helps to be able to estimate actual costs of items to be purchased, so decisions about how many programs will be provided, which performers or supplies will be used, and how many staff will be working in the department need to be made before the budget is finalized. It is also important to meet budget submission guidelines and to allow enough time to submit a reasonable and well researched budget request.

Steps in Preparing the Budget:

- Review the department's annual report and activity calendar and determine the cost of each activity for the past year. This review will verify the basic costs of running the department for a year.
- Decide what activities to keep at the same level, which should be dropped or reduced, which to enlarge, and what new programs to add.
- Calculate the cost of next year's programs.
- Relate each program or activity to how it helps meet the department's goals and the library's mission.

In addition to determining program costs it is important to determine how much staff time will be needed to carry out the proposed budget. It is not realistic, for example, to increase the collection development budget by 25 percent and not find more staff to select and process the added materials. First determine how much of each person's time is spent on each task. Staff can keep track of their activities for four or five days, over a two- or three-week period. After the personnel's time on particular tasks is determined, the cost in dollars of each aspect of service can be easily calculated. The department head can then create a program sheet listing each program and its objectives, the personnel requirements, and other costs. For example, if one-quarter of a librarian's time is spent on service to groups, the cost of providing that individual's share of this service amounts to one-quarter of his or her annual salary. Add up the portions of other people's time spent on this service to find the total personnel cost. In allocating personnel costs to various programs, the total working time of each individual must be accounted for, with no more than 10 percent of the total time listed as miscellaneous.

There are no right or wrong allocations, but the results may prompt questions. If one of the department's objectives is to provide information services and only 10 percent of the personnel time is spent on information services, while 50 percent is spent on programming, the department may want to reexamine its objectives or priorities.

Knowing how the department's time and money are spent makes it easier for the department head to plan other programs and to see how they fit into the department's overall resources. Although the procedure takes considerable time, it does supply baseline data that can be used for years in planning and developing new programming. Adjustments for changes in salaries and other costs are relatively easy to make. Time allocation can be periodically monitored by asking each staff member to keep a time diary of daily tasks for a week or two. Changes in staff often lead to changes in the allocation of tasks, so it is important to keep the information up to date.

When considering the introduction of a new program or type of service, the first thing to determine is how it fits into the department's goals and objectives. Once it has been decided that the new program will meet the needs of the community and fall within the department's objectives, the department head must prepare a specific description of the program and a budget request. The department head must determine how much professional, clerical, page, or volunteer time will be involved. Estimate the amount of collection materials and supplies that will be needed. Time requirements for resources outside of the department, such as the library's graphics or publicity departments, should also be included.

While it may be difficult to determine in advance exactly how much time each task will take, a fairly accurate estimate can be based on the time involved in completing similar tasks for current programs. Because time estimates are usually low, about 10 percent should be added to the first figures suggested. After estimating the costs of personnel and materials, the total cost can be estimated. If the program is large and will require a major time commitment, it may be necessary to indicate what other program or service will be cut back.

The same principle is true of the materials budget. A request for a new type of material, such as electronic games, requires either additional money beyond the annual increase necessary to keep up with inflation, or cutting back another type of materials acquisition. The costs of acquiring and processing the new materials should be described in specific detail.

In calculating the costs of a new program, service, or collection, be sure to include the cost of its evaluation. The evaluation will indicate whether the new program meets its objectives. Although the evaluation will require time—and, therefore, money—it is an important part of overall planning.

Finance: Managing the Budget

Specific planning for the upcoming budget year usually begins five or six months before the end of the current fiscal year, but in reality budget planning continues throughout the year. A library manager should always know where the department stands in terms of the current budget year. The library's accounting software can give an ongoing record of what has been spent and what remains. The department head should take time to master the details of the budget reports and see how closely spending matches the projections in each category. While overspending is the major threat to budgets, underspending in any category is an indication that something is wrong. This may mean the projected figures were not accurate, the need for the money was exaggerated, or the program is not being properly implemented.

With a little effort, a manager can use a simple spreadsheet program on the departmental computer to keep track of the budget. Although it takes a few hours of work to become familiar with these programs, once the process is mastered, it will cut down on both time and effort in following budgets.

Someone in the children's department needs to track book and materials orders to understand how many books ordered actually are received. It may be that as many as 25 percent of materials ordered do not arrive at the library. Materials go out of print or are unavailable for purchase. It is important the library only pay for materials that arrive and that the children's librarian orders enough books to avoid underspending the collection budget. Likewise the department needs a way to track all non-book orders to both keep track of spending against the budget and to avoid paying for items that were not delivered.

The children's librarian needs to learn and follow the library's procedures for paying performers, consultants, or other outside workers. If the library requires contracts, make sure these are in place before the work is done and follow procedures for paying non-staff workers in a timely fashion. If you hire a puppeteer, for example, sign a contract or get in writing before the event the specifics: such as, how long the performance will be; if the library needs to have a sound system; or if there will be any other costs associated with the performance. Then follow through to make sure the puppeteer gets paid promptly, or arrange to have the payment check to hand the performer at the end of the program.

Understand the rules for handling cash and follow them to the letter. If the children's department has a separate circulation desk, it will be responsible for fines, lost materials payments, and other charges. Some libraries charge for computer time, printing, use of copy machines, or sell computer disks, pencils, and other small items. Have clear rules about who will collect the money from coin-operated machines, what accounting needs to be done of that money, and where the cash is to be securely stored. Most libraries have a petty cash fund for staff to use to purchase small items from the store. This might include food for parties, craft supplies, stamps, or other items. Some libraries expect staff to purchase these items on their own and be reimbursed. Make sure to understand the rules and what receipts are required to assure that cash expenditures are carefully accounted for.

Good management of expenditures throughout the year is a requirement for all children's librarians. This assures that resources are spent as they are supposed to be according to the budget, that the children's department is getting the most out of the funds given it, and that money is not lost by negligence or theft. Learning as much as possible about the budget process will help children's librarians get support for services the department offers.

FUNDRAISING

While the regular budget process supports almost all activities in the children's department, it rarely supports all the department could or should do. Children's departments need to find other sources of income to offer the quality services the community deserves (and often demands). Libraries, like other public institutions, have recently become more dependent on outside funding. Many communities have cut back library funding at the same time the demand for library services is increasing. As Walter says "At a time when children, particularly poor children, have a growing need for the kinds of services libraries can provide, it is terrible to think that lack of resources might result in failure to meet those needs" (2001, 40).

Fundraising Activities

Although the major burden of raising funds for the library rests with the chief executive officer, the library's development officer, or the library foundation, each department has a role to play in fundraising activities. The services provided by the children's department are highly valued in most communities. This means that children's department projects should have a broad appeal for potential funders. Children's librarians owe it to their patrons to try to raise money that will enhance services. "If libraries are to sustain current levels of excellence, and if they are to grow to meet the needs of a technologically sophisticated age, they will have to discover new networks of funding" (Steele 2000, v).

Fundraising initiatives can be focused on private individuals, government and philanthropic foundation grants, or corporate sponsors.

Typical goals of fundraising:

- providing ongoing annual support
- funding capital expenditures (a new building or a computer lab)
- initiating a specific departmental project

In large- and medium-sized libraries, fundraising is likely to be done in an organized way with annual giving campaigns, fundraising events, corporate giving activities, and several grant applications a year. In these libraries the children's librarian may be asked to suggest projects that need funding, to visit potential donors, and to help write grants that support children's work. In smaller libraries the children's librarian might work with the library director and the library board to approach the local chamber of commerce or business association for funds to support a particular program or to apply for funds from the state library.

Funding from Private Individuals and Local Businesses

Many individuals, even those who frequently use the library, have never thought of giving money to a public library. They assume the funding provided by tax moneys is adequate. One of the first steps for a librarian who wants to raise money from local benefactors is to identify potential library supporters and educate them about the needs of the library. Fundraising is a business, and there is a growing body of knowledge to help the new or occasional librarian fundraiser. Expert fundraiser Ken Burnett suggests that fundraising is getting more competitive, more targeted, and donors are getting harder to find and retain. He suggests that staff who fundraise should set aside regular time for "essential reading" of books, journals, and websites about fundraising to be more effective and up-to-date (Burnett 2006).

Many public libraries have a Friends of the Library group. These groups are nonprofit organizations formed to promote a better understanding of the library's facilities, needs, and services. Often the Friends group plans and sponsors events, such as book sales, art exhibits, or performances, for the benefit of the library. Some Friends groups operate a library café or a store offering writing supplies or used books to library patrons. The group may organize volunteers to read to children or to help with special events. They also encourage gifts, endowments, and other donations. Friends groups may also have a membership fee to support the operation of the Friends and to donate directly to the library.

A Friends of the Library group provides a way for individuals and sometimes local businesses to contribute to the library and have that contribution be counted as a tax deduction. Having a Friends group provides the structure to receive money, plan for the donation use, and report back to donors on how the donations have been used. Friends' budgets are audited and the financial accounting is usually done as part of the library's money management. While most contributions to the Friends are small, total contribution to the library can be financially substantial. Friends' sponsored book sales are often the major fundraising project for libraries in small communities. A typical Friends of the Library publicity piece is shown in figure 7.2.

Friends groups are generally run by a group of its members, but their work is coordinated by library staff. Sometimes relations between the Friends and the library staff become strained because members of the Friends group have firm ideas about how their funds should be spent and are not always aware of the library staff's needs. The children's department manager should have Friends projects developed, so when asked by the Friends for ideas, the children's department will be able to explain the importance of their projects and be successful in getting Friends support. If staff does not suggest projects, funding may never be available for children's activities, or the Friends group will fund projects that are not a priority for the department.

Many libraries also have a Library Foundation in addition to or instead of a Friends group. The Foundation, which is registered as a 501(c)(3) nonprofit organization, is allowed to seek corporate and foundation grants and donations that the library as a government agency may not be eligible for. The purpose of the foundation is to raise money for the library, and it has its own board and sometimes its own staff. As with Friends groups, the children's librarian should be prepared to suggest projects to be funded and work with Foundation staff to meet with potential donors and help write and manage grants that are awarded.

An example of how a foundation might benefit the children's department is found in Hennepin County, Minnesota. The Hennepin County Library Foundation has raised four million dollars for the library in the past 20 years, and in

Figure 7.2
Friends of the Library publicity example.

Springfield Greene County Library

FRIENDS OF THE LIBRARY

Our members and volunteers actively promote Library services and resources while sharing their love of books with the community. Our purpose is to foster a positive relationship between the Library and the community, secure volunteers and raise funds to support the Library.

Book Sales

First and foremost, Friends are booksellers extraordinaire. The first book sale was held in the parking lot of the Midtown Carnegie Branch Library in 1985. The sale has grown into an annual event greatly anticipated by thousands of people in the community. Through the years, sales have raised close to $750,000, funds which benefit the eight branches and bookmobile of the Springfield-Greene County Library District.

Here is information regarding upcoming book sales.

Wee Read

Wee Read, funded by the Friends, promotes the importance of reading to infants and preschoolers by providing books to the families of children enrolled in area Parents As Teachers programs.

Gift Shops

Friends volunteer their time as gift shop assistants at the Library Station and the Library Center. The shops feature book- and library-related merchandise plus local artwork and crafts. There's also a collection of quality pre-read books selected by the Friends. Proceeds from the shops benefit the Library.

How You Benefit

Friends gain great satisfaction from helping the Library, but they also reap rewards as patrons. Friendships develop as members share camaraderie and fun activities and bond over their mutual love of books and reading. Your membership entitles you to:

- 10% off all non-discounted books at Walden Books in the Battlefield Mall
- 10%off all items in the Between Friends Gift Shops
- "Friends Night" during the annual book sale allows you first access to thousands of books.

(continued)

Figure 7.2 *(continued)*

JOIN Friends of the Library

The modest yearly dues from members help support the organization. All additional contributions are placed into the Friends Grant Fund. Contributions are used to buy books, computers, equipment and vehicles, for capital projects and to fund the summer reading programs for children and teens.

The time you give is as important as monetary donations. Friends are indispensable to the operation of the book sales. Volunteers also help out at other Library events.

For more information, or to join the Friends of the Library, download, print, complete and mail the membership form (pdf). Or, send your name, address, phone number, city, state, zip code with a check or money order to:

Friends of the Library Membership
P.O. Box 760
Springfield, MO 65801-0760

Please indicate your library preference: Ash Grove, Brentwood, Fair Grove, the Library Center, the Library Station, Midtown Carnegie, Republic, Willard or the Bookmobile and the areas and activities you are interested in: annual book sale, mailings, mini book sales, telephoning, refreshments, publications or Wee Read.

Membership Categories:

- Junior - $2 (up to 18 years old)
- Individual - $5
- Family - $7.50
- Contributor - $25

- Special Friend - $50
- Donor - $100
- Supporter - $250
- Sustainer - $500

Source: http://thelibrary.springfield.missouri.org/donate/friends.cfm.

2007 the Library Foundation announced a campaign to support the Hennepin County Library. The press release states that "Youth Development and Cultural Literacy & Diversity are Top Priorities for 2007.... The Foundation's commitment to secure $225,000 through a combination of private donor gifts, corporate and foundation grants and sponsorships will support initiatives and programming above and beyond services and programs currently available at the Hennepin County Library suburban system of 26 libraries and two Readmobiles that serve preschoolers to older adults in the metro area" (Hennepin County Library).

Corporate Support

In addition to individuals and funding agencies, local businesses and industry are important sources of support and possible funding. Companies that sell products aimed primarily at children can be approached to support library activities through donations of materials or publicity. Toys or books for awards in summer reading programs may be obtained from booksellers, publishers, or distributors. Restaurants that want to attract families may provide publicity on napkins, place mats, or containers. Many large corporations encourage their local branches to support community activities of this kind. Members of the library board are often good contacts to reach local businesspersons.

In arranging for publicity backed by business interests, there is some danger that the library could be seen as endorsing a particular product or company. This is not permissible for a public institution, and the library must be sure that sponsorship is free of commercialism. Businesses and industries can donate to public service organizations, such as libraries, but they should view these donations as ways of promoting name recognition and good will, rather than using them to advertise their products or services. The library must maintain control over any material prepared, printed, or distributed by companies on its behalf.

In ensuring that requests are coordinated, a children's librarian who wants to approach a firm would usually begin by suggesting the idea to his or her immediate supervisor—the branch head or chief administrative officer. The children's librarian should state clearly but briefly the project that needs funding, the choice of the sponsor, and the rationale that will be given to the sponsor. If the supervisor approves the plan, the children's librarian should prepare a more formal proposal for approval by the library board. The proposal may be made to the company by the chief librarian, a member of the library board, or the head of children's services, depending on the political climate and relationships within the community.

One special form of support that some children's libraries have obtained is celebrity tie-ins for programs. Having a well-known sports or music figure give his or her endorsement and picture to a summer reading program, for example, can create exciting publicity for the library. When an arrangement is made with a celebrity for endorsement, the individual ordinarily does not contribute money but gives time for an appearance at a library event, as well as the value in the use of his or her name. Arrangements for this kind of endorsement can be made through the celebrity's agent or publicist. A librarian would usually approach someone who has displayed some interest in similar projects or who is a native of, or closely identified with, the community. Many celebrities welcome the opportunity to be identified with a valued institution because of the good will it engenders for them.

Grant Support

Grants from private foundations and government agencies are an important source of money for specific projects. Grants can pay for the provision of computers in the children's department, the establishment of a literacy program, or the development of a collection of multicultural materials. Grants are targeted funds; they cannot usually be obtained to pay ongoing library costs. Grant money allows the library to initiate a new program or service. After the project has been established, the library is responsible for its maintenance. In applying for grant money, choose projects that are central to the library's mission so that they can be continued after the grant funding is ended.

Locating Grant Opportunities

The first two steps in obtaining a grant are to identify an unmet need and to learn about available grant sources. A librarian might recognize the need for Internet access beyond what the library budget can provide, for example, and search for an agency to provide grant funding. Another librarian might learn that a large foundation is interested in funding literacy projects and recognize that the children's department could organize such a project locally. Whether the impetus comes from the library's need or from the foundation's funding interests is not as important as how well the two aspects match.

Many resources are available for locating funding agencies. The first are individuals within the library system or region who have been successful in obtaining grants. State agencies and associations usually have listings of agencies that have given grants to libraries. Members of the library board and individuals from other community agencies are also good sources of information. The local United Way or community donors group may also have lists of funds available locally.

The source of funding for many youth services in libraries is the Library Services and Technology Act (LSTA) grants. These funds come from the Institute for Museum and Library Services (IMLS) and are administered through state library agencies. Many state libraries use LSTA funds to provide summer reading programs, programs for teens, and to support preschool programs. State libraries also have funding for individual library programs through a grant application process. Many state libraries hold grant workshops for librarians to explain grant guidelines and answer questions. State libraries may also have privately donated funds to distribute, such as the Gates Foundation funds to support electronic services or Target Store literacy funds.

There are two other federal grant programs for public libraries. IMLS funds demonstration and research projects that innovate, document, and evaluate library service. IMLS leadership grants can cover a period of several years and involve a major effort for the library. The other federal program that benefits public libraries is the E-Rate program that funds telecommunications and Internet access. The E-Rate application is very demanding, so not all public libraries apply for it. Libraries serving low-income communities will be eligible for the most E-Rate funding as the purpose is to provide connectivity for people unable to pay for Internet access. If the children's staff wants to expand or develop Internet services, E-rate can help reduce the communication costs.

The Foundation Center, a clearinghouse for information about foundation funding, has an informative website (http://foundationcenter.org) that provides a wide range of resources, including information on individual foundations, lists of the largest foundations, reports on trends in grants, articles on how to write a grant proposal, and individuals to contact for further information. In addition to the website, the Foundation Center maintains libraries in several U.S. locations, offers workshops, and publishes books to help nonprofit organizations to apply for grants. Another important Internet location is the Chronicle of Philanthropy website (http://www.philanthropy.com). While this is not a library specific site, it gives current information to nonprofits on fundraising techniques and opportunities.

The librarian who has an idea for a fundable project but does not know which foundation to approach can search for a foundation through a subject approach, a geographical approach, or by using individual contacts. If a project falls within a specific subject area, such as developing a family health information collection, for example, locating agencies that have a mandate to give to health information or, more generally, to health research is a good starting point. A more general project, especially one that involves collaboration with other institutions, such as a literacy program for new immigrant families, might call for a geographic approach. The librarian could look for foundations that focus on promoting the development of a particular community or region.

Several books listing foundations and their patterns of giving grants can be found in any large library. The newer, online listings are more up-to-date and are a better source of current information. Most large foundations have their own websites with descriptions of the kinds of projects they seek and guidelines for proposals. The online resources (most of which are available on the Foundation Center's website) can be searched by name, by subject, or by geographic location.

Personal contacts with a funding agency are always useful, so if someone in the library, on the board of trustees, or in the community has a link to a foundation, this can be a great benefit. A grant will not be given on the basis of personal friendship, but an individual who knows the foundation from the inside can give valuable advice about the approach to take, the kind of proposal to write, and the amount of money likely to be forthcoming. Foundation staff are also a good source of advice as you prepare to apply for a grant.

Planning the Grant Proposal

The first step in preparing a grant proposal is to think through the project for which funding is being requested. Specific questions, such as the following, may be asked:

- Does the project fill an unmet need?
- What group of people will benefit from the project?
- What will be the result of the successful project? (e.g., more children prepared for school; better integration of an immigrant group into the community)
- Do the children's librarians have the expertise to carry out the project?
- Does the project duplicate or complement other social projects in the community?
- How will you know whether the project is successful? How will it be evaluated?
- How much will the project cost? What is the project's budget?
- How will the project activities continue in the future?
- Is there a specific time period during which the project must be undertaken?

Answering these questions will usually involve meeting with other staff members and perhaps outside experts in a planning session. Granting agencies want to see documentation for claims that a project is worthwhile. Locate facts concerning the number of individuals in the target group, related activities of other social agencies, and realistic cost estimates for equipment and personnel time. Careful planning makes a grant proposal more effective.

The planning process will help in deciding which funding agency to approach. The required size of the budget is one important indicator. Many large foundations are not interested in funding small projects, and they may define these as "projects of $10,000 or less." Other grants, such as the LSTA grants, can be obtained for projects costing less than $1,000. Projects that seek to take advantage of a specific opportunity and need to be funded fairly quickly are not appropriate for large funding agencies, which usually require several months or more to make decisions. As the requirements of the project become clear, it will be easier to target the appropriate agency from which to request support.

Writing Proposals

Grant proposals normally follow a standard format. Librarians should always obtain information on guidelines from the specific foundation or granting agency that has been identified. If possible, obtain copies of grant proposals that lead to project funding in the past. The standard format includes the following parts:

- Executive summary or project abstract
- Statement of need
- Goals, objectives, and outcomes
- Project description
- Budget
- Evaluation plan
- Information about the organization

Some grants also require a plan for dissemination of the results of the project, a description of staff who will work on the project, and/or letters of support from the community or cooperating agencies. Grants may also include a cover letter that states the importance of the grant project. Follow directions for who needs to sign the grant. This might be the lead staff person who will direct the grant, the library director, or the head of the library board.

Executive Summary/Project Abstract: Although placed first in the grant proposal, the executive summary is usually written after the rest of the proposal has been completed. In a short proposal, the summary may be only a paragraph or two. A proposal of five pages or longer requires a one-page summary. The summary should express the most compelling aspects of the proposal. Key items from each section should be used in the summary. These should include a statement of the need for the project, an outline of the project itself, the amount of funding requested, and a statement about the department's ability to carry out the project.

Statement of Need: The statement of need is usually the first section written. This statement enables the reader to understand the background issues. The facts about the situation should be framed in terms of the local conditions and needs, not general statistics about national problems. Be sure that the need is stated in terms of client need, rather than library need. Explain that the problem could be helped or alleviated by some change in library service. Show that the program to be funded presents a better or different approach to the problem than those now available. If other community agencies are addressing the same problem, describe how the project complements their work or that collaboration with them may be possible.

Goals, Objectives, and Outcomes: The grant narrative usually starts with a statement of goals or objectives—the measurable outcomes of the project (see chapter 2). The objectives must be realistic. It is unwise to promise more than can be delivered because the funder will expect a final report documenting the achievement of the project's objectives. A proposal for a small grant might have only one or two limited objectives; a larger grant request might have several, perhaps extending over a period of months or years. Outcomes should relate to the audience served and how the activities will change them.

Project Description: The methods by which the project will achieve its objectives must be clearly stated. The funder expects to see a list of the specific activities to be undertaken. The method of recruiting participants, what activities will be offered and by whom, and the time lines for the project should be spelled out.

Budget: Before preparing the budget, review the project description and make notes of the costs of each aspect of the project. The budget should include the cost of staff time, additional personnel, materials, supplies, publicity, and equipment. The library's accounting department can provide information about these costs, although outside estimates on some costs may be necessary. Grant applications make clear which costs will be covered by the grant and which costs the library will have to cover. Some grants ask for matching funds from the library, often in the form of staff salaries or other key areas such as use of library space or equipment.

If a small grant is being requested for a specific purpose, such as buying materials for a special collection, including the costs of staff time might not be necessary. For large grant applications, staff time to administer the grant, evaluate it, and prepare a final report should be part of the budget request. Budget requests must be realistic. Asking for too little money may result in not completing the project. Overestimating costs may lead to a rejection of the grant; or, if the money is given, having to refund the unspent portion to the agency at the end of the project. This, too, gives a bad impression of the library's ability to handle grants. A carefully planned and clearly stated budget makes the proposal look professional and, therefore, more likely to be funded.

Evaluation Plan: The way in which the project is to be evaluated should be planned as the project is developed. An evaluation of the project is usually required in the final report to the funding agency. Some projects have obvious evaluation criteria. Other projects—for example, providing a program to help toddlers develop language skills—are more difficult to evaluate. The number of participants is one measure of success. The librarian may want to solicit anecdotes from the participating parents about their children's growing use of language. Most funding agencies like to see quantitative evaluation measures of a project's success, but qualitative, anecdotal evidence, particularly if collected by survey or in a focus group, can also be impressive.

Information about the Organization: Though libraries are well-established institutions in the community, the funding agency may want specific information on library programs that relate to the grant. Many agencies require that specific information be attached to a proposal—a listing of the library board, the staff, annual report and financial data. If the library has received grants in the past, these should be noted. In making awards, funding agencies also look for a successful track record in handling grant projects. Information on other agencies which are partners in the project may be required. Qualifications of staff to do the project may be included as well as the qualifications of consultants hired to work on the grant.

Proposals for small projects, those for less than $1,000, often require only a two or three page letter rather than a formal proposal. This is especially true if the agency has previously funded library projects. No matter how brief the letter, it should include the elements of a proposal as outlined in the previous sections. No matter the length, it is important to read the grant proposal guidelines carefully, follow the directions and meet all deadlines.

Although preparing proposals for a grant is time consuming and difficult, the process reaps rewards beyond the value of the grants themselves. Even if the grant proposal does not receive funding, the process of writing it forces library staff to think about their objectives and the way they may be attained. Often, an unsuccessful grant application can be sent to another agency and eventually find funding. Occasionally, community officials may recognize the value of the project and authorize its funding from regular tax sources.

Being awarded a grant by a government agency or respected foundation is a tribute to the strength and value of the library. Even though the monetary value of the grant may not be large, the award means that an objective agency has analyzed the proposal and acknowledged that the library is doing important work. Each successful grant helps add to the library's image as a successful community agency.

Library Marketing and Fundraising

Marketing and image building is often considered essential homework for successful fundraising. A good image is a necessary asset for success. "Libraries, like other not-for-profit institutions, base their successful fundraising culture on outstanding service, appropriate marketing and detailed attention to developing, cultivation and soliciting donors" (Holt and Holt 2007, 13). Beyond asking specific donors for funds, the children's librarian should work to build a good image for the department and the library. Using a variety of marketing techniques (see chapter 15) and seeking good coverage in the press are prerequisites for successful fundraising. Individuals, corporations, and grant-giving agencies are more likely to give to libraries that have a positive image and to librarians who are known to be successful in serving the community. Having a good track record and projecting success is a key to successful fundraising.

In addition to print and personal contacts with the community and with possible funders, public library web services help the library become more visible. Many nonprofit organizations find this visibility is useful for informing the public about their programs and for reaching potential members and donors who discover them on the web. Fundraisers find that the Internet offers a way to reach individuals who pay little attention to traditional fundraising techniques. "The Internet is an important tool for fundraising. While no one would recommend that you base your fundraising strategy solely on the Internet, it can save you time and money" (Grobman 2000, 1).

Although some public librarians would not want to use their websites to aggressively pursue funding, these sites can open the door to donors in a number of ways. Inviting visitors to the website to join a Friends of the Library group is one way to attract individuals. A membership form can be available on the website so an individual can immediately send the information to the

Friend's group mailing list. Newsletters can be mounted on the website and messages sent to email addresses to supplement the printed information that the Friends group distributes.

Several nonprofit organizations include a donor solicitation page on their website. Raising money for a specific project, such as enabling the library to subscribe to databases useful for homework help or to develop a computer club for children, might be particularly appealing to Internet users. Donors may prefer to give money for a particular purpose rather than to give to general library funds.

In order to get donations electronically, sell items on the Internet, or to allow the collection of Friends dues over the Internet, the library has to set up a secure website, be able to transact business done with a credit card, and have staff assigned to manage electronic donations and orders. Some libraries offer patrons the opportunity to order books for purchase from a vendor website and get a small profit off each sale. If a library has only a small number of electronic fund transfers, the secure website can be set up and maintained by an outside company at very low cost. If the library is not prepared to take donations electronically, it can still use its website to inform donors about giving opportunities and collect the money by mail or phone.

Public libraries have not been aggressive fundraisers in the past and many librarians find it difficult to ask for money. They are not alone. Many professionals working in hospitals, universities, museums, and the arts also dislike fundraising. Nonetheless, the majority of taxpayers in the United States have decided to cut back tax funding to nonprofit groups. The only way to maintain services is to obtain money from the private sector. Because most librarians believe strongly that the services they provide are valuable to the community, they should be willing to take on the task of asking for money. The discomfort of asking disappears when the funding arrives and the project is accomplished. The satisfaction of seeing the library live up to its potential makes the effort of fundraising worthwhile.

REFERENCES AND ADDITIONAL READING

Burnett, Ken. 2006. *The Zen of Fundraising: 89 Timeless Ideas to Strengthen and Develop Your Donor Relationships.* San Francisco: Wiley.

Chronicle of Philanthropy, The. *Fund Raising.* www.philanthropy.com/fundraising.

Deerr, Kathleen. 1995. Budgeting. In *Youth Services Librarians as Managers: A How-to Guide from Budgeting to Personnel,* eds. Kathleen Staerkel, Mary Fellows, and Sue McCleaf Nespeca, 11–21. Chicago: American Library Association.

Foundation Center, The. *Knowledge to Build On.* http://foundationcenter.org.

Grobman, Gary, Grant, Gary, and Roller, Steve. 1999. *The Wilder Nonprofit Field Guide to Fundraising on the Internet.* St. Paul, MN: Amherst H. Wilder Foundation.

Hartsook, Robert. 2005. *Closing That Gift: How to Be Successful 99% of the Time.* Englewood Cliffs, NJ: Prentice-Hall.

Hennepin County Library. "Press Release." Hennepin Public Library. www.hclib.org/pub/info/support/whatsnew.cfm.

Holt, Leslie Edmonds, Holt, Glen, and Stratton, Lloyd. 2006. *Library Success: A Celebration of Library Innovation, Adaptation and Problem Solving.* Ipswitch, MA: EBSCO Publishing.

Mutz, John M., and Murray, Katherine. 2000. *Fundraising for Dummies.* Foster City, CA: IDG Books Worldwide.

Prentice, Ann. 1996. *Financial Planning for Libraries.* Library Administration Series. Lanham, MD: Scarecrow Press.

Steele, Victoria, and Elder, Stephen D. 2000. *Becoming a Fundraiser: The Principles and Practice of Library Development.* Chicago: American Library Association.

Swan, James. 2002. *Fundraising for Libraries: 25 Proven Ways to Get More Money for Your Library.* New York: Neal-Schuman.

Walter, Virginia. 2001. *Children and Libraries: Getting It Right.* Chicago: American Library Association.

8

Planning Facilities

A public library building is a visible symbol of a community's commitment to provide educational and cultural services to all of its residents. As library services change and become more varied and community expectations for public space change, library space needs to be designed, managed, and changed to meet the needs of many users during the library's service hours. Buildings that effectively provide for the wide range of interests and tastes of users are not easy to design. "The development of library building concepts should be evolutionary with new designs and features appearing as the needs of the people they serve change. As technology and logical infrastructure of the library changes in response to new needs, to new ways of providing service, to new material formats...a particular building will evolve for specific purposes" (McCabe 2000, 3).

Specifically children's librarians need to create space that is inviting and useful to a variety of children. "In order for the child to thrive, the physical setting and the social interactions within that setting must be suitable for the age or the child and right for the particular individual. This premise is basic to the design of developmentally appropriate environments for children. A clear understanding of developmental changes and the relationship of these changes to children's action patterns in public places is the foundation for providing appropriate library early childhood programs, spaces and services" (Feinberg 1998, 4). In other words the children's room should encourage use and positive activities for all the children who are served by the department.

While new buildings or major renovation projects are infrequent, children's librarians will often spend time with modifications to space as technology is added and subtracted, as collections grow and change, and as service patterns change. If nothing else, children's librarians need to keep the children's room clean, safe, and attractive so children, families, and school groups want to visit the library.

MANAGING THE CHILDREN'S DEPARTMENT SPACE

Day-to-Day Issues

Most libraries have custodial service or employ workers to clean the entire library and most libraries have contracts for repair of the library building, computer equipment, and furnishings. Some libraries even have preventive maintenance and cleaning programs that provide regular upkeep of machinery, carpet cleaning, and ventilation and lighting repair, for example. So why should children's librarians have to worry about dealing with cleaning or repairs?

One reason is practical, at the very least children's librarians have to let cleaners and repair workers know when there is a problem and make sure that problems are corrected in a timely fashion. The other is that children and children's activities in libraries may be messier than the adult counterpart. A storytime art activity with glue and glitter will likely be messier that an adult book discussion. Children's librarians should be prepared to clean minor messes or tidy up after kids have used the department for homework when necessary. It is also important to remove broken furniture and keep clutter off floors so kids won't trip, or make the problem worse. Young children can't read out-of-order signs, so hazards and frustrating malfunctions need to be removed and children supervised carefully.

Children's librarians should work closely with cleaners and others to keep the department space clean and in working order. Children are less knowledgeable about healthy behavior. Toddlers climb over all surfaces, teethers put everything in their mouths, and many older children believe in the popular five-second rule and will eat food off the floor, if they pick it up fast. Cleaning staff may not have experience with children's behavior so will need to work with the department to keep it healthy for the children who use it.

Looking Good

In addition to the basics of keeping the department clean and in repair, it is also important to keep the room looking attractive. "One way to achieve this is through the use of interesting displays that are appropriate to the space in the children's area. In addition to creating inviting space, displays can also be tools to promote the use of the children's collection, to define space, to promote activities, and to encourage children to use their own creativity" (Steele 2001, 52). This means that staff should display books, mount posters or other art on walls, and create bulletin boards that attract children to the department. Some children's departments also have stuffed animals or toys to use as decoration for the children's room. Staff also need to change displays and the art at least twice a year, to keep it fresh and to give children the message that there is always something new at the library.

Some children's areas are big enough to divide by age group, so the use of art and displays help all children feel welcome and help them find the area that has material specifically for them. Younger children need to have at least one cute focal point in the department that will attract them and help them remember the library as a happy place. This could be stuffed animals or posters only a few inches off the floor. Older children need some part of the children's department that is not babyish, so they feel comfortable. This could be as simple as having full-sized furniture, age appropriate book displays, or bulletin boards with children's art.

Adult Friendly

The children's department should also have adult friendly features. If the department welcomes parents and teachers to the department, it needs to have adult-sized furniture, so adults will be comfortable. Some libraries have rocking chairs or reading nooks to encourage adults to read with children, or at least be comfortable while their children use the room. Some libraries have posters and book displays about children's literature and child development in the children's department to further attract parents and teachers to the children's area.

The children's room should also have comfortable and useable staff space. Staff need work areas that are ergonomically designed for adults, that are approachable by children and adults and that provide good visual control of the children's area. While children's staff may be on the move most of the day, they need a reasonable work area. Children's staff need space out of the public eye where they can work on program planning, collection development, and displays, and where they can store materials for outreach. Staff should keep work areas tidy and set up storage areas so work and desk space can be shared by all staff. Secure storage is needed for coats, purses, and other personal items and these areas need to be kept clean. Staff used computers and machinery need to be kept in working order, stored out the reach of children and have secure storage when not being used.

RENOVATING THE CHILDREN'S DEPARTMENT

Changes in the children's room are most often made to accommodate additional computers or technology, but renovations may also include changes in shelving to accommodate more books, book displays, and new media, or for upkeep, such as new floor covering, replacement of old and worn furniture, or new paint on the walls. Since the size and basic design need to stay the same, the amount of change possible may be limited, but redecorating or renovation of the interior design gives the children's staff a chance to re-evaluate their space and make changes to better serve the children who use the area. Or a library might go for a whole new look. For example the Mount Laurel (NJ) library decided on a themed environment for the children's room. Tall shelving was replaced by slat wall panels, colorful paint went on gray walls, and comfortable, colorful seating was added. Users asked "When did you buy all these new books? When did you put in these new windows?" (same books, same windows). One Mom said, "Now I come into the library and just shop the wall" (book display) (Bernstein 2006, 66).

Furnishings

Many libraries budget for changes in furnishings on a regular basis. Even if the children's department has the sturdiest of chairs and tables, day-to-day use wears all furnishing out. Nothing can do more to make a room more welcoming and comfortable than to replace damaged and worn furniture. *Library Journal* has an annual review of the best of new furniture and display design (Spring Design Supplement) and this may a good place to start when looking to upgrade furnishings. Many library supply vendors exhibit at library conferences and have information on products both in catalogs and at their product websites.

New furniture should solve the immediate problem of replacing old or broken chairs, tables, desks, displayers, and other equipment, but it also can be used to add color, update the look of the children's room, and to make children more comfortable.

Other relatively simple changes can include new paint (and possibly a new color) on the walls, adding a new storytime rug, or changing signs. Other individual changes that are more disruptive such as getting new floor covering, shelving, or computer furniture, need to be done when the current materials are worn, stained, faded, or just dated. These changes give children's department staff a chance to upgrade and update as well as replace furnishing of the room.

Staff should consider the following when evaluating the children's room furnishings:

- If you were a child would you like thus environment?
- Are shelves, furniture, and the convenience facilities scaled for children?
- Does staff have visual control over the area?
- Has space been provided for display of materials geared for children? (Murphy 2007, 135)

Department Makeovers

Occasionally the children's department gets a complete makeover. Because of cost this does not happen often, but many libraries think interiors need to be totally redone every 10 to 12 years.

Infrastructure upgrades needed every 10 years include:

- electrical wiring
- telecommunications infrastructure
- ventilation
- repair of structural flaws
- changes needed to comply with changes in building codes

Rarely does the children's staff deal directly with these issues, but the need for large changes gives the department an opportunity to make more significant changes to the space than can be done on an annual basis.

Planning Interiors

Before making major changes to the children's room, staff must know how the library will be used by staff, patrons, and the community. Perhaps the most effective way to assess this use is to keep a record of the patterns of current use over a period of weeks or months before formal planning starts. Use of the children's department can be considered in terms of activities. Activities can be categorized as group activities and individual activities (see figure 8.1). By looking at this pattern of activity, a librarian can understand how the space and furniture is currently used in the children's department. For instance, choosing materials as in figure 8.1 requires space for 65 patrons at one time. Seating is needed for adults reading to children, groups of students working together, children doing school work, and children using audiovisual materials. Study tables and probably carrels are needed, as well as chairs or cushions for leisure reading.

As in assessing patron needs, the needs of staff must be judged on the basis of systematic observation of their activities over a period of time. Librarians may know, in general, the amount of space and equipment they need to do their work, but correcting a lack of space or facilities for one task can lead to the creation of new problems. Noting staff activities and needs for several weeks will provide a more accurate record of what is necessary than asking staff members to estimate needs. Some common types of staff activity are shown in figure 8.2.

Figure 8.1
Patron activities in the children's department.

Group Activities	Age of Participants	Numbers
Storytime	Preschool	20–25
Books for Babies	Toddlers + adults	10 dyads
Film showing	8–12 year olds	30–35
Group studying	8–12 year olds	4–6 each
Programs	6–12 year olds	20–25
Playing games	6–12 year olds	2–4 each
Using computers	6–12 year olds	2–3 each
Summer Reading Club	All ages	Small groups
Socializing	All ages	Small groups
Parties/Open House	All ages	100–150

Individual Activities	Age of Participants	Numbers
Choosing materials	Preschool	10–15 total
	School age	25–45 total
	Adults	4–5 total
	(Maximum total)	65 people
Reference	All ages	Individual
Reading	Preschool/adult	2 or 3 each
	School age	Individual
Using electronic resources	School age	Individual
Doing school work	School age	Individual
Storing outer garments	All ages	Individual
Washroom use	All ages	Boys & girls
Using telephone	School age	Individual

Figure 8.2
Staff activities in the children's department.

Activity	No. of Personnel at Any One Time	Facilities Needed
Administration	One	Private office Telephone/ fax Computer
Reference	One or two	Desk visible to public, telephone, computer
Programming	One	Desk or table, storage for craft supplies & books
Selection	One or two	Desk, shelving journals, & computer
Circulation	One or two	Public desk, terminals, telephone
Shelving	Two or three	Book trucks & shelving
Meetings	Entire staff	Access to meeting room
Personal	Entire staff	Access to lounge area & wash-rooms Personal lockers or storage space

When considering how to change the children's room it is also important to get staff input on what service a program space will be needed in the future. If a program room was available how would it be used? If display cases are added how would they be filled? Or, if a coat rack was added, there would be fewer coats on the floor.

It is also possible to get some good ideas from children and families that use the children's room. Parents may have suggestions that would make them more likely to use the library and children often see space differently from adults, so they may have some important suggestions to make. One library asked different aged children to sit on the floor of the children's room with a staff member and describe what they see. Staff can also ask older children to take them a tour of the room and tell the staff what they like and don't like. Some libraries have focus groups with parents before renovation to get more systematic input from them.

Housing the Collection

The number of books in a collection is not the only factor to be considered in planning collection space for a children's department. Differences in format and in needs for access determine the type of shelving required. Some questions to be considered are:

- Will books be shelved in the traditional spine out fashion, or will books be displayed cover out?
- What is the most logical way, given the shelving space available to divide types of materials? For example, put fiction on free-standing shelves and nonfiction on wall shelving to make it easier to keep books in order.
- What is the best way to divide the collection? Children's materials have traditionally been divided into preschool materials—primarily picture books—and materials for older children. Some libraries subdivide this further by having separate shelving for board books and for early reading books. Audiovisual materials can be shelved separately from books.
- What special types of shelving are needed? Picture book shelving needs to have a different design than standard books, face-out display shelves slant books toward the user, and magazine shelving usually allows for face-out display and storage of back issues.
- How should paperbacks be shelved—with hardbacks, or in spinners?
- How will audiovisual materials be shelved? Many choices exist.
- How high should shelving be? Children cannot reach high shelves, so books become inaccessible if adult shelving is used. Low shelving also makes it easier for the librarian to see what is happening in the department and to prevent discipline problems. The tops of such shelves can also be used for informal displays of new books or other items of seasonal or special interest.

Planning for Technology

Often wiring and the location of electrical outlets governs the number and placement of computer terminals. As more libraries use wireless computer technology, there may be more flexibility as to how to plan space of computers.

Computer work stations should have good light, have good ventilation, and be easy to supervise. Many libraries keep computer areas close to the information desk, so sign up is easy and staff is available to answer questions. When planning the table area for computers, allow space for two or three children or a child and an adult to use a terminal together. Children often want help from friends or adults or they see computing as more fun when done together.

Some libraries also offer the option of computing from laptops that are either brought from home or lent from the reference desk. Study tables are wired, so laptops can be plugged in and wireless service allows access anywhere in the library. Because computer technology is likely to continue to change, space plans should be flexible, so changes can be made as computing changes.

Other Considerations

Access to the collection is important not only for various age groups but also for patrons with disabilities. Government regulations, such as the Americans with Disabilities Act, require that all new and reconstructed public facilities must be "readily accessible to and usable by individuals with disabilities" (Harrison and Gilbert 1992, 177). Whenever possible, a new room should go beyond the minimum requirements to make use by persons with disabilities as convenient and pleasant as possible. Children with disabilities especially should not be segregated from other children who are using the library.

Signs in the library should be large enough to be easily read by individuals with limited vision, and their letters should be set in a simple, clear text with high contrast between the letters and the background. If the library has elevators, they should be equipped with Braille markings as well as a sound system to announce floors. Lighting should be sufficient in all sections of the library.

Objects such as fire extinguishers and wall lighting should not protrude into passageways or rooms. The children's room should be as childproof as possible. Tables, desks, and shelving should have round edges to avoid injury to young children. Empty electrical sockets should be caped and wiring should be hidden to protect infants.

Planning should include areas for displaying library materials or special exhibits. Changing displays can add visual excitement to a department, and displays will be more effective if appropriate space has been planned. Lockable glass-front cases make it possible for the department to display valuable borrowed materials as well as library materials. Display cases placed near the entrance to the department serve as an attractive introduction to the children's room.

See the decor section below for more information on interior design.

Exploring the Possibilities

Knowing the way the library is likely to be used and knowing the collections it will house are the first steps in planning facilities. After determining the needs, the planning committee should explore ways that these needs might be met. One way to do this is to visit other libraries, both locally and while attending conferences or workshops, or by visiting new library websites. Touring other facilities allows the planners to observe both successful and unsuccessful arrangements. It is useful not only to look at the library but also to talk to staff members to learn about unseen aspects of the design. Do certain colors tend to soil easily? Does the attractive soft sculpture pose any dangers to toddlers? Librarians who have experience with various approaches can offer invaluable advice about their efficiency and practicality.

Workshops and conference programs offer more formal advice on planning library facilities. At least one staff member should attend any program available during the planning period. Periodicals and books also offer helpful advice. *Library Journal* and *American Libraries* both publish an annual architectural issue that shows examples of new library buildings and gives specifications on their sizes and facilities. Some useful additional materials are included in the publication's reference list. New materials on planning are constantly appearing; a literature search of both print and electronic sources on the topic may locate new and helpful information.

PLANNING NEW LIBRARIES

Although planning and building new libraries or making extensive renovations to existing structures are not done frequently, librarians may find themselves involved in such planning at some time during their career. Decisions made at the crucial early stages of planning will affect the working conditions of current staff and of a future succession of librarians. Careful planning requires hard work over a period of time but the result can be a department that is both esthetically pleasing and that provides a setting for efficiently organized services.

Because of the constraints on spending for public buildings, an increasing number of communities are converting buildings designed for other purposes into library facilities. These buildings include schools, churches, supermarkets, post offices, banks, and private houses. Some library advocates believe that the conversion of existing structures offers advantages over new buildings "in terms of donations, rent-to-own, lease backs, joint use, and neighborhood improvement and redevelopment incentives" (MacDonald 1996, 288). A reuse project, if approached in a positive spirit, can often generate more community support than a new building because taxpayers perceive it as offering tax savings while it results in a valued facility. Although conversion projects take less time than the construction of a new building, both require careful and time-consuming planning.

Community Needs

Planning an effective facility requires that the planners know the community in which the library is being built and the community's uses for the building. Among the factors that affect planning are

- the number of people expected to use the building
- the demographics (including age, education level, and income) and growth pattern of the community
- the proportion of residential, business, and industrial use in the community
- the presence of other libraries and information services
- the availability of related institutions (e.g., museums, cultural institutions)
- the geographic location
- the community's social climate

The size of the community affects the size of the library, but the community's current population is not as important as the growth pattern. In a well-settled neighborhood where little space is available for new housing, the number of patrons may be stable. A new or expanding suburb, however, can be expected to grow over a period of years, and the clientele may strain the facility by the time it is opened. In a city where zoning regulations allow multiple housing to replace single-family homes, the population may dramatically increase. Most communities' planning offices can provide projected figures for the growth of specific neighborhoods. Schools may also project how many students will be entering school in the next decade.

The small-scale geographic differences of building sites include the presence of public transportation, sidewalks on adjacent streets, and the location of highways or major traffic arteries, which often make it easier for people to drive to the library but less easy to walk there. Adequate parking space is necessary, and access for bicyclists and pedestrians should be provided.

The proximity of other types of buildings affects library use patterns. A library in or near a shopping mall is likely to have a different pattern of use—more unattended children and shorter patron visits—than a library located in a residential area. Being situated in or near areas that parents think are unsafe, such as parks or industrial sites, may limit library use unless special efforts are made to provide appropriate lighting and security.

The social climate of the community, especially a small community, should also be taken into account in designing a library building. If families tend to engage in recreational activities together, the children's department will need more extensive adult/child reading areas than in a community where children tend to come alone to the library. Libraries in communities with extensive day care facilities will likely need more group activity space than those in communities where most preschool children are cared for at home. If many children in the community are homeschooled, provisions should be made for children's study areas. History also plays a role; a library that has traditionally hosted an end-of-school program for children will want to ensure that new facilities offer space to carry on the program.

During the early stages of planning, the library staff should make a conscious effort to list aspects of the community that might affect building plans. A file of suggestions from various staff members may give the planning committee insights it would not otherwise have.

Creating the Building Program

Decision Points

One of the early decisions to be made in designing a children's department is its location within the building. This decision will be based on how much separation from the adult department is desired and on the practicalities of staffing and use.

Preparing Plans

Most libraries built in recent years have had an open plan, with the children's section visible and accessible from the adult circulation department, but clearly indicated by decor and signage as a special area for children. The nature of the community can influence the desirable level of separation. If parents, children, and teenagers are the main users of a library branch, the traffic between adult and children's section is likely to be heavy, and noise from the children's department is unlikely to offend adult users. If, on the other hand, many adults are using the library for business or study, they may prefer to have the children's department out of sight and range of hearing. Usually, it is best to have the browsing shelves closest to the children's department and to place the adult reference and study areas at the furthest distance.

The placement of washrooms and other public facilities deserves careful thought. The best solution is to have children's washrooms within the department, with the entrance to them visible from the librarian's desk. This allows the library staff to monitor their use. If washrooms are available only in the adult department, children may disturb adults as they walk through the area, and the washrooms must be kept locked to protect children's safety. Washrooms in the entrance hall or on a corridor, out of sight of library staff, are particularly undesirable for children's use.

Lighting is a major factor in planning, as it can add to the comfort level of the library. Natural light is one way to light a library, but direct sunlight can damage materials and make the building uncomfortably warm. Windows that bring light into the room without occupying too much wall space are ideal. Strip windows located across the top of wall shelving are practical, although they usually require drapes or blinds to prevent the sunlight from fading the interior or blinding library users. Windows not only provide light but keep both staff and patrons aware of weather situations—snowstorms or rain—and may enhance the beauty of the room by providing a view of the sky, trees, or a cityscape.

Artificial lighting is necessary in a library, regardless of the number of windows. Most children's departments are busy in the evening because many parents and school-age children find this the most convenient time to visit the library. Since most library activities involve close viewing of print or nonprint materials, sufficient lighting should be available throughout the department. Standards of lighting have changed in recent years as scientists have come to understand that the glare of bright light on paper may make reading more difficult than a lower level of lighting. Consultation with lighting experts and vision specialists can help library planners choose the most effective lighting for a particular facility.

Sound control is important in children's departments because children tend to work and play together when they are using library resources. Ceiling materials, drapes, and carpeting can deaden the sounds of library use and make the atmosphere more pleasant, especially when the library is crowded. The area to be used for programs should be designed so that a reasonable number of children can hear a storyteller's or reader's voice. If the area is clearly marked and has doors to close it off from the rest of the department, it is much easier for the library staff to present programs that include music or sound effects without disturbing other library users.

Spacing is another important consideration. The most practical shape for a room is generally a square, and space arrangements should be determined by traffic flow. The most heavily used resources are best located closest to the center of the room. Librarian's desks should be centrally located for easy access and to allow the librarian to keep an eye on all activities. Usually the librarian's desk is located near the reference section and computer terminals because children often need help with these items.

Some planners believe that wall space should be reserved for people, and stacks should be placed in the center of the room. However, center stacks can prevent the librarian from visually monitoring the room. Wall shelving makes a small room look larger and can permit greater flexibility in the use of space. When working with the architect, the librarian should try to ensure that the space will allow flexibility in furnishing. Electrical outlets should be placed so that terminals and AV equipment can be used in any area of the room. Structural designs, such as a story pit, should be considered carefully because they are permanent and limit the use of space. Built-in features may determine the location of various sections for many years. It may be preferable to impose few structural limitations on the space allowed for the children's department.

Presenting Plans

As part of the planning process, each department will probably be asked to make suggestions about the department's needs and desires. This is the time when the initial work of observing and documenting library use will pay dividends. The department head who knows the average number of patrons in the department at various times, the activities of the patrons, and the needs of patrons and staff will be in a better position to present credible requirements than one who relies on intuition. The representative of the children's department who attends planning committee meetings should go prepared with written documentation of the department's concerns. Because all demands cannot be met, the department head should be flexible but make as strong a case as possible for planning an ideal facility. In addition to knowing the department's present uses and possible future trends, the department representative can provide examples of other children's departments that incorporate the requested features. Finally, the department should establish priorities for equipment or space that may be relinquished in case of cutbacks.

The planning committee usually includes members of the library board, but sometimes department representatives are expected to present their cases to the entire library board. Because the board members are less familiar with the day-to-day operations of the library than staff members are, the documentation given to board members should be complete and persuasive. At the same time, it is important not to waste board members' time with lengthy oral presentations. A clear, concise handout for each board member can provide the basic facts. The oral presentation should be brief and devoted primarily to answering questions about the plans.

Planning the Layout and Decor

When the library board has decided on an architectural firm, the department head may meet with architects to discuss the plans. At these meetings, the librarian should make clear the requirements for maintaining an efficient department. The architects may have valuable and innovative suggestions for meeting these requirements, but it is the librarian's task to ensure that these requirements are met. As discussed above, librarians need to plan the best use of space including patron use, staff needs, collection storage, and program and computer space. Every suggestion should be tested by asking such questions as the following:

- How will this suggestion help us provide better library services?
- Could this suggestion cause extra work for the staff?
- Could this suggestion cause a danger to children? (Attractive seating arrangements and sculptures, such as castles and dragons, have had to be dismantled in libraries because of their potential danger to young children.)
- Has this suggestion been tried in other libraries, and if so, how successful does the staff consider it to be? (See figures 8.3, 8.4, and 8.5.)

Once the building plans have been finalized, attention will turn to the library's interior decor. Some architectural firms have design departments that work with clients in this type of planning. Or, the library may work with individual

Figure 8.3
**Inside the ImaginOn children's library in Charlotte, NC, work stations for the
youngest children are sized and decorated to attract users. Photo by Glen E. Holt.**

designers to coordinate color schemes, choose furniture and floor coverings, and add the finishing touches.

The goal of interior design for a children's department is to produce a space that is friendly, approachable, and welcoming for all users. The overall effect should be lively and appealing, with sections that visually indicate whether they are planned for toddlers playing with toys and board books, or for school-age children using computers and reference materials for school projects.

Informal seating should allow for a variety of postures while reading or taking notes but should somewhat limit conversational groups. For children, carpeting and cushions can take the place of chairs or carrels. However, study carrels are good for children who have a difficult time concentrating. The ideal room provides a variety of types of seating and work areas. Children, as a rule, like to sit closer to one another than do adults. Furniture should be scaled for children but should also allow for adult use as adults frequently accompany children. Comfortable seating arrangements should be available for parents that read to their children.

Figure 8.4
**In Springfield, MO, the Library Station branch has a transportation theme that cel-
ebrates Springfield's history as a transportation hub. The children's area's centerpiece
is a train that children use as a reading area. Photo by Glen E. Holt.**

Usually the colors used in the children's department are brighter than those
in other sections of the library. The staff can gather ideas for effective color
schemes by visiting other libraries. Some librarians are tempted to carry their
personal color choices over into the library setting. This is unwise, because
public spaces have different purposes than private spaces. It is better to look at
public buildings—theaters, museums, and shopping malls, in addition to other
libraries—for ideas about colors for walls, carpets, and furniture.

Signage is another important aspect of planning. Many new users, both
young children and their parents, will be coming to a children's department, so
signs should be large, clear, and well placed. Pictures that reinforce the meaning
of the printed words help young readers. There are many commercial signage
systems to choose from. Some libraries get creative with signs, fitting them into
the theme of the room. Signs can be hung from the ceiling, mounted on shelves,
or put on the wall. The decorator can plan the colors, lettering, and style of the
signs to fit in with the overall decorative plan.

Artwork adds color and interest to a department and should be incorporated in the department's design. Permanent works of art, such as murals, add
color and interest to walls. Some libraries have three dimensional objects such
as trains, story panels, or play houses in the children's room. However, they
limit the amount of display space available for temporary exhibits and may
lose their charm over time. Many libraries have found that changeable displays
and exhibits are preferable to permanent, built-in art. Glass-front display cases

Figure 8.5
When the Barr branch in St. Louis, MO, was renovated the new entrance included the tortoise beating the hare in a race to the library. Photo by Glen E. Holt.

in which pictures, art objects, and books can be placed offer flexibility. Space for hanging posters, children's drawings, and seasonal decorations is also useful. Areas of corkboard or other soft surface make it possible to hang pictures and other items easily and safely. The decorator can suggest practical ways to achieve flexibility in the display of artworks.

Moving into New Facilities

A department head normally does not decide the procedure for the move to a new facility, but everyone on the planning committee should know the options and make suggestions. Although a professional moving company usually takes responsibility for transporting books and equipment to the new location, the library staff will need to plan every detail of the move. Public libraries may use volunteers to help in moving a collection, with the library staff supervising these volunteers.

To prepare for a move, the librarian must know the current collection, its space requirements, and its arrangement in the new facility. Computer programs are useful in planning the amount of space for housing a collection and in determining the best layout for the collection in the new facility. Sufficient time (several months) must be spent in determining the exact requirements and how they can best be met.

Evaluating the New Building

It is always desirable to allow staff some transition time to get used to a new building. A week may be needed to re-shelve the collection, get computers to work, and finish up last minute installations. Even a weekend for staff to settle in saves time in the end. Regardless of how efficient the move may be, some unexpected problems will occur in settling into a new facility. All of the equipment should be tested as quickly as possible so that any failures can be noted and corrected. Staff members may have some difficulty in adjusting to new conditions, so additional time may be required to handle routine tasks. However, this situation should rapidly improve. Although the new facilities should be an improvement over the old building, it is wise to keep notes on any miscalculations or desired changes. Notes about disappointments and failings in the new building will make it easier to plan for the inevitable day when yet another change will be needed.

Although few new facilities are systematically evaluated after they have been built or renovated, a strong case can be made for including evaluation as part of the overall plan. As Lushington and Kusack (1991, 117) claim: "No matter how excellent the architect or how diligent the planners are in evaluating the plans, the true test of the building comes when it is built, occupied, and used. Plan evaluation is abstract and primarily an intellectual exercise; post-occupancy evaluation is concrete and involves the natural complexity of real life. Both types of evaluation make important contributions to the improvement of library buildings."

Evaluation should not begin until at least six months after the new building has been occupied. By that time, staff and patrons will have had time to become used to changes. Even if the entire library is not planning an evaluation, an individual department can carry out a small-scale study of how its particular service has been affected by a move.

The first step in an evaluation is to collect observations and evidence about visible problems. Providing a notebook in which any staff member can record observations will facilitate the collection of information. A roof that leaks or a heating system that delivers uneven warmth are examples of obvious problems that should be recorded. Notable successes, such as a doubling of circulation or an increase in library card registration, are also part of the record. Statistics of performance measures in the old building should be compared with those of the new facilities. These measures will indicate changes in service to the community. If time and resources are available, questionnaires may be administered to individuals using the children's department to determine their satisfaction with the facility. All of these efforts will result in a collection of useful data to indicate directions for planning future changes.

REFERENCES AND ADDITIONAL READING

Bernstein, Joan E., and Schalk-Greene, Kathy. 2006. Extreme Library Makeover: One Year Later [April]. *American Libraries* 37: 66–69.

Brown, Carol R. 2002. *Interior Design for Libraries. Drawing on Function and Appeal.* Chicago: American Library Association.

Feinberg, Sandra, Kuchner, Joan, and Feldman, Sari. 1998. *Learning Environments for Young Children.* Chicago: American Library Association.

Harrison, Maureen, and Gilbert, Steve eds. 1992. *The Americans with Disabilities Act Handbook. Landmark Laws Series.* Beverly Hills, CA: Excellent Books.

Lushington, Nolan, and Kusack, James M. 1991. *The Design and Evaluation of Public Library Buildings.* Hamden, CT: Library Professional Publication.

MacDonald, Gregory. 1996. Building ReUse: Right for the Times. *Public Libraries* 35: 288–291.

McCabe, Gerald B. 2000. *Planning for a New Generation of Public Library Buildings.* Westport, CT: Greenwood Press.

Murphy, Tish. 2007. *Library Furnishings: A Planning Guide.* Jefferson, NC: McFarland.

Steele, Anitra. 2001. *Bare Bones Children's Services.* Chicago: American Library Association.

Sullivan, Michael. 2005. *Fundamentals of Children's Services:* ALA Fundamentals Series. Chicago: American Library Association.

Taney, Kimberly Bolan. 2003. *Teen Spaces: The Step-By-Step Library Makeover.* Chicago: American Library Association.

9

Keeping Children Safe and Problem-free in the Library

Public libraries are public spaces that should be welcoming and accessible to all members of the community. The American Library Association proclaims "Libraries in America are cornerstones of the communities they serve. Free access to the books, ideas, resources, and information in America's libraries is imperative for education, employment, enjoyment, and self-government" (1999).

When children visit the library to find materials or information, their families expect them to be safe and protected from danger and harassment. Well-run libraries are usually problem-free, but librarians must be prepared to cope with threats to people or property if they are to serve their communities well. Problems can be divided into those caused by natural disasters and those caused by individuals or groups of people. The keys to maintaining a safe and problem-free library are organization, balancing individual needs, and handling emergencies.

ORGANIZING TO MAINTAIN SECURITY

Developing Policies

Although problems occur in even the best-run library, sound planning can minimize the damage. Every library should have a board-approved policy outlining the steps to be taken in various emergencies. These plans must be reviewed and updated frequently and every department should have a current copy of the plan easily available for all staff (Baltimore County Public Library 1987). Electronic copies of contingency plans are usually available online and print copies are often kept in a loose-leaf notebook for quick and easy reference. At least one electronic copy should be stored off-site where it can be retrieved if the library building is inaccessible. All staff members should be aware of the contingency plans and should know what they will be expected to do in various situations. In addition to the general library plans, children's departments often develop their own policies for problems specific to young people.

Developing plans for appropriate action in emergencies requires input from outside agencies as well as from library staff. The general principles of planning are similar in most libraries, but the implementation may vary depending on local conditions. It is important to know how local agencies such as the police, medical, and fire services prefer to be informed of emergencies and which agency is the appropriate one to be notified of particular occurrences.

Contingency documents are usually divided into a number of sections:

- physical emergencies
- medical emergencies
- security problems
- difficulties with patrons

A committee of staff members will write each section in consultation with appropriate outside agencies. Each section should include general principles governing the event (emptying the building quickly in case of suspected fire, for example) and then list the specific procedures to accomplish those goals. Contact information for individuals to be notified must be specified. While the principles of dealing with emergencies may remain relatively constant, the specific procedures must be reviewed and updated at least twice a year and whenever a change of personnel occurs in a relevant department.

After the planning document has been drafted, it should be reviewed by the library administration, appropriate civic agencies, and the library board. The board will give final approval to the document and take responsibility for actions carried out under the plan. Individual librarians who are acting in accordance with the accepted contingency plans are thus relieved of liability for injuries that might occur during an emergency.

Taking Responsibility

A basic principle of good administration is that any time the library is open, one designated person is in charge. One of the weaknesses in the emergency procedures of many libraries is the failure to specify the staff member in charge when an emergency occurs (Curry 1996, 182). This can lead to confusion and occasionally may put a staff member or patron in danger. Normally the department head or another professional staff member is the person in charge. During meal hours, coffee breaks, or on Sundays or evenings, when the professional staff may not be on duty, someone in the department should take responsibility for observing and handling emergencies and notifying the proper authorities if something out-of-order occurs. Most minor problems, such as a leaking roof or broken furniture, can be handled by contacting the maintenance staff promptly or taking such common sense actions as putting a waste basket under a dripping roof. The major reason for having one individual officially in charge of the department at all times is that when a more serious problem occurs, staff members immediately know to whom they should report.

Chain of Command

The individual in charge of the department must be aware of any unusual happenings in the department and make a decision about who needs to be notified. Small problems such as a burned out light bulb or a non-functioning computer can be reported to the maintenance or technical staff in a routine way. Most other problems, especially those involving patrons in the library should be documented and reported to the building supervisor. These would include

- loud or boisterous behavior by children or teenagers
- complaints about materials or staff
- accidents
- medical problems
- violence or threats of violence

The senior building administrator should be notified whenever the department implements emergency procedures. If a problem is not serious, the report may be a memo after the event, but it is important that the branch head or chief librarian know about unusual occurrences in every department.

Reporting Problems

Frequently a difficulty in one department is noticeable throughout the building, but this is not always true, especially if a department is somewhat isolated from other departments. Communication is one of the keys to avoiding crises in libraries especially those involving patrons. The first people who need to know that something unusual is going on are the staff in the department. This can be done by using simple signals. For example, the staff may keep the form for reporting complaints about materials on a bright green or yellow clipboard. When staff members see a colleague take out this clipboard, they are aware a complaint is being made and can be alert for the possibility of abusive language or behavior from the patron.

Telephones are the obvious way to communicate with another department or with the security office. If police or other community departments should be called, this is usually done by the building supervisor or a delegate. Instant messaging or a pager may be appropriate to reach someone who is away from her desk. The method of communication is not as important as having a plan describing what will be done.

A written memo or report may be the best way to report an incident that was successfully resolved in the department. These incidents should be documented because unless the librarian in charge of a department knows about past patterns of behavior, he or she may be caught unawares by an unexpected crisis. An example of this cited in one article is a staff member becoming emotionally upset as the result of being stared at persistently by a member of the public (Curry 1996, 186–187). An earlier discussion of this behavior at staff meetings might have avoided an unpleasant reaction.

Any problem that necessitates calling in outside authorities should be reported not only to the building manager but also to administrators at the system level. A continuing series of lower-level problems such as disruptive children or teenagers usually is a matter for systemwide monitoring. Often, problems in one branch move to another; good communications can help prevent their spread.

Libraries need support from community resources such as the police and fire departments, utility companies, and occasionally schools or other social agencies for many problems. The library's contingency plan specifies when an outside agency should be contacted. Most fire departments want to be notified whenever a fire occurs, but police departments have varying policies about what kind of disturbance they will respond to. The library needs to consult with the agency and keep the contingency plan up to date on their latest advice. When a sudden serious incident occurs, of course, calling 911 or other emergency numbers is the fastest and most appropriate action.

BALANCING THE NEEDS OF ALL PATRONS

A public library provides open access for all members of the community, but not everyone uses the library for the same purposes and these differences can cause tension. Issues can range from the minor irritation of noisy babies or teenagers to the serious threat of violence or drug dealing. Librarians must know how to cope with any of these diverse difficulties.

Unattended Children

Children who come to the library for periods of time before or after school each day while their parents are at work are often called latchkey children or self-care children. The presence of these children in the library offers librarians an opportunity to encourage reading and the use of other materials, but the length of time children spend in the library may cause problems. Some parents tell the children to stay in the library until there is someone at home to take care of them. This means that after school and on holidays the library may be host to many children who would rather be someplace else. Although they may not be disruptive, many of the children are not content to read or use library materials for the entire time that they are in the library. A lack of other kinds of activities may lead them to play boisterous games or socialize loudly. They may monopolize the computers and try to keep other children from using them.

Most children's librarians are committed to providing the best possible service to latchkey children. Most self-care children come from homes where no adult is available to supervise the children in the afternoon. Parents want to find a safe place for their children, but many do not realize that too many children in the library every afternoon may cause problems. Libraries have discovered that "after-school programs for unattended children reduce behavior problems and risks to children's welfare, and they provide the personal gratification of seeing a 'problem child' succeed in a structured environment" (*Unattended Children* 25).

Many libraries have tried to meet the needs of these children by providing organized after school and school break activities. Among these have been:

- Survival skills workshops (cooking, home safety, emergency preparedness)
- Homework help and tutoring
- Drop-in programs

- Reading programs
- Volunteer opportunities
- Outreach (*Unattended Children* 22)

Providing these services is expensive in staff time and money, but the benefits in increased child literacy and a decrease in troubled behavior make the expense worthwhile. Costs may be reduced by cooperating with other community organizations to share staff time as well as direct costs. For example, the library could provide programming one afternoon a week with the understanding that other community groups will handle the other four afternoons.

Some libraries have rules requiring that children under a specified age must be accompanied by an adult. This discourages library use by preteen children and may lead to a decline in library use by many families. A less confrontational policy can set out the kind of behavior and responsibility acceptable to the library. This policy should build on the current library policies for all patrons. Steps in drawing up such a policy include

- Reviewing existing patron behavior policy so that any new policy will not single out children for special treatment
- Becoming familiar with local and state laws regarding children
- Getting input from staff members who have experience with unattended children
- Looking at the policies of libraries in your area and asking librarians how well they have worked

Library policies vary considerably. This is a small sample:

The Beloit Public Library encourages children and families to use its facility together. When children are left unattended at the library problems can arise. Young children may become frightened or confused and wander away. Older children cannot be expected to deal with a small child who is frightened, tired or ill. Older children left on their own for extended periods may become bored and disruptive. Since the library is a public building, strangers might approach children. If an unattended child has a medical emergency, the library staff cannot take legal responsibility. Therefore to protect children while using the library and to provide all customers with a facility that is safe, pleasant and conducive to library use, the following guidelines must be observed:

1. A caregiver over the age of fourteen (14) must accompany every person under the age of twelve (12). The caregiver is responsible for the behavior and supervision of children in their care while at the library.
2. The library reserves the right to contact parents, guardians or proper authorities if minors are left unattended and require supervision.
3. The library requires that caregivers of children under the age of eight (8) stay within the line of sight of the children. (Beloit Public Library, Wisconsin)

Children age 6 and under may not be left alone without adult supervision. If children under 6 are left unattended, library staff may call the police to locate parents. Children

---

older than 6 who enjoy using the library on their own are welcome. We encourage them to visit for a reasonable period of time—that is, a length of time that they can remain comfortable, interested and involved with using the library. Most children reach their limits in about an hour. If children older than 6 are unattended and become disruptive to service, library staff may ask them to leave the building (Manhattan Public Library, Kansas).

Children up to age 10 must have a parent/caregiver in the immediate vicinity of, and in visual contact with them. The assigned caregiver must be a responsible person and must carry emergency contact information. An exception would be children attending a library program without the parent or caregiver in the room, but the parent/caregiver is expected to remain in the library building and to immediately join the child at the end of the program. If a child in this age group is found unattended, library staff will attempt to locate the parent/caregiver in the library and inform him/her of the rules. If the parent/caregiver cannot be found, or if the child is found unattended again, the Sheriff's department will be called for assistance (Calcasieu Parish Public Library, Lake Charles, Louisiana).

For the safety and comfort of children, a responsible adult or caregiver should accompany children while they are using the Library. While in the Library, parents and caregivers are responsible for monitoring and regulating the behavior of their children (Seattle Public Library, Washington).

Decisions about the appropriate age at which an unattended child in a library is acceptable will vary from one community to another. This kind of decision should be made after discussion with library staff and a consideration of the location of the library. Do many children walk to the library? Is the library close to an elementary school, so that children could stop into the library for an hour or so after school? Are there many adults in the library during after-school hours? These factors and others will affect the policies that librarians devise for unattended children.

Disruptive Children

Young people who are left in the children's room while their caregiver looks for books in the adult department or leaves the library for a short time, may become disruptive. Some unattended child policies, as shown above, require an adult to have the child in line of sight at all times in the library, although this is a difficult rule to enforce. Some three- or four-year-olds can browse contentedly in the picture book section for an hour or so, but younger children are likely to start pulling books from shelves, crumpling pages of magazines, or interfering with other children who are playing games or reading. The only recourse for the library staff is to prevent the child from continuing disruptive behavior while watching for the return of the adult who brought the child. If that is too slow, a staff member may take the child to the adult in another section of the library. A polite but firm explanation that young children cannot be left alone in the library may prevent future occurrences, but occasionally firmer action is needed. The adult should be informed that they will not be permitted to use the library unless the child remains under supervision. If a policy exists, a copy should be given to the adult.

Older children frequently like to work on school projects or homework in groups. This often causes considerable noise in a children's department, which is not a problem as long as it does not disturb other patrons. However, when children begin fighting or pushing and shoving in a disruptive way, the librarian should take some action.

- First step: a reprimand and a reminder of the need for reasonable noise levels in the library
- Second step: a warning that if the behavior does not stop the individuals involved will have to leave the library
- Third step: the children should be asked to leave and told they may return when they are prepared to behave appropriately

If the same group of children continues to be disruptive in the library, they may be barred from using it for a period of time—a week or so. Barring children from the library should be done with caution, because public libraries are meant to encourage, not discourage, use. Sometimes groups of children who are not allowed into the library will hang around outside and harass library users. If the situation persists, it is usually best to try to gain the group's cooperation by meeting with them to discuss causes and possible solutions to problems. Allowing the youngsters to make suggestions about developing library rules may help to make them cooperative patrons. If the children habitually use the library and stay in its vicinity, it is clear that they see the institution as a place where they want to be. The library should make it possible for children to use the library without disrupting service to others.

Serious Delinquency

Occasionally children or teenagers go beyond merely causing annoyance to other patrons. Vandalism may include damaging or defacing books and other materials or library computers, building, or grounds. If library staff identify the culprits, their parents should be notified because parents or guardians are responsible for restitution for costs of vandalism. If parental intervention does not put a stop to the activities, the police must be notified. Police generally take damage to computers, buildings, or grounds of the library more seriously than damage to materials. Persistent tearing or defacing books can be a serious problem, but it is often difficult to trace the offender. Carefully monitoring materials as they circulate can narrow the field of suspects and lead to identification of the offender. Usually, if the offender is a young person, notifying the parents and requiring payment for the damage are the most effective deterrents to further vandalism.

Theft and mutilation of books or other materials—CDs and DVDs are particularly vulnerable—can be a major headache. A study of small- and medium-sized libraries in British Columbia revealed that library managers consider mutilation of more concern than theft, because the rates have been increasing. (Curry et al. 2000, 19). Children's books and magazines are often mutilated by children searching for pictures to use in class projects, although the increasing availability of images on the Internet may change that. (Use of images taken from the Internet, of course, raises the issue of copyright infringement, which librarians also worry about.)

Even with an effective security system, a library can expect to lose a certain percentage of materials each year: two to four percent loss has been suggested as average (Lincoln 1984). When the figures go much higher than this, librarians should institute more effective measures of security. CDs and DVDs may be kept behind the circulation desk. The patron selects from the empty cases on display and receives the actual item at check-out. This helps to cut down on the loss of material from the shelves, but does not solve the problem of borrowers who fail to return items. Days or weeks of amnesty sometimes produce a flood of overdue materials, but many librarians feel that amnesty is unfair to patrons who do return materials on time.

Libraries have not found a comprehensive solution to the problem of theft. Some frequently used methods include

- Publicizing the severity of the problem though media releases
- Visiting schools to inform teachers about difficulties of requiring illustrations in reports
- Installing security systems or security guards at exits
- Notifying police if problem becomes severe

In addition to the common problems of vandalism and theft, some libraries have problems with the use or distribution of illegal or controlled substances in the library. While these offenses are most often perpetrated by teenagers or adults, school-age children are sometimes involved. Following are ways to minimize the opportunity for distributing illegal or controlled substances:

- Make sure all areas of the children's department can be observed by library staff.
- Keep bathrooms locked and give key only on request.
- Except for young children, allow only one individual at a time to use bathroom.
- Monitor the length of time any one person has the restroom key.

Problem Adults in the Children's Department

Adults who use the children's department of a public library are usually parents, teachers, college students, or members of professions involved with children's materials. Occasionally, however, adults in the children's department may pose a danger to children. Some public libraries, especially those in large cities, have made it a policy not to allow adults to remain in the children's department unless they are accompanying a child. Adults who wish to consult materials from the children's department are asked to use them in another area of the library. This approach may be necessary in some urban libraries, but smaller systems often prefer a more open policy. Generally, librarians should assume that every individual has a reason for using the library and may do so unless his or her behavior impinges on the rights of other patrons. However, the person in charge of the department needs to be alert to potential difficulty (Baltimore County Public Library 1987).

Pedophiles are attracted to places where children congregate and that of course includes public libraries. Library staff should be alert to what is happening in the department and keep an eye on adults in the children's room. They should pay attention if an adult approaches a child who did not come into the department with him or her. Frequently the child's reaction will indicate that the adult is a family member, but if it appears to be a stranger addressing the child, the librarian should intervene. This can be done by offering to help the child, thus forcing the adult to come up with some plausible explanation of what is going on. Usually this will be enough to frighten away a person whose intentions are inappropriate.

Most children learn while quite young to be wary of adults who might harm them. Books and courses that street proof children are popular with parents in many communities. Sometimes, however, children have difficulty knowing whether an adult in the children's department works in the library or is a stranger. For this reason, many departments provide nametags for staff members; children know that staff members wearing nametags can be trusted. This can be especially important for male children's librarians, because most children are taught to be more suspicious of men than of women.

In contrast to adults who like children for the wrong reasons, some adults are annoyed or irritated by children in the library. If a children's department is adjacent to the adult department, or if the library is small, children's voices may be heard clearly in the adult department. Some adults are disturbed by this noise, especially if they are trying to work. Sometimes the problem can be solved by placing tables where adults might do concentrated work as far away as possible from the children's area. Adults who are browsing probably will not be disturbed by the children's noise. Added sound insulation, including carpeting or sound baffles such as felt or fabric hangings, can be useful too in reducing noise.

The library staff must set limits for noise in the children's department and not allow unreasonable demands for quiet. A subdued buzz of noise and conversation, punctuated occasionally by short periods of wailing or crying, is acceptable. Other patrons must learn to accept these sounds. An adult who is particularly irritated by noise may be offered the use of headphones to block out sound.

Children running around the adult department, shouting exuberantly or crying for long periods, disturb many adults. Librarians should require school-age children to restrict their noise to an acceptable level. Adults accompanying young children who cry for an unreasonably long time can be asked to take noisy children outside until they have quieted down. In any public facility the comfort of the majority of patrons and staff must be given due consideration.

COMMON EMERGENCIES

Fires, storms, power outages, and medical emergencies are some of the most common disasters that strike libraries. Less sudden, but equally serious problems, can be caused by insects and animals. To avoid severe consequences from each of these, planning, preventative action, and emergency reactions are necessary.

Fires

Although most libraries are in fire-resistive buildings, the danger of fire still exists. Fire may damage materials and cause injuries. Consultation with the library's insurance agents will be necessary for developing plans for dealing with fire emergencies. In addition to having contingency plans, libraries should spell out preventive measures including

- fire alarms or detection systems that relay to a fire station
- fire extinguishers located in areas where small fires might occur (around electronic equipment, waste baskets, etc.)
- signs adjacent to fire exits advising the staff and public about steps to take in an emergency
- fire drills for the staff so that they are prepared to take appropriate action when a fire occurs

Actions to be taken when the fire alarm goes off or a fire is discovered may vary depending on the local situation, but the first priority is to evacuate the building. Patrons must be urged to leave the building immediately without stopping to pick up clothing or other possessions. School-age children are usually familiar with fire drills in school and can often be counted on to follow the directions given by an adult in authority. Patrons with disabilities, young children, and elderly patrons may need help. Deaf children cannot always hear alarms or directions, and blind children cannot see where danger lies. These children can be partnered with a child who is not disabled or with an adult who can lead the way to safety. Children in wheelchairs may be able to walk with assistance or may be carried outside. Wheelchairs should be left behind unless there is an exit without stairs immediately available. Very young children should be led or carried out of the building. The librarian must be sure that every child is included in the evacuation. After a room has been emptied of people, the door should be closed but not locked.

Once outside the building, children should be kept in a designated area until emergency personnel indicate it is safe to reenter the building. If the building remains dangerous for long, children who are old enough should be encouraged to go home. The librarian will have to arrange for preschoolers or disabled children to be picked up by parents or taken home by volunteers.

Storms

In areas where severe storms—blizzards, tornadoes, or hurricanes—occur, plans should be made to cope with these disasters. A designated staff member should monitor weather reports and emergency warnings and follow established procedures for disseminating the information to staff when necessary. A decision to close the library is usually made by the chief administrative officer, although occasionally the children's department may urge patrons to go home before the library is officially closed. If the storm threat is severe enough to make the streets dangerous, children should be encouraged to remain in the building. During severe electrical storms or high winds children are probably safer in the library than outside.

In regions where tornadoes occur, the library will have designated areas where patrons should take shelter when a tornado is imminent. Everyone on staff should know the procedures to follow when a storm occurs. Regular storm drills should be held for library staff, and new staff members should receive appropriate instruction.

Medical Emergencies

Medical emergencies affecting either staff or patrons must be handled quickly and decisively. These events may include heart attacks, seizures, psychotic episodes, choking, falls, and injuries ranging from a paper cut to a gunshot wound. Less acute medical problems may arise when a child in the library develops a fever, a rash, or starts throwing up. One effective contingency plan for medical emergencies is to have as many staff members as possible trained in first-aid techniques. For staff members who do not take formal courses, brief training in emergency procedures should be given periodically at staff meetings.

The staff member in charge of the department must decide what procedure to follow immediately. When any serious medical event occurs, 911 services should be called. If there is doubt about how serious the problem is, it is better to be over-cautious than careless.

While waiting for medical assistance to arrive, the library staff should keep the affected person comfortable and isolated from curious patrons. The department should have a blanket to keep the person warm, and a first-aid kit. Only first-aid that cannot wait should be attempted. This includes resuscitation if breathing stops, treatment for choking, and stopping dangerous bleeding.

When a child in the library appears to be sick but does not require emergency treatment, the librarian must use judgment in deciding what to do. If the child is with an adult but appears to have a contagious disease, the adult can be asked to take the child out of the library for the sake of other patrons. If the child is without an adult and appears to be ill, the librarian may call the child's home and suggest that a parent or other adult fetch the child. The most annoying, but probably least serious medical difficulty occurs when a child vomits. If the child is alone, a staff member can help her to the washroom, ask the janitor to clean up the mess, and notify the parent or guardian about the situation. This unpleasant but common duty, like similar situations when a child urinates or has a bowel movement, is part of the pattern of working with children.

Animals and Other Creatures

Problems with animals include pets that are brought or smuggled into the library and wildlife that wanders in. Most libraries require pets to be left outside the building, except perhaps for special programs. (Guide dogs for patrons with disabilities are an exception to this rule.) Dogs tied outside the building can be a nuisance if they bark and can become a problem if the owner leaves them for too long, especially in bad weather. If an animal is obviously uncomfortable, the child should be asked to take it home and to return to the library at another time. Children need to be encouraged to treat their pets humanely.

A variety of wildlife—birds, bats, skunks, raccoons, mice, stray cats, and squirrels—may occasionally be found in the library. Sometimes a bird or animal that has blundered into the building will leave quickly if given the opportunity (an open door or window). If this does not happen, the animal control department should be called. A wild animal may carry rabies and can endanger staff and patrons alike. Unless a staff member has special expertise, it is unwise to try to catch a wild animal without help, and children should never be allowed to try to catch wild creatures. Amateurs may frighten the creature and cause it to injure itself or to attack a person. Most animals that invade a library will stay out of the way of people if not disturbed and can be left in peace until the authorities arrive.

Some pests that invade libraries do not create immediate emergencies but pose long-term problems. Insects that attack books are not a major problem in most children's departments, where turnover is high and books are not kept in storage for long periods. Household pests such as ants, roaches, beetles, and silverfish are generally kept in check by regular pest control and by good maintenance.

Allowing food in public libraries can bring problems with insect infestations. The most effective way to avoid these is to enforce firm rules against food in the library, but this may not fit with library priorities. Several public libraries now have a designated area where patrons can obtain coffee, soft drinks, and snacks. These facilities are extremely popular with patrons who have grown used to bookstore cafes. It is probably wise, however, not to allow food in the children's department. If a program for children features food, it should be confined to a limited area that is cleaned soon after the program is over.

REFERENCES AND ADDITIONAL READING

American Libraries Association 1999. *Libraries: An American Value*. http://www.ala.org/ala/oif/statementspols/americanvalue/librariesamerican.htm.

Baltimore, County Public Library. 1987. *STEPS: Staff Training for Emergency Procedures at the Baltimore County Public Library*, Second Edition. Baltimore, MD: Baltimore County Public Library.

Curry, Ann. 1996. Managing the Problem Patron. *Public Libraries* 35: 181–188.

Curry, Ann, Susanna Flodin, and Matheson, Kelly. 2000. Theft and Mutilation of Library Materials: Coping with Biblio-Bandits. *Library and Archival Security* 15: 9–26.

Lincoln, Alan Jay. 1984. *Crime in the Library: A Study of Patterns, Impact, and Security*. New York: Bowker.

Unattended Children in the Public Library; A Resource Guide. 2000. Chicago: Association for Library Service to Children; Association for Library Trustees and Advocates; Public Library Association.

Section III

Managing Services

10

Collection Management

One of the children's department's primary roles is to provide materials for circulation and for use at the library. Creating and maintaining the department's collection is an essential responsibility of children's librarians. The task is often a natural one, as children's librarians enjoy children's literature and like spending time learning more about it. But collection management involves more than buying good books. Collection management is the process of providing the best collection over time. It includes selecting, purchasing, cataloging, weeding, and replacing materials. It is ongoing, systematic, and efficient. Good collection management is good stewardship of the library's resources.

COLLECTION MANAGEMENT INCLUDES

selection of all materials in all formats,

collection policies,

collection maintenance (selection for weeding, storage, preservation and serials cancellation),

budget and finance,

assessment of needs of users and potential users,

collection use studies, and

collection assessment and evaluation. (Johnson 2004, 2)

Generally all these tasks can be grouped in three activities: collection development, materials acquisitions, and cataloging and collection access. In addition to the fun of buying good books for children, librarians need to perfect their skills at the business side of collection management to get the most out of the time and money spent on the collection.

COLLECTION DEVELOPMENT

The provision of a collection of materials is a basic task of a library. A children's department collection includes fiction and nonfiction books, magazines, and non-print materials such as videos and DVDs and music and spoken word CDs. Unlike adult collections, children's collections are usually divided by reading level and include

- board books for toddlers
- picture books for non-readers
- beginning readers for children just learning to read
- easy chapter books
- nonfiction books

Many children's departments include books of interest to parents and teachers that have information about children and some may provide textbooks, tutoring materials, and multimedia kits. Materials in formats for special needs children—large print, Braille, or audiobooks—may also be part of the collection. Some libraries have collections in languages other than English. Libraries may also have historical children's literature collections or special collections on local or regional history for children.

Books and other materials currently make up the majority of the collection. However, developments in information technology have made the idea of a collection more fluid. Access to electronically stored information can be as important as the provision of physical packages of information (books, magazines, recordings). At the present state of technology, a children's department will typically try to combine the provision of on-site materials with that of access to off-site information. Collection development can include selecting databases, linking to Internet sites from the library webpage, or purchasing reference materials that include print and electronic services.

Managing the children's collection involves setting priorities, purchasing materials based on library policies, and weeding, or getting rid of materials that no longer fit in the collection because physical condition, date of publication, or lack of use by children. In addition to this regular upkeep, children's librarians must be aware of changes in format and in electronic products available.

Selection

Whether a library has a large materials budget or a very small one, it is important to develop and use selection criteria, a selection policy that defines the scope of the collection, and selection procedures that describes the process used to select materials. That is, the children's librarian needs to make some decisions before looking at specific books or reading book reviews:

- selection criteria: what makes an individual book or item valuable
- selection policy: what items will be included in the collection
- selection procedures: how materials are ordered

Even in a small library, it is important to set up a system of selection. This insures that a small budget is spent on the best and most useful materials, that the collection has strengths and is more than "books in a room" and that time spent selecting materials is used efficiently.

In medium or large libraries selection rules may be set for all selectors including children's librarians. Even in this setting there will be some special issues to be included in collection planning. Children's librarians generally worry more about the ability of child users to read and understand materials than selectors for adults, and the attractiveness and durability of materials may be more important when selecting for children. (See figure 10.1.)

For librarians who are particularly interested in supporting student learning additional considerations might include more criteria that acknowledge multiple learning styles or intelligences (see figure 10.2).

Most libraries also consider the physical quality of materials, the attractiveness of covers, packaging and book layout, the quality of illustrations, and the literary merit of written works.

After setting criteria for selecting individual books or material, it is important to describe what the collection should be like. Selection policies often include procedures used in selecting, acquiring, and weeding materials, as well as selection principles. Because the library board should approve the basic selection policy, it is usually wise to keep the procedures in a separate statement for staff use. In this way, the entire document does not have to be brought to the board each time a change in procedures is made.

Whether contained in one or in several documents, selection policies and procedures for materials should cover such areas as:

- goals (meeting recreation and information needs)
- intellectual freedom statement
- balance of collection
- age of potential clientele
- type of service to adults
- relationship to school media center collections
- provision for needs of special groups (e.g., disabled, immigrants)
- materials excluded (by format and content)
- gifts
- collection levels for various content areas
- method of selection
- selection tools used
- basis for evaluation (e.g., reviews, personal inspection)
- individuals involved in selection
- obtaining input from the community
- special methods for specific materials (e.g., non-English language)
- special procedures for particular formats (e.g., software, databases)
- method of acquisition
- dealers and other suppliers
- procedures (usually systemwide)
- weeding

Figure 10.1
Selection considerations. (Hughes-Hassell 2005, 46).

Criteria	Questions to Consider
Appropriateness	Is the content appropriate for my learners? Does it match their developmental level? reading level? social development? learning style? ethnic or cultural background? Will the work be of interest to my learners?
Scope	What is the purpose of the work? Is topic useful? Does it support the school curriculum or interests of the students?
Accuracy	Is the material up-to-date and accurate? Are opinions and biases, if they exist, acknowledged as such? Does the creator of the work identify the sources used to create it? Does the creator cite credible sources, including specialists or experts in the subject area?
Treatment	Is the style of presentation appropriate for the subject matter and does it have appeal to my learners? Does the creator avoid stereotypes dealing with race, gender, age, region, and socioeconomic level? Does the resource reflect our diverse society?
Arrangement and organization	Is the information arranged and organized so that students can understand it? Is the resource organized so that students can easily locate information?
Authority	What are the creator's qualifications? How knowledgeable is the creator about the subject? Does the creator cite credible sources, including specialists or experts in the subject area? Has the creator published or produced other materials on this topic?
Comparison with other works	How does this work compare with others in the same genre and format on the same subject? How might my learners use this work? How might educators use it with students?

Figure 10.2
Multiple intelligences and the selection of literacy resources. (Hughes-Hassell 2005, 39).

Intelligence	Characteristics of Resources
Linguistic	Demonstrate the beauty and power of the written word (for example, books on tape or videotapes of poetry, short stories, or novels; guest storytellers and poets)
Bodily-kinesthetic	Allow students to physically interact *with* them (for example, software programs that allow students to interact with text by making notations, manipulating bookmarks, *and* putting sticky notes on favorite passages)
Spatial	Allow visual interaction (for example, pop-up books, three-dimensional books, and books that come apart into puzzle pieces and can be reconstructed)
Musical	Include songs, rhymes, raps, alliteration (for example, CDs, videos, software, and websites that focus on the rhythmic nature of language)
Logical-mathematical	Focus on numbers (for example, online *databases* and websites that present sports statistics or recipes)
Intrapersonal	Deal directly with emotions and emotionally charged issues such as racism, sexual abuse, and drug use (for example, nonfiction resources that deal specifically with feelings)
Interpersonal	Demonstrate the power youth have to affect social change (for example, websites that provide opportunities for students to interact in writing with others who are interested in social action and change)
Natural	Appeal to those that are naturalistically inclined (for example, nature guides, maps, and field guides to specific regions, parks, or landmarks)

- appropriate copyright date to discard (obsolete materials)
- appropriate length of time since last circulation to discard
- decision on mending materials
- procedure for systematic weeding

The first part of a selection policy describes the overall philosophy of the department. It sets the stage for the specific procedures by stating the audience for whom the collection is designed and the professional commitment to intellectual freedom and a balanced collection. This part of the policy spells out the basis for selection, and therefore, can be used as a defense against censorship attempts. If the library is officially committed to providing a balanced collection of information for all children in the community, the librarian is in a better position to defend the purchase of materials with subjects such as homosexuality, intelligent design, or witches.

General statements about the relationship of the public library to schools also makes it possible to justify not buying materials that are adequately supplied by the schools. Although some overlap is always expected among collections, the differences in the aims of the two collections should be clearly stated in the policy.

The gift policy is important as an explanation to would-be donors of unsuitable material. This section should state that any material accepted as gifts should meet collection standards.

The development of standard collection levels for different content areas is a useful way to ensure that a balanced collection is acquired. The levels chosen should reflect:

- the composition of the community; for example, the predominant age level of children, or the presence of specific language groups;
- the adequacy of the provision of school media resources;
- the strength or weakness of local interest in certain topics.

Collection Assessment

There are several ways to assess the collection in the children's department. The most used is the informal assessment of the children's staff based on their successfully filling requests for materials, in providing reference services, and using books and other materials in library programs. Librarians often keep a list of materials requested that the library does not own, or they buy added copies of popular titles if there are too many reserves on it. Through weeding, children's staff remove books and materials no longer in use.

Occasionally a more formal assessment is done on the whole collection or part of the collection to identify needs, update titles, and adjust buying priorities. This might include systematically checking circulation of books, removing materials that have not been used for years and checking for titles on recommended or award lists to assure that quality materials are in the collection. This more global approach may also identify new subjects that need better coverage and parts of the collection that are of particular need of updating.

Another consideration in assessing the collection is to match the needs of the community to the collection provided. If a new immigrant or ethnic group has moved into the community, it is important to identify materials that the library needs to serve these families. If the school curriculum changes the public library may have to adjust its collection to continue to support students who use the library. If more teachers are using the library, the collection may need to include books and resources that help teachers plan and that contain activity ideas for them to use in the classroom. A systematic consideration of community needs will help the children's librarian set priorities for collection development and help change the collection to meet the communities changing needs.

Libraries may also employ specific measures of use to evaluate the collection. This might include circulation per capita (circulation of children's materials divided by the number of children in the community), circulation per card holder, and number of books used at the library. A library might also measure turnover rates (the percentage of books in the collection that circulate). These output measures take some effort to collect, but can signal the need for changes in the collection. If this information is available it can be used by staff to focus on parts of the collection that are less used and in need of attention.

Informal, formal, and statistical assessments should be used to plan for collection development. Collection planning includes setting priorities for purchase of new materials, identifying areas of the collection for weeding and replacement buying, and new areas of collection building needed to serve the community. According to Doll and Barron "evaluation of the collection falls into two categories: (1) evaluation of the collection itself, usually in terms of numbers, quality, currency, or similar measures. . . .(2) how well the collection serves the needs of the users" (2002, 3).

Typically this is done as part of the annual budget setting. The collection plan, then, would dictate how available collection development funds would be spent. Children's librarians should participate fully in planning and budgeting to get the most from their budget and to spend their time selecting the most effectively.

Weeding the Collection

Weeding is the process used to withdraw materials from the collection. For most children's departments weeding is an ongoing activity. Damaged and worn books need to be disposed of, and materials that are no longer useful need to be withdrawn to make room for newly purchased items. Nonfiction books that are old may give children incorrect outdated information. Because weeding is often considered a housekeeping issue, some libraries put off doing it as long as possible. Librarians don't like throwing materials away for fear that they may be useful some day. The problem with not weeding is that children find it more difficult to find the good books in the forest of old, damaged, or unattractive books left in the collection. If the shelves are full, it may be more difficult to justify a adequate collection development budget to purchase new materials.

The concept of weeding is simple enough. Library staff set criteria for such things as last circulation, copyright, and physical attractiveness, and then, the materials in the collection are systematically examined using the weeding criteria. Books that no longer circulate, are too old, or are not attractive, are withdrawn from the collection and thrown away, sold in book sales, or offered to other agencies in the community.

Because even small libraries have a variety of materials in the collection, the criteria needs to be tailored to each type of book or nonprint category. For example many libraries consider the following:

- Weeding based on condition or appearance: torn pages, poor audio quality, uneven video projection, dirty covers or pages, dated and unappealing illustrations
- Weeding of superfluous or duplicate volumes: need only one copy of a once popular book, subject no longer of interest, newer editions now available

- Weeding based on poor content: information is dated, poorly written or incorrect or cultural norms have changed so material is now considered biased or offensive
- Weeding of periodicals and serials: periodicals that are not indexed, magazines that have ceased publication, incomplete runs of series
- Weeding based on use patterns: books not circulated in 3 years, books not used by staff in five years, old books that are not classics (Slote 1997, 21–26)

Many state libraries provide guidance for public libraries when they weed including how best to gather use data, how to dispose of books, and what criteria is best to use for weeding. For example the State Library of Arizona has excellent weeding information on its website (http://www.dlapr.lib.az.us/cdt/weeding.htm). Weeding is an important part of collection management as it gets rid of the least used, least useful materials, and gives the children's collection room to grow.

MATERIALS ACQUISITION

Once materials are selected for the collection, they must be purchased. Acquisition is the process of ordering and obtaining materials after they have been selected (Intner 2006, 111). Acquisition also can include the considerable financial bookkeeping needed to account for money spent on materials purchased. In many medium and large libraries acquisitions is centralized or at least done by a single person rather than by the staff who select materials. This makes the process of ordering and receiving materials more efficient and problem solving more effective. Because of this practice of centralizing acquisitions, procedures are the same for the children's department as for the rest of the library.

Acquisitions for children's materials fall into four categories. The first are materials that are purchased from vendors or materials wholesalers. Often the library negotiates standard discounts (usually based on the size of the book or materials budget) and sets terms of service that includes rules for back ordered materials (books or other items that are out of stock), material returns, processing standards, and other terms of service. Libraries might pick one vendor to supply books, another to supply audio and video materials, and another to supply all the libraries periodicals. Most vendor orders are placed and tracked electronically, so order forms and billing practices are also set with each vendor. Using these vendors simplifies the order process and makes the billing easier than dealing directly with each publisher.

Many public libraries are required to bid out contracts with major vendors at regular intervals of time. Usually contracts last several years and the same vendors are used again and again. This bidding allows libraries to negotiate better discounts and better service. Most libraries have two or three materials vendors with which they do the majority of the materials purchasing. It is important for the children's librarian to be sure that at least one of these vendors has a good selection of children's materials.

Another type of purchasing done by the children's department includes specialty companies that sell children's music, DVDs, software, puppets, games, toys, and other items that are unique to children's work. Often the contract arrangements are similar to those with larger vendors, but discounts are less likely to be given and a standard library purchase order is used to track purchases. Often the children's librarian has to identify these specialty companies and then work with the acquisitions staff to conduct business with them. Another specialty company used by the children's department includes alternative and diversity publishers. These include small presses that sell foreign language materials for children and cultural and political groups that publish materials for children. It is important to seek out these publishers if the community has immigrants or cultural and ethnic groups, or if the library has requests for alternative political viewpoints.

The third type of acquisitions is the use of approval plans. These plans allow the library to set a profile for the vendor to use to send titles to the library. The library does not order individual titles under the plan and there is usually a restriction on how many approval plan books can be returned. Libraries often use an approval plan if there is no children's librarian to select books or to get books that are sure to be selected. Libraries that buy all the new titles from a specific publisher would find it easier to set up an approval plan that sends all new books as a group from this publisher rather than having to manage individual orders. Approval plans are less used now than in the 1970s and 1980s because librarians need to be more selective to get the materials they need for their specific community.

Most publishers and vendors offer similar services that allow local librarians more opportunities for selecting or tailoring group orders to the libraries specific needs. Vendors will generate lists on topics (mysteries for middle school, materials for parents, books about the Olympics, etc.) and allow the children's librarians to select and order books as a group. Vendors also allow libraries to have standard orders for types of materials (books on the *New York Times* bestseller's list, top 20 music albums, or book award winners). These orders allow the library to get materials in a timely manner and to avoid having to order individually materials that library users will be sure to enjoy.

The last kind of acquisitions is purchasing materials from retail stores and retail online companies. The advantage of using local stores is that the children's librarian gets to see the actual item before purchase, it is a way to get materials needed immediately and a way for the library to support the local economy. It is also time consuming to shop for individual books; even the selection of good retail stores is limited when compared to national vendors and often the discount is less than using library vendors. Some libraries set up accounts with local stores and allow librarians to purchase from them. Children's librarians need to know how and when to use retail outlets to buy materials for their collections.

Many libraries also set up online accounts with national retail companies rather than use local book, music, or video stores. Such companies as Amazon or Barnes and Nobel Online allow libraries to set up accounts and offer discounts and free or reduced rate shipping. Smaller libraries may find the discounts of these companies similar to those offered by library vendors and that the selection of materials is very broad. Retail companies are less well set up to track large orders than library vendors, and the billing and returns may be a little more trouble for libraries, but this provides a good alternative to the book store, a wider selection, and generally good customer service. For children's librarians these companies offer customer reviews that might help them understand which books are really popular with children and why.

When acquiring databases the process is not purchase but rather licensing agreements. In essence the library rents access for library users rather than purchasing a database. Databases can be purchased by the company that produces them, or they may be sold in packages that combine products. For example, many encyclopedias sell both the print version and the electronic database access for one price. There may also be fees to access Internet sites that are especially useful or interesting to children. Prices are often determined by how many potential users of the site the library has, whether the site can be accessed from home or school, and how many simultaneous users of the site the library can support.

Children's librarians need to understand and follow their library's acquisitions policies and procedures and work to get the most for the least amount of time and money. Most libraries need several ways to purchase materials to get the collections they need, so the children's librarians need to research companies that can be used to purchase materials for children.

COLLECTION ACCESS

A collection of materials is of little value unless users can find the specific items they want or browse books and materials of interest to them. The services for making resources accessible include cataloging and classification of materials to ensure that individual items can be located within a collection. Shelving schemes and signage also help users browse for "just the right" book. The library staff may create bibliographies or display recommended books to help children find what they need.

Cataloging and Classification

Electronic catalogs provide access to information about where and in what format materials are housed and if materials are on the shelf and available for circulation. Electronic catalogs facilitate resource sharing among locations by allowing reciprocal borrowing between branches in a single system or between separate library systems. Electronic catalogs also facilitate requests through interlibrary loan. Online catalogs may include access to electronic information such as full text magazine articles, specific Internet sites, or specific data bases. Another important access point is the library's webpage. This allows users to access the catalog and other electronic information from home or school as well as within the library.

Most public libraries provide an electronic catalog available at the library as well as accessed online from remote locations. These catalogs are maintained by at least one professional staff member with specific training in cataloging rules and standards. Some libraries are part of a system of independent libraries that have joined together to provide a catalog. Some libraries purchase cataloging from the jobber or book wholesaler that sells the materials the libraries buy. Publishers and the Library of Congress have cooperated for decades to provide cataloging for each title sold through the Cataloging in Publication (CIP) that provides classification (assigning location) and cataloging (identifying and describing the item) for titles before publication so it can appear in the material when it is published.

In a library that has a specific staff person responsible for cataloging and classification, or one that buys these services from a vendor or cooperative regional system, what is the role of the children's librarian in providing a useful catalog for children? The first role is to help set specifications for cataloging and classification that best serve children in the community served. Cataloging and classification is rule based using a classification schedule (Dewey Decimal or Library of Congress system); the Anglo-American Cataloging Rules (AACR2 2002, and updates); machine readable cataloging (MARC format); and subject heading rules (Library of Congress or Sears). Even with all these rules, there are decisions to be made that will make the library's catalog more useful to the children it serves. The children's services manager should be involved in setting and reviewing cataloging specifications.

Some decisions are basic. Should cataloging be in English only, or should other languages be included? Should the catalog include icons or pictures to help children find what they are looking for? Authors Pamela Newberg and Jennifer Allen outline specific concerns for children's catalogs, as shown in figure 10.3.

Once catalog specifications are developed the children's librarian needs to be sure there is a system to check that these specifications are followed and that the specifications create the catalog that is needed. Also remember that as publishing trends change, so does cataloging. For example, should graphic novels be classified separately from traditional books? If so, a separate classification will need to be created. While the children's librarian may not control cataloging decisions, oversight of the catalog and participation in library-wide cataloging discussions are important to get the best catalog possible for the children served.

A second responsibility of children's librarians is to develop services that help children, parents and teachers understand and use the library's catalog. No matter how user-friendly a library's catalog is, catalogs are difficult to read and understand. Young readers need staff help to use the catalog, and older children and adults often do not understand the catalog and need help. Library staff should be available to help all users find what they need in the catalog and then on the shelf. Staff should be trained to give individual catalog instruction as needed and explain how to do advance catalog searches to help users find everything they need.

Many libraries offer group catalog instruction to school or other groups of users. This is particularly helpful for students doing research for reports if the instruction is tailored to the specific needs of the students. It is also important to respect the developmental level of students so as not to provide information beyond their learning level. It is useful to explain how to access the online catalog from school or home and to describe library procedures needed to access the computer as well as to use it. Most instruction includes helping students understand catalog vocabulary (what is a call number?), techniques for searching, understanding the catalog entry, and how to locate the actual material found in the catalog. If the local school teaches information literacy in its library media center, it is helpful to coordinate catalog instruction at the public library with this instruction.

Figure 10.3
Catalog specification decisions.

Call Numbers

Questions regarding call numbers involve policies covering the assignment of classification numbers and the addition of book numbers.

If Dewey is used, should the source be the abridged edition or the unabridged edition?

Are the numbers carried to the first slash? Two digits past the decimal? Four digits past the decimal?

Are author letters or Cutter numbers used? If so, how many characters or digits will be assigned?

Where are the biographies? 921? B? Will they be shelved in a separate section or mixed with other nonfiction?

Where are easy books? Are they marked E or P, or something else?

Are there special collections that require a prefix (Reference, Professional collection, Foreign language, Story collections)?

If automated, in which tag and subfield divisions do the call numbers belong?

Subject Headings

Questions about subject headings include the following:

What subject authority will be used: LC adult headings, AC headings (LC children's headings), or Sears?

Are the numbers of subject headings used limited in some way?

Reading Programs

Special treatments to facilitate reading programs require asking the following:

If a reading program is used, how are the books identified? If automated, are there special requirements for this tag?

Physical Processing

Choices about physical processing include decisions about the following:

Covers or not?

Cards and pockets?

Bar codes? If so, where will they be placed on the materials?

(Intner, 2006, p. 109)

Shelving Materials

Most children's librarians work in libraries where the shelving pattern is set and where signage is uniform throughout the library. Some children's room managers may get the opportunity to design new interior schemes as part of renovation or new building projects. Whatever the situation, it is the responsibility of the children's librarian to evaluate how well the shelving plan works for child users and whether the directional signs are effective in helping children find what they want. If shelving is confused or signage inadequate, the children's librarian should suggest changes that will make the best use of the space available for the children's collection, display the collection in an attractive manner, and make it easy for children, parents, and teachers to find materials of interest.

The number of books in a collection is not the only factor to be considered in planning collection space for a children's department. Differences in format and in needs for access determine the type of shelving required.

Children's materials have traditionally been divided into preschool materials—primarily picture books—and materials for older children. Some libraries subdivide this further by having separate shelving for board books and for early reading books. Audiovisual materials are usually shelved separately from books, and so are Braille, large print, and other formats designed for special needs children. Award winning books may be shelved together as a collection. Although this arrangement may help the librarian choose books for a child by going to the most appropriate shelf, it can make it more difficult for patrons to choose books on their own. The goal of most departments is to enable young patrons and their parents to select materials for themselves, rather than having to ask library staff for help. Unless a clear need for segregated collections is apparent, the simplest system is usually the best—picture books in one visible area, fiction in alphabetical order, and nonfiction in one sequence of Dewey decimal order.

Both fairy tales and graphic novels can cause special problems in shelving. While collections of fairy tales are shelved by Dewey number, some libraries choose to shelve fairy tales in picture book format that are appropriate for young children with the other picture books to make the fairy tale picture books more available to the intended audience. Often children want to read graphic novels because they like the format, so it is easier for them if the library has a separate section for them rather than integrating them into the fiction section. Whatever shelving scheme used will need good, clear signage and helpful staff to direct library users to the materials they want.

Special types of shelving are needed for picture books. Because most of these books are oversized and thin, with little information on the spine, the most effective shelving is face-outward. Slanting shelves, which allow browsers to see the front cover of the books and to open them easily, are highly desirable, but most collections are too large to allow all books to be displayed this way. One solution is to have most of the books shelved spine-outward on a set of low shelves and to have one row of slanted shelving above these to display a constantly changing selection of books. Some libraries have experimented with keeping picture books in large baskets, in bins, or on book trucks for easy browsing. Although these methods make it difficult to find a particular book, most children choose their books by browsing. Whatever shelving is used, estimate the number of picture books that are likely to be collected and house them separately from other materials.

Periodicals are similar in format to paperback books. Because most libraries do not bind children's periodicals, back issues soon become tattered and unsightly. The most frequently used system allows current issues to be shown face-outward and provides shelf space to stack back issues. Most periodicals are used in-house, so the shelving should be placed near comfortable seating for easy browsing.

Paperback materials are usually stored separately from hardcover books. Many libraries use spinners, revolving book racks, which allow books to be displayed face-outward. Spinners tend to attract several children at a time and may cause congestion if not allotted sufficient space.

The standard collection of children's fiction and nonfiction takes up more space than an adult collection of similar size because usually only low shelving is used. Children cannot reach high shelves, so books become inaccessible if adult shelving is used. The tops of such shelves can also be used for informal displays of new books or other items of seasonal or special interest. When predicting an increase in the size of the collection, the children's department's needs for easy access should be taken into account.

Nonprint materials require special types of storage: trays or spinners for cassettes and compact discs, shelving for games, cabinets for toys, and files for software.

Marketing the Collection

After a collection has been developed, a plan for collection growth has been adopted (and funded!), and materials are shelved, it is important to let library users know what the collections hold and how to use them. Traditionally children's librarians have done topical and seasonal book displays and created bibliographies on topics of interest to library users. Some librarians do bibliographies on demand from teachers or other childcare workers to help the users find books or materials that meet their needs. With the development of nonprint materials and electronic media, bibliographies now include books, audio materials, magazine, and web addresses or other electronic sources on a topic.

Beyond these basic recommendations, librarians often have the opportunity to promote materials that have value but may be overlooked by users. It is also good to remember that even if the collection does not change many parts of it will be new to children as they grow and mature. Preschool children will find it exciting to be able to use beginning reading books, and third and fourth graders need to be introduced to chapter books as they gain the ability to read books of more than 100 pages. Children need recommendations of nonfiction books as they broaden their personal interests and as they have more complex homework assignments.

Children with special needs and their parents and teachers need to know what materials the library has for them and how to find them in the library's collection. Special lists or information on the library's website will help attract these users who might not think of the library as having materials they will find useful. If the library has foreign language collections, it is also important to find ways of highlighting non-English materials and by providing foreign language cataloging and getting library materials translated into other languages.

As well as including reader's advisory services as part of children's reference, libraries can plan displays, programs, and booktalks to help children move through the collection as their needs grow. Many children's librarians also provide specific transition from the children's collection to the young adult and adult collections, so young teens will feel comfortable with the library's entire collection. It is also fun to figure out ways to attract children to all parts of the collection. Whether it is providing ways for children to review and recommend books to their peers, designating a star book of the week, a website of the month, or booktalking good books about Italy to a fourth grade class working on an Italian festival for parent's night, librarians should always be aware of the potential for marketing the collection to the community of users.

A good collection meets the needs of users and will attract children to the library, but providing both a good collection *and* services that expand children's knowledge of what is in the collection and how it will help them will better meet the needs of children served by the library.

REFERENCES AND ADDITIONAL READING

Baumbach, Donna J., and Miller, Linda L. 2006. *Less Is More: A Practical Guide to Weeding School Library Collections.* Chicago: American Library Association.

Doll, Carol A., and Barron, Pamela Petrick. 2002. *Managing and Analyzing Your Collection: A Practical Guide for Small Libraries and School Media Centers.* Chicago: American Library Association.

Hughes-Hassell, Sandra and Mancall, Jacqueline. 2005. *Collection Management for Youth: Responding to the Needs of Learners.* Chicago: American Library Association.

Intner, Sheila S, Fountain, Joanna F., and Gilchrist, Jane E. 2006. *Cataloging for Kids: An Introduction to the Tools,* 4th edition. Chicago: American Library Association.

Johnson, Peggy. 2004. *Fundamentals of Collection Development and Management.* Chicago: American Library Association, 2004.

Slote, Stanley. 1997. *Weeding Library Collections: Library Weeding Methods.* Englewood, CO: Libraries Unlimited.

Taylor, Arlene G. 2006. *Introduction to Cataloging and Classification,* 10th ed. Westport, CT: Libraries Unlimited.

11

Electronic Resources and Services

Helping children find information is one of the most important tasks of children's services. The Association for Library Services to Children (ALSC) list of competencies includes: "Understands and applies search strategies to give children full and equitable access to information from the widest possible range of sources" (ALSC 1999). Public libraries provide many print reference sources as well as access to databases and the Internet, and the methods librarians use to help children find information have changed. In addition to face-to-face conversation in the library, reference services are delivered by electronic means. Each of these reference technologies has value but each also poses problems.

- Telephone service is available to almost every school-age child and offers a convenient way for a librarian to search for information and give answers. It is time-consuming, however, and unless one librarian is assigned to telephone duty, the staff may find it difficult to serve the patrons in the library.
- Email service is available to most children, but not all. It is convenient for librarians because emails can be answered when the library is quiet. Unfortunately, questions are not always written clearly and several iterations must be used to clarify what is being asked.
- Instant messaging appeals to teenagers, but many librarians are not comfortable with it. It requires attention and time from the librarians often during busy periods in the library.
- Social networks have been used by a few libraries, but the service may be difficult for children to find; also, some parents object to using social networks.

As with any other service, libraries must make their electronic services easy for patrons to find and to use. Announcements of formats for reference service may include

- Announcements of new types of service in local media outlets
- Information in print and electronic form to local schools
- Flyers and posters in the library
- Information on bookmarks
- Large, clear links to reference services from the children's department webpage

Before a new type of service is publicized, library staff should discuss the implications for staff time. In some libraries, it may be most efficient to have one librarian handle all email reference. Because afternoon and early evening hours are the busiest for children's departments, responses to email questions may be written during the morning when the library is quiet. If this plan is followed, the library should make it clear that email questions will be answered within 24 hours, but not immediately. If a quicker turnaround can be made, patrons will appreciate it. Another way to plan email reference service is to limit it to specific hours, such as 4:00 to 8:00 P.M. and assign one individual to field all queries during that period.

Whenever a new technology-based service is used, the tech support staff should be consulted. All computers malfunction occasionally, but too-frequent closures of the system suggests that a library is not serious about providing service. There should be enough fully equipped computers to handle up to 50 percent more traffic than is expected. If the service is good, traffic will increase over time.

CREATING A CHILDREN'S DEPARTMENT WEBSITE

A public library website has become one of the primary contact points for patrons, so the design and content of the website deserve careful attention and thought. The website for a children's department is usually a part of the overall library website. In large library systems, the technology department may handle the design and implementation of the website, often with only minimal input from individual departments. Children's librarians who want their site to be of greatest benefit to children, however, should try to influence the design and content. To do this, you need a plan based on your knowledge of your clientele and services. The components of this plan determine what your site will look like and should include:

- Purpose
- Design
- Content
- Features

The purpose of the website determines what content and services you want to make available online, so it is worth taking some time to decide exactly what you want your site to accomplish. It may seem obvious that the website should publicize the library's activities and attract children and families to the library, but, depending on what you make available online, the website may mean that fewer people visit the library.

Library websites can serve many purposes:

- Give information about the location and hours of the library, making visits easier
- Allow access to the catalog from outside the library
- Announce library programs
- Supply registration forms for programs
- Facilitate placing reserves and renewing materials
- Provide stories online for listening
- Make full text reference materials available for downloading
- Provide interactive homework help
- Serve as a portal to information sources
- Provide access to games and activities and blogs

These services range on a continuum from providing basic information to help patrons find their way to the library to portals that make a visit to the website a substitute for visiting a bricks-and-mortar library. If a library serves a limited population in a compact geographic area, helping people find their way to the library may be sufficient, but the trend is toward making the website an integral part of library service, and an extension of and substitute for the permanent library building. Providing this kind of service requires a major commitment of resources and staff time. A children's department in such a library should try to make the website a component of every service they plan and should allocate appropriate personnel time to this effort. This chapter will consider the possibilities of designing a website on level one (basic services) and level two (enhanced resources), although the two levels overlap at many points.

Design

No matter how much a library website may offer for children, it will not be useful if the children and their parents cannot find it easily. There should be a clear and simple entry point on the library's homepage. If the website is aimed at young children whose reading skills are limited, it is useful to have a graphic entry point in addition to text.

The entry page for the children's department should be different from the one designed for adult patrons. Research has shown that children have distinctive preferences in web design (Nielsen). One example is that children like animation and sound, both of which encourage them to linger on a page and explore it. They usually react well to features such as information popping up when the curser is rolled over a graphic or heading. Adults often find these features distracting, but the children's page should be designed for its own audience.

The text should be in a font that is clear, easy to read, and visually appealing. Several studies have shown the children have definite preferences about font type and size. Figure 11.1 shows how children ranked some commonly used fonts.

Fourth and fifth graders consistently rated the Comic Sans MS 12 their favorite, and Arial 14 was preferred to Times New Roman and Courier New (Bernard

Figure 11.1
Font types for websites.

Arial 14 pt	Everytown Public Library
Times Roman 12 pt	Everytown Public Library
Comic Sans MS 12 pt	Everytown Public Library
Courier 12 pt	Everytown Public Library

and Mills 2001). Librarians are often tempted to put as much information as possible on a page by using blocks of text in a rather small font, but this approach is not attractive to children. They prefer an attractive page with graphics that can be clicked to provide more information.

Design features should vary according to the age of the intended user. Preschool children need larger fonts and simpler language than school-age children, but if the page is designed for them, older children will not want to use it. Four specific age groups have been identified in the book *Weaving a Library Web:*

- Pre-readers (3- to 5-year-olds) who may recognize some letters, but rely on graphics for most information. They need short, simple activities and appreciate audio to accompany text.
- Beginning readers (5- to 8-year-olds) can handle longer blocks of text in a large, clear font. They enjoy graphics and can understand a wider range of picture references.
- Intermediate readers (9- to 12-year-olds) read chapter books and general fiction. They still enjoy graphics, but also like to interact with the website by means of surveys, email, and the like.
- Young Adults (13- to 17-year-olds) do not think of themselves as children. Most are heavy users of the Internet, so designing a site for them presents special challenges. (Blowers and Bryan 2004, 61–62)

Content

The more you understand about your audience and the purpose of the site, the easier it will be to determine the content needed. Most library websites combine practical user information including schedules of programs and procedures for obtaining a library card with promotional material such as booklists, games, and amusing surveys. Most often, a department should start with the basics and add additional elements when staff can handle them.

Components of a website for children:

- Access to library catalog
- Interface for reserving or renewing materials
- Information about programs

- Suggestions for reading
- Instructions on how to obtain a card

Catalog Access

Children are often looking for a specific book or author, so access to the library catalog is an important element of the website. There is no need to call it a catalog. The website can have an icon with a simple direction such as *Search for library materials*. A direct link to the library catalog from the children's page is useful because children do not like to have to click through several levels to get to their target. Depending on the system in use, catalog access might be customized for the children's department allowing children to access only materials designated for them.

Direct access to research databases designed for young people is far preferable to linking to the list of all the databases offered by the library. Because school-age children prefer online information sources to print materials, access to relevant databases is important. Links to tutorials that help children learn how to use the database save many questions to the library staff.

Programs

Information about programs should be prominently listed on the front page of the children's department website. A calendar listing at all the programs for a month or longer is convenient for many families. To avoid clutter, the age level and program name can be given with a link to more detailed information about time and place. Keeping the program listing updated is vitally important. Nothing makes a website look more irrelevant than a list of events that are over. If registration is required for programs, patrons should be given a choice to register online or by telephone.

Links

Another basic component of a children's department webpage will be links to sources inside and outside the library. These links should include:

- Library homepage
- Public school websites (perhaps non-public schools too)
- Community recreation information
- Homeschooling sites
- Homework help sites

Library Blogs

Maintaining a library blog linked to the website enables staff members to post information quickly and easily. Librarians can let patrons know about new materials and programs or can comment on summer reading programs or other events. Sometimes a children's department has its own blog, and sometimes it shares the general library blog (see figure 11.2 for an example from the Marin County Public Library).

Figure 11.2
Library blog from Marin County, California.

Source: http://www.marincountyfreelibrary.blogspot.com/. Accessed May, 4, 2007.

A blog requires frequent attention; patrons will quickly lose interest in a blog that is not updated at least several times a week. An individual staff member may take responsibility for posting almost every day on the blog, or that duty may rotate among the staff. If library users are allowed to post comments on the blog, a staff member must monitor posts to be sure the material is appropriate.

Before starting a blog you need to determine your audience and decide which content will appeal to them. You might want to consider a bilingual blog, especially if the parents of child patrons are not fluent in English. Blogs can be embellished with video and audio files, perhaps of children reading their reviews of books. While you want to have consistency in the design and format of your blog, variation in content increases the interest of readers.

Library Wikis

Wikis—interactive, communally edited information sites—have also been used in many libraries. The structure of a wiki allows any reader to edit and change the information posted. (The name comes from an Hawaiian word for quick.) Wikis have been used by public and school libraries to allow input from librarians and patrons.

Types of patron input:

- Create booklists
- Post reviews
- Comment on library materials or services
- Volunteer to help library projects
- Types of librarian input
- Post directions for use of library copiers, scanners, or other equipment
- Announce programs
- Create lists of new materials

An important feature of a wiki is its interactivity. Blogs are usually written by one individual or a small team but wikis are created from the input of many community members. The arrangement of material in a wiki is generally by subject, just as in an encyclopedia or other reference work. Unlike a blog, most people access a wiki by subject rather than by date, and do not often read straight through to get the latest news as they might with a blog.

WEB 2.0 AND LIBRARIES

Libraries in the twenty-first century have had to become flexible, ever-changing service organizations as technology affects the way we communicate with patrons and deliver information and materials. Librarians were among the first professional group to integrate electronic technology with their traditional services, starting with automated catalogs and expanding into databases, online information provision, websites, and blogs. As other technological tools became available, some public libraries began offering new types of service. The difference between earlier technological innovations, such as catalogs and websites, and the more recent interactive sites, sometimes called Web 2.0, is that librarians become partners in an ongoing conversation rather than providers of carefully selected information and resources. While this offers the possibility of enriched services, it may also threaten the role of librarians as information experts. Characteristics of Web 2.0 library applications are

- It is user-centered.
- It provides a multimedia experience.
- It is socially rich.
- It is communally innovative. (Maness 2006)

Social networking sites such as MySpace achieved great popularity with young people starting in 2003. Their popularity has led to two different strands of reaction. Some parents objected to having their children access these sites in the library or elsewhere. Some of the censorship issues connected with social networking sites are discussed in chapter 12. While some libraries saw these sites as problems, however, others saw them as offering a new way for libraries to connect with young people. Several public libraries set up MySpace profiles to distribute information and publicity about library services. One of the first to take advantage of this new service was the Hennepin County Public

Library in Minnesota. Other public libraries as well as school and college libraries have also found it worthwhile to create a profile on social networking sites.

KEEPING UP WITH TECHNOLOGY

Because technology changes quickly, librarians have to search actively for
new ideas and techniques. Print sources lag behind in their coverage of what
new technology is available and how libraries are adapting new technological
tools. Professional journals are helpful, but the best way to stay on the cutting
edge is to be active in professional associations. Conferences offer a mix of personal interaction for information exchange, demonstrations of new tools and
techniques, and resources to examine and purchase. Time and money spent on
conference attendance provide great benefits for the library.

Technology itself helps in the exchange of information. In late fall 2006, the
Association for Library Service to Children of the American Library Association
(ALA) announced the start of a wiki for children's services librarians. This is
linked to other wikis sponsored by the ALA, which provide current information
on technology in libraries. The ALA also has a wiki on Interactive Web Applications for Libraries (http://wikis.ala.org/iwa/index.php/Main_Page), which compiles information from libraries around the country.

Not every children's department will have the resources to offer an expanding
array of new technology applications to its community. Besides keeping up with
what libraries are doing, an individual library must be alert to the needs of the
community and decide which services will be welcomed. The librarian needs to
balance their knowledge of people and their knowledge of innovative new resources, in order to provide the most appropriate service plan for a library.

REFERENCES AND ADDITIONAL READING

The Association for Library Services to Children. 1999. *Competencies for Librarians Serving
Children in Public Libraries,* Revised Edition, 5. Chicago: American Library Association.

Bernard, Michael L. 2003. *Criteria for Optimal Web Design (Designing for Usability),* 4. Wichita, KS: Wichita State University.

Bernard, Michael L, and Mills, Melissa. 2001. *Which Fonts Do Children Prefer to Read Online?*
5. Wichita, KS: Wichita State University.

Blowers, Helene, and Bryan, Robin. 2004. *Weaving a Library Web: A Guide to Developing
Children's Websites.* Chicago: American Library Association.

Jurkowski, Odin. 2005. Schools of Thought: What to Include on Your School Library Web
Site [Spring 2005]. *Children and Libraries* 3: 24–29.

Krug, Steve. 2006. *Don't Make Me Think: A Common Sense Approach to Web Usability,* Second Edition. Berkeley, CA: New Riders Publishing.

Leighton, H. Vernon, Jackson, Joe, Sullivan, Kathryn, and Dennison, Russell F. 2003. Web
Page Design and Successful Use: A Focus Group Study. *Internet Reference Services
Quarterly* 8: 17–27.

Magid, Larry, and Collier, Anne. 2007. *MySpace Unraveled: A Parent's Guide to Teen Social
Networking from the Directors of BlogSafety.com.* Berkeley, CA: Peachpit Press.

Maness, J. 2006. Library 2.0 Theory: Web 2.0 and Its Implications for Libraries. *Webology* 3:
Article 25.

Shipley, David, and Schwalbe, Will. 2007. *Send: The Essential Guide to Email for Office and Home*. New York: Alfred A. Knopf.

Stephens, Michael. 2006. *Web 2.0 & Libraries: Best Practices for Social Software, 68*. Chicago: ALA TechSource. Library Technology Reports: Expert Guides to Library Systems and Services. Vol. 40, no. 4.

Wibbels, Andy. 2006. *Blog Wild! A Guide for Small Business Blogging*. New York: Penguin (Portfolio).

Young Adult Library Services Association. 2005. *Teens & Social Networking in School & Public Libraries: A Toolkit for Librarians & Library Workers*. American Library Association. http://www.ala.org/yalsa

12

Intellectual Freedom and Censorship

Intellectual Freedom is one of the foundations of librarianship. The American Library Association (ALA) has defined this concept for the profession:

Intellectual Freedom is the right of every individual to both seek and receive information from all points of view without restriction. It provides for free access to all expressions of ideas through which any and all sides of a question, cause or movement may be explored. Intellectual freedom encompasses the freedom to hold, receive and disseminate ideas. (http://www.ala.org/ala/oif/basics/intellectual.htm#ifpoint1, Accessed Sept. 9, 2007)

In practice, however, it is not always easy to figure out how libraries should operate to support this freedom, especially when serving children. Questions arise when librarians make decisions about purchasing materials:

- Will a comic story about a blundering school principal make children less respectful of their teachers?
- Should we purchase a book that includes stories about witches even though some parents object?
- Will the religious context of this story make children of other religions feel marginalized?
- Is the story of a boy with two lesbian mothers appropriate for a picture book?
- Should sex education books for children be kept on open shelves in the children's department?
- Do children who read books that include profanity learn to use this language in the classroom or at home?
- Should a book portraying a happy family living in a totalitarian country be removed from a children's collection?

Over the years, standards of what is appropriate in books for children have changed greatly. Language and situations that would not have been published 20 years ago are commonplace now, but these changes are not accepted by all members of the community. Challenges to books and other materials occur frequently.

Ten Most Often Challenged Books of 2006 (compiled by ALA)

- *And Tango Makes Three* by Justin Richardson and Peter Parnell, for homosexuality, anti-family, and unsuited to age group
- *Gossip Girls* series by Cecily Von Ziegesar for homosexuality, sexual content, drugs, unsuited to age group, and offensive language
- *Alice* series by Phyllis Reynolds Naylor for sexual content and offensive language
- *The Earth, My Butt, and Other Big Round Things* by Carolyn Mackler for sexual content, anti-family, offensive language, and unsuited to age group
- *The Bluest Eye* by Toni Morrison for sexual content, offensive language, and unsuited to age group
- *Scary Stories* series by Alvin Schwartz for occult/Satanism, unsuited to age group, violence, and insensitivity
- *Athletic Shorts* by Chris Crutcher for homosexuality and offensive language
- *The Perks of Being a Wallflower* by Stephen Chbosky for homosexuality, sexually explicit, offensive language, and unsuited to age group
- *Beloved* by Toni Morrison for offensive language, sexual content, and unsuited to age group
- *The Chocolate War* by Robert Cormier for sexual content, offensive language, and violence. (http://www.ala.org/ala/oif/bannedbooksweek/challengedbanned/challenged-banned.htm#mfcb [Accessed April 13, 2007])

From the beginnings of public library service to children, there have been arguments about the amount of freedom children should be given in choosing books to read. As a public institution in a pluralistic society, libraries have an ill-defined relationship with children. Unlike public schools, they are not compulsory and are not charged with providing formal education. Because they are funded by tax money, they are not free to cater entirely to majority taste but are expected to provide services that are a social good. They must offer recreation and entertainment to entice children to use their facilities, but at the same time serve as quasi-educational and cultural institutions.

Because children do not have the knowledge or power to choose books and other materials for themselves, adults do it for them. Many people believe children are likely to accept false information and false values presented in books and other media. Most parents, librarians, and teachers want to give children materials that uphold social values such as honesty, compassion, tolerance, and love of family, community, and country. These values are widely held throughout society; authors, publishers, and printers tend to produce materials that reflect them. Librarians, most of whom make their materials selections from mainstream selection aids, rarely make choices that cause problems. Nonetheless, there are always some materials on which people do not agree. Almost every librarian has heard objections raised to materials at one time or another, and the number of complaints has not diminished in recent years. The way librarians handle these objections can have a marked effect on the library's relations with the community and on the effectiveness of its programs.

AREAS OF CONCERN

The major area of concern for parents and other adults are shown in the list of the most challenged books. The chart in figure 12.1, prepared by ALA'S Office of Intellectual Freedom, shows the basis for challenges over the past several years:

BASIC INTELLECTUAL FREEDOM DOCUMENTS

The ALA has prepared a number of documents explaining the professional attitude toward aspects of intellectual freedom. These offer helpful information to help the media and the general public to understand the reasons for the library's choices of material and policies. The basic position on Intellectual Freedom is stated in the Library Bill of Rights (see figure 12.2; ALA 2006, 55–56).

This document has been updated several times in the years since its initial approval. One of the interpretations especially relevant to children's librarians is that on allowing children and teenagers free access to libraries (see figure 12.3).

When the ALA took the position that children should be allowed to use materials in any part of the library, some adults thought that special children's departments would no longer be allowed. The interpretation does not go that far. Libraries may set up specialized collections for any group of people provided those people (including children) can also obtain materials from the

Figure 12.1
OIF censorship database 2000–2005: Challenges by type.*

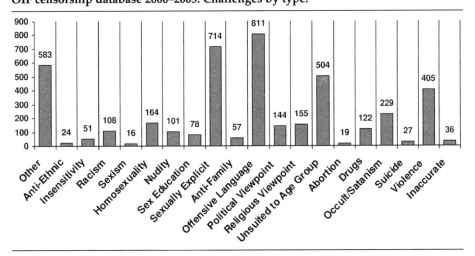

Source: (http://www.ala.org/ala/oif/bannedbooksweek/bbwlinks/challengesbytype20002005.pdf; Accessed March 1, 2007). Reprinted by permission of the American Library Association.
* Out of 3,019 challenges recorded between January 1, 2000, and December 31 2005, by the Office for Intellectual Freedom. The Office for Intellectual Freed does not claim comprehensiveness in recording challenges. Research suggests that for each challenge reported there are as many as four or five which go unreported.

whole collection. Not all libraries have embraced the idea of setting no age limits on access to materials. Many parents have complained to libraries that their child borrowed unsuitable material. The professional response has been that "parents—and only parents—have the right and the responsibility to restrict the access of their children—and only their children—to library resources." (See figure 12.3.) This position includes nonprint as well as print materials.

Figure 12.2
Library Bill of Rights.

The American Library Association affirms that all libraries are forums for information and ideas, and that the following basic policies should guide their services.

I.   Books and other library resources should be provided for the interest, information, and enlightenment of all people of the community the library serves. Materials should not be excluded because of the origin, background, or views of those contributing to their creation.

II.   Libraries should provide materials and information presenting all points of view on current and historical issues. Materials should not be proscribed or removed because of partisan or doctrinal disapproval.

III.   Libraries should challenge censorship in the fulfillment of their responsibility to provide information and enlightenment.

IV.   Libraries should cooperate with all persons and groups concerned with resisting abridgment of free expression and free access to ideas.

V.   A person's right to use a library should not be denied or abridged because of origin, age, background, or views.

VI.   Libraries which make exhibit spaces and meeting rooms available to the public they serve should make such facilities available on an equitable basis, regardless of the beliefs or affiliations of individuals or groups requesting their use.

Adopted June 18, 1948.
Amended February 2, 1961, and January 23, 1980,
inclusion of "age" reaffirmed January 23, 1996,
by the ALA Council.

Reprinted by permission of the American Library Association.

Figure 12.3
Free access to libraries for minors: An interpretation of the Library Bill of Rights.

Library policies and procedures that effectively deny minors equal and equitable access to all library resources available to other users violate the *Library Bill of Rights*. The American Library Association opposes all attempts to restrict access to library services, materials, and facilities based on the age of library users.

Article V of the *Library Bill of Rights* states, "A person's right to use a library should not be denied or abridged because of origin, age, background, or views." The "right to use a library" includes free access to, and unrestricted use of, all the services, materials, and facilities the library has to offer. Every restriction on access to, and use of, library resources, based solely on the chronological age, educational level, literacy skills, or legal emancipation of users violates Article V.

Libraries are charged with the mission of developing resources to meet the diverse information needs and interests of the communities they serve. Services, materials, and facilities that fulfill the needs and interests of library users at different stages in their personal development are a necessary part of library resources. The needs and interests of each library user, and resources appropriate to meet those needs and interests, must be determined on an individual basis. Librarians cannot predict what resources will best fulfill the needs and interests of any individual user based on a single criterion such as chronological age, educational level, literacy skills, or legal emancipation.

Libraries should not limit the selection and development of library resources simply because minors will have access to them. Institutional self-censorship diminishes the credibility of the library in the community, and restricts access for all library users.

Children and young adults unquestionably possess First Amendment rights, including the right to receive information in the library. Constitutionally protected speech cannot be suppressed solely to protect children or young adults from ideas or images a legislative body believes to be unsuitable for them.[1] Librarians and library governing bodies should not resort to age restrictions in an effort to avoid actual or anticipated objections, because only a court of law can determine whether material is not constitutionally protected.

The mission, goals, and objectives of libraries cannot authorize librarians or library governing bodies to assume, abrogate, or overrule the rights and responsibilities of parents. As "Libraries: An American Value" states, "We affirm the responsibility and the right of all parents and guardians to guide their own children's use of the library and its resources and services." Librarians and governing bodies should maintain that parents—and only parents—have the right and the responsibility to restrict the access of their children—and only their children—to library resources. Parents who do not want their children to have access to certain library services, materials, or facilities should so advise their children. Librarians and library governing bodies cannot assume the role of parents or the functions of parental authority in the private relationship between parent and child.

Lack of access to information can be harmful to minors. Librarians and library governing bodies have a public and professional obligation to ensure that all members of the community they serve have free, equal, and equitable access to the entire range of library resources regardless of content, approach, format, or amount of detail. This principle of library service applies equally to all users, minors as well as adults. Librarians and library governing bodies must uphold this principle in order to provide adequate and effective service to minors.

(continued)

Figure 12.3 *(continued)*

[1] *See* <u>Erznoznik v. City of Jacksonville</u>, 422 U.S. 205 (1975)—"Speech that is neither obscene as to youths nor subject to some other legitimate proscription cannot be suppressed solely to protect the young from ideas or images that a legislative body thinks unsuitable [422 U.S. 205, 214] for them. In most circumstances, the values protected by the First Amendment are no less applicable when government seeks to control the flow of information to minors. *See* <u>Tinker v. Des Moines School Dist.</u>, *supra. Cf.* <u>West Virginia Bd. of Ed. v. Barnette</u>, 319 U.S. 624 (1943)."

Adopted June 30, 1972; amended July 1, 1981; July 3, 1991, June 30, 2004, by the ALA Council.

[ISBN 8389-7549-6]

REACTING TO A CHALLENGE

The first responsibility in reacting to any challenge to library materials is for the librarian to handle these complaints respectfully and fairly. Most complaints come from concerned local residents who care about the welfare of children, their own, and others. The librarian's job is to explain the library's philosophy and procedures.

As normal operating procedure, each library should maintain:

- a materials selection policy
- a library service policy
- a clearly defined method for handling complaints
- in-service training
- lines of communication with civic, religious, educational, and political bodies of the community
- a vigorous public information program on behalf of intellectual freedom
- familiarity with any local municipal and state legislation pertaining to intellectual freedom

Following these practices provides a base from which to operate when concerns are expressed. When a complaint is made, the librarian should listen calmly and courteously. Good communication skills can help the librarian explain the need for diversity in library collections and the use of library resources.

If, after discussion, the person is not satisfied, advise the complainant of the library procedures for handling statements of concern and provide a form for requesting a reconsideration of the materials. Figure 12.4 shows an example of the type of form used.

If the individual submits a written complaint, make sure a written reply is sent promptly.

Inform the administrator and/or the governing authority (usually the library board) of the complaint. Send full, written information about the nature and source of the complaint to the immediate supervisor promptly so appropriate individuals can be briefed without delay.

Figure 12.4
Sample request for reconsideration of library resources.

[*This is where you identify who in your own structure, has authorized use of this form—Director, Board of Trustees, Board of Education, etc.—and to whom to return the form.*]

Example: The school board of Mainstream County, U.S.A., has delegated the responsibility for selection and evaluation of library/educational resources to the school library media specialist/curriculum committee, and has established reconsideration procedures to address concerns about those resources. Completion of this form is the first step in those procedures. If you wish to request reconsideration of school or library resources, please return the completed form to the Coordinator of Library Media Resources, Mainstream School Dist., 1 Mainstream Plaza, Anytown, U.S.A.

Name _____

Date _____

Address _____

City _____

State _____

Zip _____

Phone _____

Do you represent self? _____ Organization? _____

    1. Resource on which you are commenting:

        _____ Book _____ Textbook _____ Video _____ Display

        _____ Magazine _____ Library Program _____ Audio Recording

        _____ Newspaper _____ Electronic information/network (please specify)

        _____ Other _____

        Title _____

        Author/Producer _____

    2. What brought this resource to your attention?
    3. Have you examined the entire resource?
    4. What concerns you about the resource? (use other side or additional pages if necessary)
    5. Are there resource(s) you suggest to provide additional information and/or other viewpoints on this topic?

Revised by the American Library Association Intellectual Freedom Committee
June 27, 1995

http://www.ala.org/ala/oif/challengesupport/dealing/dealingconcerns.htm#samplerequest
(Accessed March 1, 2007)

If the complaint becomes a public issue, the library should inform local media and civic organizations of the facts and enlist their support. The person or group making the complaint should not be allowed to dominate community information sources. Contact the ALA's Office for Intellectual Freedom and the state or provincial intellectual freedom committee to inform them of the complaint and to enlist their support and the assistance of other agencies.

WHEN CENSOR AND LIBRARIAN AGREE

Occasionally librarians are embarrassed to discover that they agree with an objection raised by a library patron. This can occur when shelves have not been weeded, and outdated and offensively sexist or racist material has been found. Such material should be reconsidered in the light of current selection policies and, if it does not meet standards, it should be discarded or moved to the adult collection to represent a historical point of view. Material that a librarian finds offensive but which has been recently selected through the normal channels should not be removed. The selection process in a library represents the overall library viewpoint rather than that of any one individual, so there will always be some controversial selections.

On average one complaint in ten results in the removal of library materials after a complaint (Wirth 1996, 44). Either the librarians agreed the material was offensive or they did not want to become involved in an argument about it. Removal or restriction is the easiest way to resolve a censorship challenge, but it is the most dangerous. Once librarians have given in to the people who want to limit library materials, they have given up the responsibility for maintaining their professional standards and ethics. "If the keepers of books, journals, films, compact disks, and software do not vigilantly defend free expression and intellectual freedom, who will?" (Hauptman 1988, 66). While parents and other community members have a right to challenge materials in the library, they do not have the right to take away the professional responsibilities of librarians. A strong stand against unwarranted interference with library practices is the only way for a library to retain the respect of the community as a professional institution.

PROBLEMS WITH ELECTRONIC RESOURCES

Information in electronic format is not immune to challenges. In fact, many of the most publicized controversies in recent years have been over Internet access for children. Almost as soon as public libraries began offering Internet access to patrons, debate started over what kind of access was appropriate for children (Minow 1997). In 2000, Congress passed the Children's Internet Protection Act designed to prevent children from having access to inappropriate online materials. This act requires all libraries receiving federal funding for electronic services "adopt a policy and employ technological protections that block or filter certain visual depictions deemed obscene, pornographic or harmful to minors" (Children's Internet Protection Act (CIPA), Pub. L. No. 106–554 (2000)). In 2003, the Supreme Court upheld this law, although some libraries protest that it infringes the intellectual freedom rights of patrons. The law has spurred many libraries to develop an "Acceptable Use of the Internet" policy to clarify the ways in which both children and adults are allowed to use library computers.

The ALA and its Divisions have developed resources to help librarians deal with these policy issues. The ALA section on The Children's Internet Protection Act (http://www.ala.org/ala/washoff/WOissues/civilliberties/cipaweb/cipa. htm, Accessed March 7, 2007) provides a wealth of resources for libraries seeking guidance on how to comply with the Act and provide services for their patrons.

Four questions a library may address in developing an Internet policy are

1. Does the library offer unfiltered access to the Internet? Why?
2. Does the library offer filtered access to the Internet? Why?
3. What resources may be accessed using library-provided personal computers?
4. How does providing access to the Internet support the library's goals and objectives? (Nelson 2003, 180)

An important part of an Internet policy is distinguishing between adult use and children's permissible use of the Internet and defining who falls into each use. One example of a clarification of age levels of use is given in the Multnomah County Public Library's policy:

Public Internet computers are equipped with commercial filtering software. The library's filtering policy upholds the principles of intellectual freedom, allowing adults to make their own choices regarding filtering. The policy also aims to ensure that our libraries are safe and welcoming places for children, and it affirms the right and responsibility of parents to make choices for their own children and teens.

- Adults (18 years and older) may choose filtered or unfiltered searching at each login.
- Teens (13–17) have the choice of filtered or unfiltered Internet access unless their parent or guardian designates filtered access.
- Children (12 years and younger) have filtered Internet access unless a parent or guardian designates they can choose between filtered and unfiltered access.

Because parents have differing views on how much freedom children and teenagers should have on the Internet, there are likely to be complaints about too much or too little filtering. Librarians should be prepared to defend the library's policy and adhere to it.

Libraries do not monitor patrons' use of the Internet, but they have a legitimate interest in encouraging responsible use. Another approach taken by many librarians is to provide lists of appropriate websites where children can find information relevant to school assignments or other interests. If the time child can spend on the Internet is limited by library policy, as it is in many libraries, children can locate useful sites for their assignments, but do not have time to aimlessly cruise the Internet and find objectionable materials. Librarians can also provide copies of guidelines for children's use of the Internet to help parents set limits to home use of this medium.

Websites are accessed in a more public way than other library materials and this has led to complaints about the sites other people are viewing. To protect privacy, some libraries place terminals close to a wall or provide screens that make it difficult to others to observe what is being viewed. Computers used by adults can often be placed far away from the children's room, so children do not see the sites that adults are visiting.

Web 2.0 Applications

One of the striking changes in the use of the Internet during the first few years of the twenty-first century has been the increasing interactivity. Social networking technologies have fueled the development of some of the most popular websites online. Social networking websites provide an opportunity for participants to send emails, post comments, build web content, and take part in live chats (YALSA 2005). Although several social networking sites like MySpace and Facebook were created for a specific audience, such as students enrolled in a university, they changed their policy and offer membership to others. Social networking sites serve many purposes and are being integrated into school projects and assignments.

Examples of use of social networking tools in libraries

- Creating reading blogs for summer reading programs
- Creating a wiki for a group assignment
- Posting reviews of library materials
- Exchanging opinions and voting on literature awards

Concerns about Social Networking

Parents and other adults are often concerned about social networking tools and sites because they are interactive and inappropriate people may communicate with teens and children. There have been cases when sexual predators have contacted young people and arranged to meet them in the community. As a result of these cases, legislatures have been pressured to enact laws to ban these sites from schools and libraries. The library community in general, led by the ALA, has opposed much of the legislation as being overbroad and preventing all use of social networking tools despite their value in schools and libraries.

The ALA has recommended education about online use as a way for children and families to avoid potential problems.

Rules for online safety for teens

1. Keep your identity private.
2. Never get together with someone you "meet" online.
3. Never respond to email, chat comments, instant messages, or other messages that are hostile, belligerent, inappropriate or in any way, or make you feel uncomfortable.
4. Talk with your parents about their expectations and general rules for going online. (Doyle 2006)

Educating the community about social networking

Libraries that allow children and teens to use social networking tools may want to build support for this policy by

- inviting parents and other adults to participate in a workshop where they learn to use the tools
- providing brochures about what the library is doing to keep young people safe online
- host a community debate about local or national legislation to regulate social networking
- develop a demo which parents can use to try out the tools

MAINTAINING INTELLECTUAL FREEDOM IN THE LIBRARY

Because of changing tastes and changing technologies, issues that touch on intellectual freedom often arise in the children's department. Books that have been part of the collection for years may be challenged as well as new techniques of delivering information or entertainment. Librarians must be aware of what is going on in their community, their state, and the country to be ready for unexpected complaints or demands. The best way to do this is to be active in professional associations and keep up with what is happening in other libraries. The many electronic mailing lists that associations and other groups offer are invaluable resources when questions arise. By being a participant in a professional network, a librarian can be prepared for challenges and gather ideas about ways to respond to them.

Three vital principles of maintaining a free provision of materials are

- Develop policies to define library positions.
- Respond to challenges respectfully and promptly.
- Maintain communication with the library community.

REFERENCES AND ADDITIONAL READING

American Library Association. 1996. *Access to Electronic Information Services, and Networks: An Interpretation of the* Library Bill of Rights. Chicago: American Library Association.

American Library Association. 1997. *Access for Children and Young People to Videotapes and Other Nonprint Formats: An Interpretation of the* Library Bill of Rights. http://www.ala. org/ICONN/ICONN-website/video.html.

American Library Association. 2006. *Intellectual Freedom Manual: Compiled by the Office for Intellectual Freedom of the American Library Association.* Chicago: American Library Association.

Doyle, Robert P. 2006. The Current Legislative Challenge: DOPA and the Participation Gap [October 2006]. *The ILA Reporter* XXIV: 16–21.

Hauptman, Robert. 1988. *Ethical Challenges in Librarianship.* Phoenix, AZ: Oryx.

Jaeger, P. T., Bertot, J. C., and McClure, C. R. 2004. The Effects of the Children's Internet Protection Act (CIPA) in Public Libraries and Its Implications for Research: A Statistical, Policy, and Legal Analysis. *Journal of the American Society for Information Science* 55: 1131–1139.

Magid, Lawrence J. 1996. *Child Safety on the Information Highway.* Produced by the National Center for Missing and Exploited Children and Interactive Services Association: http://www.missingkids.org/information_superhighway.html#rules.

Minow, Mary. 1997. Filters and the public library: A Legal and Policy Analysis. *First Monday* 2, no. 12. http://www.firstmonday.org (accessed March 7, 2007).

Minow, Mary, and Lipinski, Tomas. 2003. *The Library's Legal Answer Book.* Chicago: American Library Association.

Mitchell, K. J., Finkelhor, D., and Wolak, J. 2003. The Exposure of Youth to Unwanted Sexual Material on the Internet. *Youth and Society,* 34: 330–358.

Nelson, Sandra, Garcia, June, and Association, For the Public Library Association. 2003. *Creating Policies for Results: From Chaos to Clarity: PLA Results Series.* Chicago: American Library Association.

Peck, Robert. 2000. *Libraries, the First Amendment and Cyberspace: What You Need to Know.* Chicago: American Library Association.

Wirth, Eileen. 1996. The State of Censorship. *American Libraries,* 27, 44–48.

Young Adult Library Services Association [YALSA]. 2005. *Teens and Social Networking in School and Public Libraries: A Toolkit for Librarians and Library Workers.* Chicago: American Library Association. http://www.ala.org/ala/yalsa/profdev/SocialNetworking Toolkit_March07.pdf.

13

Organizing Special Events and Ongoing Programs

Celebrations and events present an opportunity for a department to generate publicity from local media and alert the community to library services. Events may include:

- the opening of a new branch or department
- a visit by an author, illustrator, or performer
- the opening of a special collection
- the inauguration of a new service

Any event not foreseen in the normal program planning of a library department is to some extent a special event. To take advantage of the public relations value of events, librarians must plan carefully. Well-organized events run smoothly and appear effortless, but they are usually the result of careful planning on someone's part. Special events generate excitement among patrons and staff but because they take considerable time and planning, as well as costing money; no library department can expect to handle a great many of them. A realistic goal would be for a department to have one special event every six months.

Programs such as summer reading programs, book clubs, and special interest groups can also be a source of good publicity for a department. Programs that are repeated every year, summer reading programs, for example, are not quite special events, but the planning and preparation involved are very similar.

PREPARING FOR AN EVENT

The first question to ask before taking on a program or special event is "What is the objective?" Librarians should not spend time and money with only the vague hope that the public will notice and appreciate the event. While thinking about the objectives for an event, librarians should also devise evaluation measures to see whether these objectives are achieved. Some possible objectives for special events include:

- obtaining favorable publicity
- attracting a large audience
- bringing non-users into the library
- presenting a quality experience for committed library users
- serving a particular target audience, an ethnic group, or age category
- offering civic information or voter education

Each of these objectives requires a different approach.

Attracting the Whole Community

If the objective of an event is to attract as large an audience as possible including people who do not currently use the library, librarians should try to blanket the community with publicity. This can be done by

- Finding community partners to co-sponsor an event—Local civic groups, parent-teacher associations, and ethnic and religious groups can publicize the event through their membership and encourage participation.
- Enlisting the aid of prominent media figures—A local television personality or sports figure will attract community members simply by attending an event.
- Working with community leaders—Members of the city council, executives of local businesses, and prominent supporters of local charities have wide networks of friends and colleagues who will be influenced by their support of an event.
- Using varied channels of publicity—Utilize flyers and posters in the library; news releases for newspapers; public service announcements for television and radio stations; notices on the library websites; messages on listservs and mailing lists; ads in buses. Each channel can reach a different audience.

Targeting a Specific Audience

Some events, such as the visit of a children's author or illustrator, aim to provide a more intensive but smaller program. If the author writes difficult books for older children, it would be unwise to send out press releases inviting everyone in the community to attend a reading. Preschool children might be disruptive, whereas children who have read the author's books would be able to have an exciting, reasonably intimate interaction with the author. The steps to providing a rich experience include:

- Identify the appropriate audience. Talk to the author or illustrator and find out what kind of program will be offered and decide on age limits.
- Insert invitations to the event in copies of the author's books, so borrowers will be aware of the visit.
- Contact teachers and invite their students to attend.
- Call your local bookstore and arrange for notices to be available there.

- Invite youth groups from community centers or churches.
- Post notices on the library website and link to school websites.

Initial Planning

The first step in arranging a visit from an author or illustrator or other notable person is to brainstorm about the choices. Staff members and the children themselves can be asked which author or illustrator they would most like to have visit the library. Choosing a visitor whose books are popular with your clientele ensures a large audience, but widely popular authors are difficult to schedule and are often expensive.

Authors and illustrators who have some connection with your community are easier to attract than national figures. If the visitor lives within an easy driving distance to the library, both costs and time commitment will be kept down. People who lived in the community when they were young, or who have visited it before, may be particularly interested in returning. Other attractions are a regional interest or a relationship to an ethnic group within the community. Try to think of why the visitor would want to come to your community as well as why you would want to have him or her come.

If after considering the possibilities, you and your staff decide you want a nationally known figure, try to find other groups in the community to cosponsor a visit. This not only limits the cost that each participating group incurs, but also gives the visitor a wider audience and greater potential sales growing out of the visit. You can contact schools, universities, bookstores, community or religious groups, and museums as potential partners. You may also be able to write a grant to finance an appearance by an author or illustrator if the event is a workshop that offers an educational opportunity for children.

After you have drawn up a pool of potential candidates, try to find out whether they are dynamic speakers. Colleagues who attend state and national conferences may have heard some of them. Library mailing lists such as PUBYAC or the ALSC lists also serve as forums for gathering opinions about the appeal of potential speakers.

Checklist of information about potential speaker:

- Does the library have the author/illustrator's books? If not, buy them.
- Where does the speaker live? Long distances and inaccessible locations make transportation more expensive.
- Has the speaker appeared at other local institutions recently? Has he/she appeared on television? This may build an audience.
- Is there a new book coming out that the publisher would like to publicize?
- Has the speaker won an award recently?
- Are there any connections between your chosen author/illustrator and a specific community ethnic or interest group?

Armed with this information, a department head can approach the chief librarian for permission to implement the visit and provide funding. Authors and illustrators can be contacted through their publisher. A preliminary letter should lead to a telephone call in which the proposed dates, the type of presentation the library would like, the honorarium, and   , and expenses to be covered can be discussed. It is important to be realistic and honest with the speaker and the publisher about the amount of publicity to be given to the event, the size of the anticipated audience, and the number of the author or illustrator's books that are likely to be sold. It is in the interest of all the parties concerned that expectations for the event are likely to be met.

Constructing a Budget

Preparing a budget for a special event is not much different from the budgeting for regularly scheduled programs, but it requires organized thought. A special event may appear to be free or inexpensive, but the costs in money and staff time can mount up quickly. It is useful to estimate the costs before a final commitment is made, because the decision whether to have the event or not should be based on the importance of the objectives in relation to costs.

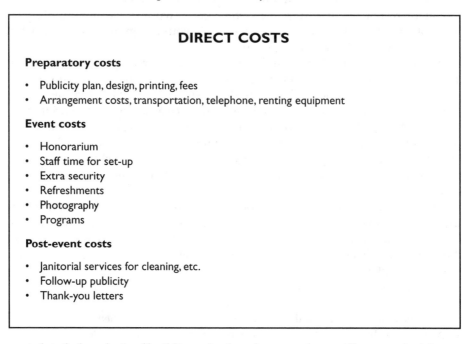

DIRECT COSTS

Preparatory costs

- Publicity plan, design, printing, fees
- Arrangement costs, transportation, telephone, renting equipment

Event costs

- Honorarium
- Staff time for set-up
- Extra security
- Refreshments
- Photography
- Programs

Post-event costs

- Janitorial services for cleaning, etc.
- Follow-up publicity
- Thank-you letters

A detailed analysis of building a budget for an author or illustrator's visit can be found in *Inviting Children's Authors and Illustrators* (East 1995).

Because the time spent in preparing for and carrying out the event must be taken from other duties, it has a dollar value. Cost of staff time can be estimated by the category of worker carrying out tasks.

Department head will need the full day of the event and some preparatory meetings.

Librarians will require the equivalent of one individual spending three or four days in correspondence, preparing publicity, supervising preparations, and attending meetings, as well as the full day of the event and a half day afterwards for wrap-up.

Clerical staff often spend the equivalent of a week's time preparing for a special event. Because clerical staff time is less expensive than professional time, as many tasks as possible should be allocated to them. Clerical staff members should be told which tasks can be postponed or eliminated to make time for event activities.

Volunteers can be used to lessen the amount of staff time needed for special events. A Friends of the Library group may supply volunteers, especially if the routine work is balanced by the opportunity to meet a well-known person. Older children and parents of library users are sometimes willing to contribute time to mailing publicity, decorating the children's room, or preparing and serving refreshments. In addition, adult volunteers may be willing to meet visiting dignitaries at the airport and to entertain them for a few hours while the library staff is busy with other preparations.

Although volunteers are not paid for their work, they should receive other rewards. Often the opportunity to meet an admired author or other guest is the major impetus for volunteering, but other incentives may be added. Librarians owe volunteers the courtesy of including them in planning sessions and listening to their suggestions. A volunteer who has given considerable time to welcoming and entertaining a guest, might like to be included in publicity pictures and be mentioned in publicity releases. The volunteer would almost certainly appreciate an invitation to a luncheon or dinner for the guest. Any program prepared for an event should list the names of volunteers. The librarian's opening or closing remarks should mention volunteers who have given considerable time to the project. After the event, each volunteer should receive a letter of appreciation from the librarian. Children may receive a small gift such as a paperback copy of an author's book. Gracefully acknowledging the library's gratitude to volunteers will help to ensure a continuing supply of help for future events.

PUBLICITY

Who prepares the publicity? Large library systems have public relations (PR) or publicity departments to prepare news releases and arrange media contacts for all library events. Librarians who plan a special event should work closely with the PR department and give them all the relevant information. This information includes

- Biography of visiting speaker
- List of publications and awards
- Target audience of published books (age level, characteristics, etc.)
- Curriculum tie-in with books
- Connection with community
- Adult audience (e.g., parents, teachers, local history groups)

Publicity Channels

People have different patterns of gathering information, so information about the event should appear in as many different formats as possible.

- Newspapers (including neighborhood weeklies and ethnic press)
- Television (both commercial and public channels)

- Radio
- Flyers (in library, schools, and community)
- Library website (with link to author/illustrator's website)
- Community bulletin boards (electronic and physical)
- Postcard invitations to target audience
- Local bloggers who cover similar events

News Release

The news release contains the basic information about an event and can be adapted for use in various formats. The key to writing a successful release is to be clear, concise, and lively. The release should open with the most important, eye-catching information so the person who first sees it will not toss it aside without realizing its potential interest for readers. The news release includes the five *W*'s of newspaper reporting: who, what, when, where, why (see figure 13.1 for an example of a new release).

ELEMENTS OF A NEWS RELEASE

- Catchy introductory sentence
- Who the speaker is to be, including photo
- What the topic of the event will be
- When—the date and time
- Where—location, including directions for walking, driving, and public transit
- Why—benefit to the audience and possibly to the library
- Contact for further information (telephone, email, and website)

Public Service Announcements

New releases will give the basic information about a program for print media, but for radio and television media, public service announcements (PSA) are important. PSAs are short messages that nonprofit organizations can broadcast without charge on radio and television stations.

BASIC FACTS ABOUT PSAS

- PSAs for radio shows may be prerecorded or read by an announcer.
- PSAs for television may be read and videotaped or may be shown as text announcements at station breaks or as a crawl on the bottom of the screen.
- PSAs should run 10, 20, 30, or 60 seconds. Most stations prefer them to be 30 seconds or less.
- A 30-second PSA for radio should contain about 75 words.

The first step in developing a PSA is to identify the media outlets that will broadcast the message. Most libraries have a list of public broadcast channels and commercial stations that are receptive to nonprofit organizations. In

Figure 13.1
Sample news release.

Valley View Public Library

---

432 West Ridge Drive
Valley View, CA 45062
(369) 732-6000
Fax: (369) 732-6222

NEWS RELEASE
FOR IMMEDIATE RELEASE
Contact: Agnes Geary, 369-732-6023, fax: 369-732-6224, e-mail a.geary@valleyview
pl.org

February 17, 2008 What did all those hopeful miners eat while they were searching for treasure during the California gold rush? Children's author Gloria Esquivel has searched old letters and diaries and found a dozen recipes for her latest book, *Gold That Melts in Your Mouth.* On Wednesday, March 1, 2008, from 4:00 to 6:00 Ms. Esquivel will be at the Valley View Public Library to demonstrate how gold rush miners cooked on the trail. Children ages six and older are invited to hear the talk and sample some authentic gold mining food, including deep fried grasshoppers and pine nut pancakes.

Ms. Esquivel is the author of six previous books for children. Her historical novel *Mystery at the Mission Dolores* won the Hector Protector Prize in 2006 and has been translated into six languages. Her earlier series, *Tales of the Traveling Tortillas*, remains a favorite with girls throughout the world.

Copies of Ms. Esquivel's books will be on display at the library. Children may bring their own copies of the books for autographing.

###

---

compiling such a list, do not forget to include stations broadcasting in non-English languages. Check with each station about the length of PSA they prefer and the format for submission. Some media outlets enable users to submit PSAs through their websites, which is a quick and easy way to get them sent out; others prefer text files sent by email or fax. Be sure to call the station to identify the individual to whom the information should be sent. (For an example of a PSA, see figure 13.2.)

Information to be included in a PSA:

- Heading to indicate that the script is for a PSA
- Name of library and contact information
- Length of PSA
- Dates on which the PSA should be made available. It is especially important to indicate the date after which it will be stale.
- Double or triple space the text

Figure 13.2
Sample public service announcement (PSA).

Public Service Announcement
Cypress Public Library
Contact: Daniel Leong
                    Children's Services Manager
                    Tel: 432-857-5050
                    Fax: 432-857-5030
                    D.Leong@Cypresspl.org
10 seconds
For use through March 28, 2008
ENJOY A SPACE ADVENTURE WITH OTIS PENDAR, ASTRONAUT AND
SCIENTIST. AT CYPRUS PUBLIC LIBRARY FRIDAY, MARCH 28 AT 4:00. MORE
INFORMATION AT HTTP://WWW.CYPRESSPL.ORG

Website Announcements

The library website is one of the best places to call attention to a library program. Whenever a program is coming up, an announcement with a picture should be placed on the front page of the website. That can link to the children's page, which can give further information and links to the websites of an author, illustrator, or performer involved in the event, as shown in figures 13.3 and 13.4.

Tips for an effective website announcement:

- Use a button or graphic with the word "new" to call attention to your announcement.
- Use the information in your news release as a guide to content, but make it brief.
- Be sure to include a picture of the performer or a book jacket or illustration.
- Animation or blinking announcements will get attention, but don't overdo the clutter.
- Links to related websites will increase the value and interest of the announcement.
- Ask a couple of children to look at your announcement before you post it. If they don't find it attractive and clear, redo it.
- Caption graphics for accessibility (see chapter 11).
- If the library has a blog, ask the visiting speaker to contribute a message for potential audience.
- Remove the information *promptly* when the event is over. Announcements about long gone projects make a website look stale and useless.

Continuing Information

Library staff should be prepared to answer questions and give further details to patrons and reporters. Information about the event and the speaker should be available near department telephones and at the circulation counter so any library employee can give quick and knowledgeable answers to simple questions. Calls from the media should be referred to the librarian in charge of events. If the information requested is not immediately available, a follow-up telephone call should be made as soon as possible. Replies to email messages should be sent quickly. Media people work on short deadlines, and a story may not be covered if the

Figure 13.3
Homepage of Newark Public Library announcing program. Reprinted with permission of Newark Public Library.

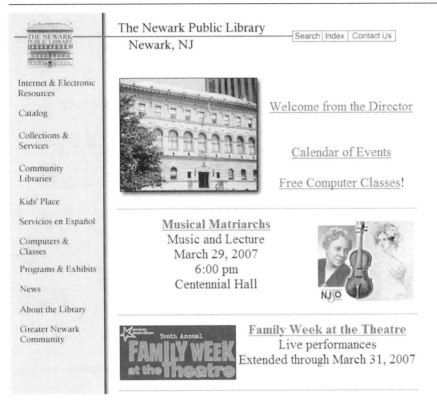

library does not answer questions quickly. Requests for interviews with a librarian about the program, either in person, by email, or on the telephone, should be encouraged. Not only does the program receive greater publicity, but the library's reputation as an informed and responsive institution is enhanced.

Media representatives, both writers and photographers, should be invited to attend any special event. If an event is particularly visual—a magician or artist, for example—invitations should mention that fact so that photographers will be sent.

Electronic notices sent to libraries and schools in the region as well as to bookstores, community groups, and appropriate electronic mail lists are effective. These notices not only attract an audience, but also let other librarians know about speakers who might be available for other visits.

Publicity in the Library

The most obvious pool of potential attendees for a library program is people who use the library, so publicity there should include

- Large posters in both the adult and children's department several weeks before the program.
- Flyers on the circulation desk or a publicity table near the library entrance.

Figure 13.4
Further information about program on children's page. Reprinted with permission of Newark Public Library.

Kids' Place

At The Newark Public Library

All programs free and open to the public!
Seating is first come, first served.

Saturday, 03/03/2007

Genies, Lamps and Dreams: Tales of the Arabian Nights

Produced by:	A Young Audiences of New Jersey production
Presented by:	Newark Public Library / Springfield Branch
Performance Time:	11:00 AM
Description:	Imagine yourself on a flying carpet traveling back in time! In this all-new telling of the tales of the Arabian Nights, Youth Stages will transport you to the Sultan's palace in the Persian Empire in 803 AD. Debby Stewart and Jim Folly recreate the tales of The Genie and the Fisher Woman, Sinbad the Sailor, Aladdin and the Genie, and Ali Baba and the Sticky Thieves! With a great deal of audience participation, Youth Stages makes these tales accessible to young children as they become bakers and birds, fish and frogs, and doors that say "Open Sesame!"

- Bookmarks announcing the program placed in each book circulated for a month before the event.
- Notices on staff bulletin boards so the entire staff is aware of the program.
- Email messages sent to staff and friends-of-the-library groups.

STAFF PREPARATION

Any special event will go more smoothly if staff members are enthusiastic about the event and think it is worthwhile. Staff members will be more willing to work hard on an event they see as a united effort than one the administration forces upon them. Many staff members, from librarians to pages, will have ideas about publicizing and facilitating an event. Encourage willing staff members to take responsibility for specific tasks, with the department head coordinating the overall plans. One person might design publicity materials, another coordinate distribution of publicity, a third supervise physical arrangements (e.g., seating, cloak room, and decorations), and a fourth arrange housing for the guest. Distributing tasks among a number of persons lessens the burden on any one individual, although it means the department head or a designate must monitor progress in each area.

Because time spent on a special event is taken away from regular duties, the department head should discuss which regular tasks must be done and which can be postponed. The department head and staff should agree in advance on priorities. In a large department, the agreement should be in writing to avoid later arguments or recriminations.

Volunteers should be recruited about six weeks before the event. By this time library staff will have made the major decisions, but there will still be time to solicit ideas for details. Many volunteers, both children and adults, cannot make firm commitments of time more than four to six weeks in advance, so recruiting volunteers too early may cause some to drop out later.

Usually volunteers will be recruited from regular library users or Friends of the Library groups. Because the library staff has frequent and informal contact with these people, the librarian need only make informal inquiries until an appropriate number of volunteers are found. Occasionally, the librarian may ask an organization or other group to volunteer for a particular program. Recruitment on this level requires a more formal approach through telephone calls or letters to a contact person in the group. A notice on the library website can be an excellent way to attract volunteers.

All volunteer commitments should be in writing. Note the dates and time specifically: "taking tickets between 2:00 and 3:00 on Sunday April 18th" or "distributing flyers to the Heather Hill retirement residence on April 10th," for example. Written agreements make it easier for volunteers to remember what they have promised, and for the library staff to identify other necessary tasks.

WORKING WITH VISITING CELEBRITIES

Several months may elapse between making arrangements for a visit and the event. The visitor should be kept informed of plans as they develop. The department head will probably speak to the visitor by telephone several times in order to confirm housing and speaking arrangements. These arrangements should be confirmed in writing to avoid misunderstanding.

Checklist of details to be confirmed at least two weeks in advance:

- Details of travel arrangements and housing
- Honorarium and payment procedures
- Permission for taping or photographs
- Arrangements for selling autographed copies of books

- Detailed itinerary with directions to the library
- Information about meals provided

Out-of-town authors or performers sometimes expect a staff member or volunteer to meet them at the airport. If the library cannot provide this service, the visitor should be given clear instructions about ground transportation and whether to go to a hotel or to the library. When a visitor is to drive to the community, clear directions and a map should be provided. Never assume that visitors prefer to make their own arrangements for housing and meals, although that option should be available. Occasionally a visitor may stay at the home of a librarian or board member. Some visitors prefer this arrangement because it is more personal than a hotel, but the host should ensure that the visitor has enough privacy to prepare the program and to prevent fatigue from constantly meeting new people.

The department head should try to meet the visitor as soon as possible after arrival. This first meeting gives the librarian a chance to discover the guest's personal requirements. Some speakers prefer solitude for several hours before their presentation; others like to visit the library or a local attraction. Most visitors want to see the where they will speak and check any equipment they will be using.

Meals provide opportunities to introduce the guest to library staff or community members. One staff member or volunteer should be responsible for the visitor during each meal. This person should ensure that the meal meets the visitor's preferences for food and drink, including dietary restrictions. The staff member or volunteer must also ensure that one or two guests do not monopolize the visitor's attention and that the meal does not drag on so long the visitor becomes tired.

During the visitor's stay, whether it is for a day or for a weekend, a designated contact person should answer questions and handle contingencies. These may range from laundry, dry cleaning, or a midnight pizza to the loss of cash and valuables, an illness, or accident. The visitor should never feel friendless while visiting the library community.

On the day of the presentation, the visitor should be taken to the library in ample time. Even the most sophisticated speaker can develop stage fright and want the reassurance of being close to the scene of the event. Equipment and facilities should be retested just before the event. Everything should be done to meet the needs of the speaker whether for solitude, the company of several people, or a glass of water.

The end of the program can mark the beginning of a difficult period for the speaker. No matter how successful the event and how warm the applause, the speaker may experience a letdown. The host librarian can alleviate this by ensuring there is a follow-up. If a reception is planned, the speaker should be shepherded around so that he or she is neither monopolized by a few guests nor ignored.

After the public reception, the library staff usually take the speaker out to a meal or for a drink to allow the excitement of the occasion to subside gradually. Even famous and sophisticated speakers may feel uncertain after a performance and wonder whether the occasion was a success. They enjoy hearing that the library appreciates the speaker and is happy with the event. Librarians may hesitate to praise a famous guest, assuming that the visitor hears this all the time, but everyone likes to hear well-earned praise and appreciation.

Finally the department head must see that the visitor is paid as soon as possible. If receipts are needed for expenses, the host should remind the guest to present them before leaving the community. If for any reason payment might be delayed, the letter of thanks sent to the guest after the event should mention the reason for this and give a date by which payment can be expected. The library's financial officer will handle the processing, but the department head should be sure that the honorarium and expense money are paid. It is embarrassing for a speaker to have to write to an institution to remind them of an unpaid obligation.

POST-EVENT TASKS

Assign the task of cleaning up after the event before the day itself. Maintenance staff will do most of the cleaning. If volunteers are expected to help clean up, their responsibility should be clearly explained. Staff members should have specific tasks assigned; cleaning up goes better if the department head participates, unless she is busy taking care of the visitor. As part of the cleanup, remove all outdated notices about the program from bulletin boards.

Immediately after the event, send a news release to local media. The event's publicist can write the release in advance, adding final details afterwards. The library should send out the release even if local media representatives have attended the program. The release may help reporters prepare final copy and may result in an extra story. News releases should be sent to regional and state library publications and to national publications if appropriate.

The notice on the library's website should be changed from an announcement to a report on the event. Photographs are an attraction, especially if they include patrons. A list of the speaker's books should remain, so audience members will remember which ones they want to read. If the visitor has given permission, a streaming video of at least part of the event, or an audio file may be posted on the website.

Within a week after the event the department head should write thank-you letters to

- Speakers
- Publishers or booksellers who participated
- All volunteers
- Staff members who helped

The department head should prepare a written report of the event, even if the administrator does not require one. Reports are useful for planning future events and in documenting activities for annual reports or grant applications. Reports usually include

- planning process
- time commitment
- any problems that arose
- suggestions for improving the event

PLANNING ONGOING PROGRAMS

Special events bring a library good publicity and attract new users, but ongoing programs build a loyal group of patrons. Almost every children's department offers storyhours for preschool children and most also have summer reading programs.

Popular Programs

Public libraries now offer many kinds of programs and a great range of materials designed to bring people into the library. Yet, surveys of library services consistently indicate that the old-fashioned storyhour is still the program most people know and care about in libraries. Even adults who do not use the library themselves often value storyhours for their children. It is important for libraries to remember the immense public relations value of programming for children.

Ten successful types of library programs:

• Traditional storyhours for children three and up
• Summer reading programs
• Lapsits for infants with caregivers present
• Toddler storyhours, often with caregivers present
• Class visits for schools and daycare programs
• Family storyhours for mixed age groups
• Media programs—film, music, and so forth
• Bilingual programs for any age group
• Caregiver programs for adults who live or work with children
• Programs for children with special needs

Decision Points for Planning Programs

• What is the target groups—infants, toddlers, preschool (3–5), or parent groups?
• How much staff time can the library dedicate to planning and giving programs?
• Will the programs be on a registration or drop-in basis?
• How frequently should programs be offered? (Weekly is the usual pattern.)
• What time of day is best—morning, after school, early evening, weekends?
• Will each session of programs have an overall theme, or will each be a separate event?
• What are the goals of the programs—to increase walk-in traffic, to raise circulation, to prepare children for school, to introduce books to non-reading parents, to encourage multiethnic participation?

Decisions should be based on knowledge of the community and the actual and potential patrons. Are parents in the community likely to register for a series of library programs or do they prefer spontaneous planning? Do many children have caregivers available to bring them to a daytime program or should daycare groups be the target? Would working parents appreciate a chance to attend evening programs with their children? Are there particular ethnic or racial groups in the community who might be attracted to programs designed for them? The more effort put into designing appropriate programs, the more successful the programs are likely to be.

Planning Cycle

Planning programs takes as much time as presenting them, but librarians often enjoy working on programming and spend even more time than necessary. Time should be budgeted so other work, such as reference service, maintaining collections, and budgeting, are not neglected. In early fall, when one summer reading program has been completed and evaluated, planning for the next one begins. This allows time to collaborate with partners and prepare professional graphics and publicity. During the summer, while the summer program is running, is a good time to plan for the storyhours offered during the school year.

Secrets of successful program planning

* Become familiar with the community demographics to select the most needed programs.
* Coordinate with larger units—summer reading programs on a systemwide, regional or statewide basis allow cost-effective graphics and publicity to be made available to all.
* Document successes and failures—after each program, notes should be made about which books and projects worked and which need to be modified. These notes should be kept and used for future planning.
* Investigate other community youth organizations and avoid offering programs that conflict in time or content with what is being offered elsewhere.
* Allow school-age children to give input into the type of programs they want,
* Publicize ongoing programs in the same way special events are publicized, outside as well as inside the library.
* Encourage participation by nonprofessional staff in implementing programs.
* Use the library website and blogs as means of publicizing programs, building on programs to encourage additional reading, and receiving useful feedback.

Library programs for children are the gateway through which future readers enter the library. Whether a special event or an ongoing series, programs are the primary showcase for libraries in the community. With imaginative thinking and careful planning, children's services librarians can make them the centerpiece of the library's marketing efforts.

REFERENCES AND ADDITIONAL READING

Banks, Paula. 1995. News Releases, Photo Releases, Public Service Announcements. In *Part-Time Public Relations with Full-Time Results*, ed. Rashelle Karp, 1–9. Chicago: American Library Association.

East, Kathy. 1995. *Inviting Children's Authors and Illustrators: A How-to-Do-It Manual for School and Public Librarians.* How-to-do-it Manuals for Librarians; 49. New York: Neal-Schuman.

Karp, Rashelle S. ed. 1995. *Part-Time Public Relations with Full-Time Results: A PR Primer for Libraries.* Chicago: American Library Association.

O'Keefe, Claudia. 2005. Publicity 101: How to Promote Your Library's Next Event [June/July 2005]. *American Libraries* 36: 52–55.

14

Serving Schools, Daycares, and Child Serving Agencies

The two major community institutions designed to help children learn and succeed should be the school and the public library. Often the library has resources and library staff that can supplement the resources the school has and schools offer access to children that the library does not always have. By working together schools and public libraries can help children be better students, readers, and independent learners. Cooperation and partnerships also serve the mission of both the school and the public library.

Most communities have additional agencies that also serve children. These include preschools and daycares for young children, out of school programs for grade school children, Y's, boys and girls clubs, 4-H, and a myriad of programs that have specific audiences or missions like scouts, juvenile correction agencies, homeless shelters, and summer camps. Each school (public, charter, or private) and child-serving agency offers the opportunity to expand the library's influence and accomplish its mission and to attract new library users by developing services to agencies. These services recognize the school or agency as deserving of library services because helping teachers and youth workers helps the children they teach and serve, *and* libraries can serve children better by using the school or agency as an effective intermediary.

The benefits of serving schools and other child agencies include:

- Reaching children who live a long way from the library or have no way to get to the library facility.
- Helping teachers and other influential adults to use library services and resources that in turn help them work with children more effectively.
- Recruiting more users and stimulating more use of the library.
- Helping the school or agency achieve success in meeting its goals.

The biggest liability for serving institutions is that it takes time, energy, and resources that may be needed to provide services to individuals. In addition, some people in the community may see service to the school and other agencies as unnecessarily duplicating services. There may also be conflicts with school librarians, teachers, and youth workers about how to use time within the school day or program.

Outreach to schools and other agencies, however, is a staple of children's library services and for most libraries it is not a question of whether to serve schools, daycares, and other agencies, but how best to serve them. The essential elements of successful outreach are

- Personal contact with teachers, administrators, school librarians, daycare staff, and youth workers. Face-to face contact helps outsiders focus on the benefits of the library. Contact also helps library staff know what happens at school, the pressures and issues faced by teachers and workers, and builds empathy for the work done by others working with children.
- A careful plan for the services offered. These should relate directly to the goals of the institution served as well as to the goals of the library.
- Patience and persistence in developing a relationship with schools and other agencies. Teachers and others may not drop everything at the first opportunity and begin using the library's services.
- A flexible work schedule that allows librarians to visit schools and other programs at times convenient to them and, in general, to have sufficient time to be away from the library and direct service responsibilities.

What follows is a discussion of the issues for each kind of outreach program.

OUTREACH TO SCHOOLS

Public libraries often grew out of the need for schools to provide materials that support student learning. Many public libraries were, indeed, part of a school system in the early part of the twentieth century, so the practice of serving students and teachers was one of the first reasons to create libraries. In 1888 Melvil Dewey, a founder of modern librarianship, said that the school is the "chisel" and the public library the "marble" and without both there can be no "statues" (Bostwick 1914, 73). While most public libraries are now separate from the local school district, this symbiotic relationship still exists. To best educate students, schools and libraries need to work together.

This work can include sharing materials both print and electronic, staff communication, planning, librarian visits to schools and class visits to the public library, and sharing facilities, as well as joint programs like writing, art, and student performance projects. Most libraries offer services to students, teachers, school librarians, and school administrators who work in public, private, and charter schools located in the library's service area. While public schools outnumber private schools in most communities, librarians should make a special effort to communicate with private schools. Some independent, parochial, and charter schools have fewer resources than the public schools and will be especially receptive to overtures from the public library. And while homeschooling families normally visit the library, some libraries offer outreach services to homeschool associations or groups where the librarian might provide stories, parent training, booktalking, or technical training to homeschoolers and their parents that meet away from the library.

Resource Sharing

Public librarians should become familiar with the general curriculum of each of the schools in the community. Although the public library does not usually build its collection around curricular needs, subjects covered in the school will undoubtedly be reflected in requests for materials. Information about the public school curricula are usually available online from local or state boards of education. Librarians should be alert to major shifts in topics covered or the introduction of new subjects. If the schools in a community begin instruction in a new language, for example, the public library will want to strengthen its collection in this language. Similarly, a new health education curriculum stressing the role of nutrition in childhood obesity will lead to heavy demand for this type of material in the public library. Information about extracurricular school activities—theatrical productions, sports, extended trips—are often reported in local newspapers. Public librarians can capitalize on this information by displaying materials related to, for example, a school trip to Hawaii or a school production of *Aladdin*.

Similarly the library should promote the use of fiction, recorded books, magazines, DVDs, and other materials that schools may not collect, but which support student learning and help to foster a love of reading. School media center budgets rarely are adequate to keep collections broad or current. Some agreement about what will be collected by the school and by the public library will help maximize the financial support of each institution. A part of any formal or even informal collection development cooperation should be agreement about how public library resources will be made available to teachers and students at school. Libraries can offer courtesy cards to teachers and tailor loan periods to meet their needs, or transport books to and from schools on library trucks.

Another possibility for resource sharing is sharing database access. Most libraries offer cardholder Internet access to databases, offering this service to teachers would be easy. Schools can provide a direct link to the public library's webpage from the school media computer, and classroom work stations. The public library might also offer staff and student training on using electronic resources.

Communication

School media personnel can be a first line of communication for public librarians. If there are no school media employees or no school library, communication can start with the principal, vice principal or an instructional coordinator who has responsibility for community relations. When dealing with large single or consolidated school districts, the children's librarian should communicate with the district media center coordinator or the superintendent's office as well as with the individual schools. By visiting with various levels of school staff and asking who is the person to contact or who has authority to cooperate with the library, the children's librarian can create a reasonable and effective list of contacts. The list will need to be updated at least annually as school staff may be reassigned or leave the school.

Regular meetings with personnel from the schools served by a branch library should help avoid problems associated with heavy school-oriented use and streamline activities that involve the school and the library. The public library should take the initiative in contacting school personnel. A coffee hour or other informal annual meeting may be scheduled at the beginning of the school year or some other convenient time. At this meeting, mutual concerns can be discussed before they become problems. The meeting should focus on finding solutions. Many school media centers have the same problem as public libraries with unexpected assignments, for example. When the school media specialists find that all of the information on a topic has been taken, they may suggest that students go to the public library. The more that each institution knows about the resources of the other, the more likely it is that appropriate referrals will be made.

Continuing contact maintains strong relations between the school and the public library. Information about relevant new acquisitions or services can supplement the annual meetings. Include the school media person in the electronic mailing list for library press releases and other publicity. An informal email message sent every few weeks provides an excellent format for efficient communication between the public library and the schools.

In addition to the school media staff, librarians will want to keep local teachers informed about the library's collections and services, as well as problems with students. Letting teachers know why the public library cannot provide some materials for school assignments is important, but negative feedback should not be the only type of communication. The library should send information about library services to schools at the beginning of each school year. This information is particularly useful for new teachers but can also remind all teachers about the hours, services, and limitations of the public library. Brief, clear information presented with a touch of humor is most effective. In the mailing, teachers can also be invited to schedule class visits to the library. Also, information about school assignments, science fair projects, and other activities that may affect the public library should be requested. Set up a feedback section on the library website to make it easy for teachers to keep the library informed. If possible, a library staff member should monitor the school library website to find information about changes, projects, and activities at the school that may affect the public library.

Not all teachers will respond to the invitations and requests. Teachers are often overwhelmed with paperwork in addition to their teaching duties, and a request from the public library adds to the burden. Many teachers will be willing to email assignment alerts, requests for materials or request for librarian visits, so the children's department may want to assign staff to read and respond quickly to teacher requests. Email is usually the quickest and easiest ways to communicate efficiently, but the library should not deluge teachers with more messages than they want. Teachers who realize that the library can make their jobs easier are likely to make their satisfaction known to other teachers. Gradually, the library may build up a solid core of teachers who keep the library informed about activities that require materials beyond the resources of the school media centers. While no public library can hope to have enough materials and staff to supply the needs of all students for all assignments, cooperation with the schools can help both agencies provide the best service possible with their limited resources.

School Programs and Services

In many communities, class visits to the public library are the principal form of interaction between schools and libraries. Sometimes these visits are formalized so all the children in a certain grade visit the library once during the year. In other communities, individual teachers or schools arrange for class visits, which may involve any grade level. Either the public librarian or the schools can make the initial contact. Once a routine is established, the practice may continue without much further input.

The purposes of class visits may include:

- A general introduction to the library
- Library registration
- A lesson in how to use the library
- A demonstration of Internet resources
- Introduction of materials for a specific school project
- Encouragement of recreational reading and booktalks
- A recreational program of story reading, films, and so forth
- Introduction of a summer reading program

The teacher and the librarian should understand and agree on the purpose of a particular visit. If a teacher expects the librarian to teach the Dewey Decimal System, while the librarian plans to read the latest Caldecott Medal-winning book, both may be disappointed, and the relationship between the school and the library strained. To avoid this problem, the librarian should always ask the teacher what he or she expects from the visit and inform the teacher about the library's plans. If the library plans to give the children library cards, the librarian should inform the teacher about any necessary documentation. If the teacher wants the children to be introduced to materials on a particular topic, the librarian should try to obtain a copy of the assignment or lesson plan for that topic. This makes it easier to gather and present appropriate material. Librarians should also ask about any special needs. Children with special needs, non-English speaking children, and those with behavioral problems may require particular care.

Librarians who are organizing a program of school visits to the library will want to consider overall department goals in deciding the objectives of these visits. If schools in the area have adequate school media centers, public library visits will probably not involve library instruction or an introduction to materials for class assignments. In such situations, visits are more likely to focus on the public library as a source of recreational reading, programs, and other services. In rural areas, where most children are bused to school, and even in urban areas, where children's parents do not use the library, many children may be unaware of the public library, unless they are introduced to it during school visits. In these situations, the library should use the class visit to introduce a range of materials and services that the child and other family members may wish to use.

Storytelling, puppet shows, film programs, and crafts are appropriate ways to introduce the library as a pleasant place to visit. The emphasis on recreational activities clearly differentiates the public library from the school media center, with its mandate to support the curricular needs of the school.

Time spent preparing for a class visit helps to make it go well. Librarians often ask the teacher to send a class list so nametags can be made for the children. This is particularly useful for kindergarten and primary grade children, who like to feel the librarian is interested in knowing them as individuals. Book lists or bookmarks (personalized with the child's name) make good souvenirs and will remind the children and their parents of the services and materials available. Brochures and newsletters aimed at parents and older siblings make useful handouts because they encourage the use of the library as a family resource. Depending on the season, information about holiday or summer programs should be available as well.

Although class visits to libraries can further cooperation between schools and public libraries, the practice should always be viewed in the light of overall departmental goals. Other types of services, such as preschool programs and service to daycare centers, should not be downgraded to provide service to school-age children unless that conforms to library goals. Because many library branches serve areas with six or more schools, encouraging all teachers to bring their classes may overwhelm the library. Many librarians find it difficult to limit service to any group, but it is unfair to other patrons to allow school visits to drain library resources. Setting parameters, such as having odd-numbered grades visit one semester and even-numbered grades the next, or limiting class visits to one per school year can help to ensure that adequate service will be provided to everyone. Local conditions are the most important factor in setting parameters for services to schools. If a school district relies upon a public library to provide library instruction and resources, it makes sense to request funding to cover the additional staff time and materials to meet this need. In the final analysis, it is better for everyone if services to children are seen in the context of the entire community, rather than just one agency.

As an alternative to class visits to the library, a public librarian may visit schools. Having one person travel to a school to visit three or four classes is more economical than having dozens of children and several teachers traveling to the library. The disadvantage is that children do not have an opportunity to see the library building and the range of materials available. If children have never been inside the library, it is important for them to have a chance to visit and see it for themselves.

Despite these drawbacks, visits to the schools can publicize library services and introduce programs. Some librarians schedule visits to the schools at the end of the school year to encourage children to register for summer programs at the library. Most teachers enthusiastically support summer reading programs and welcome the opportunity to inform children about the opportunity to continue their reading during the summer.

Visits at the beginning of the school year can focus on the public library as a source of recreational reading and information for school projects. And visits during the year can be tied to holiday programs, science fairs, or other seasonal activities.

Preparation for school visits includes obtaining as much information as possible about the class—the names of the students, current curricular projects, interests, and individuals or groups with special needs. During the class visit, most librarians give a booktalk on materials chosen to match the grade level and interests of the group. Use attractive and appealing materials and present them in an enticing way. (For suggestions about booktalks and other ways to introduce children to books, check the webpage http://www.ala.org/ala/yalsa/professsionaldev/booktalking.htm.) Children in a classroom are a captive audience and can be difficult unless the librarian quickly establishes a rapport. Primary-grade children are usually receptive to a visitor talking about books and reading, but those in the junior or intermediate grades may require skillful handling. An honest, informal presentation usually makes a better impression than one that strains at humor or relevance. The best approach is to emphasize how the library can help students without gushing or overselling library resources.

Attractive handouts help to make the librarian's visit memorable. If each child receives a personalized packet of materials to take home, the library's public image may be enhanced throughout the community. Sometimes the librarian can leave books as a long-term loan for the classroom. This allows the children to read the materials they are interested in and may increase their desire to visit the public library.

The teacher should not be forgotten during a visit, but should receive a packet of materials about the library and its services, and a list of all titles mentioned during the booktalk. The librarian should discuss the teacher's perceptions of the library and to ask about possible future needs for library services. If any problems have surfaced in regard to unannounced assignments, this can be an unthreatening time to raise the issue. Be sure to ask for an email address, so the teacher can be added to a mailing list to receive library news.

Sharing Space

The most dramatic form of cooperation is sharing space. Many communities have considered having the public library located in a school building so one facility can serve the needs of the school and the public more efficiently. The appeal of this solution lies in the apparent logic of spreading underutilized resources throughout the community as widely as possible. Communities that have tried the system have met with varied success.

Many schools are located away from major transportation routes to ensure the safety of children walking to and from school. This makes a public library in a school less accessible to the public than one located in a high-traffic area. The most effective location for a school media center is at the heart of the school, easily accessible from classrooms and labs. If a public library shares this space, the entire school building must be kept open, and security provided during after-school hours. The expense is often prohibitive.

Many members of the public do not consider schools a welcoming institution, and adult use of the public library often drops when it is housed in a school. Some adults believe that only materials suitable for children will be chosen for the collection.

Service to preschool children is particularly difficult in a school-housed public library, because the noise and activities of young children in the media center and hallways can distract students. Elderly people also may find it difficult or distracting to use a library dominated by schoolchildren.

Finding acceptable standards for the collection in a shared facility may be difficult because schools traditionally choose materials aimed at children. A school-housed library may be constrained from including adult materials that might be considered inappropriate for children. In spite of these problems, some communities have found school-housed public libraries a desirable alternative to the provision of two separate collections aimed at the same clientele. This trend toward joint-use facilities has been growing for the last 20 years (Goldberg 1996). The pressure on local governments to reduce spending levels has influenced this trend, and this pressure is likely to continue. The role public librarians can play is to document how joint-use facilities have worked elsewhere, to work with schools to clarify the goals of each institution, and to develop clear guidelines for continuing the public library's programs and services if a joint-use facility is developed.

Whatever pattern of cooperation evolves between schools and public libraries, attempts to create closer cooperation will undoubtedly continue. Information technology has made it easier for services to be provided regardless of their physical location. As this technology becomes available to everyone schools and libraries will have to work together to ensure that every member of the community has access to the widest possible range of information.

For more information on cooperation between the public library and schools go to the ALA website at http://www.ala.org/ala/alsc/alscresources/forlibrarians/SchPLCoopActivities.html. This site includes a database of model programs, a bibliography and a list of websites about cooperation.

OUTREACH TO DAYCARE

Preschool storytime has become a staple of public library service to children. Many libraries offer several sessions a week to three and four year olds who are brought by a parent, relative, or caregiver. Kids enjoy the experience, benefit from time with other children and begin to develop skills, knowledge, and attitudes that will help them become readers. Many libraries also find it useful to offer story programs at daycares, Head Start, nursery schools, and other programs in their community. According to Kids Count 2004, 59 percent of children under age six have all parents working. This means more and more young children are not home during the day and do not necessarily have individual caregivers to take them to the library. To reach the more than half the young children who are likely to be in daycare, the library needs to offer outreach services.

If the library has a goal to introduce books, reading, and the library to young children, librarians may have to take their programs to daycares as well as offering services in the library. Many of the issues and techniques described above relating to outreach to schools hold true for outreach to preschools. Personal contact, willingness to be flexible and tailoring services to the needs of children and care providers are essential for success.

There a few key differences between schools and daycares that children's librarians should realize and acknowledge. They are:

- Daycares are often independent small businesses with no district management, or unified program. This means each must be contacted individually and each program may be different from others in the community. School districts may have an early education program and Head Start and other federal and state programs are often run regionally, but communication and oversight will vary considerably from community to community.
- Daycares and nursery schools are subject to licensing by the state. Most libraries only visit licensed centers as they are likely to have a program and staff who can work with the library to arrange visits. Each state's regulation is different, so children's librarians need to understand the rules of each local community.
- Many children are cared for at home. Most states license homecare providers and keep a list by community of these licensed homes. Children are often cared for by unlicensed babysitters and relatives. Many libraries try to create a mailing list for homecare providers, so they can invite them to library programs.
- Unlike schools, most daycares and preschool programs have no library or only a small collection of books. Some states are beginning to certify early education teachers, but many childcare workers, who may have good practical skills, have limited formal education in child development and program planning.
- Daycares and preschool personnel change often and independent daycares and homecare providers move or go out of business frequently. Keeping an accurate list of early education contacts is an on-going task.

Children's librarians need to acknowledge that keeping track of daycares will require constant effort, but there are some ways to get help in locating early education programs.

- Check state lists of licensed daycares and home providers. These can be sorted by zip code. Some states provide this information free online, some charge a small fee.
- Check daycare associations. They may have a newsletter, mailing list or hold meetings where library information can be shared.
- Look at online listings of daycare facilities in your community.
- If all else fails, checking the phone book, asking young families, and kindergarten teachers who may know where their students were cared for before coming to school are ways to make contacts with early education programs in the library's community.

Outreach services at daycares are similar to those in schools. Many libraries offer loans of books and other library materials as well as visiting daycares with story programs. Some libraries have special materials like puzzles, toys, or picture sets that are particularly useful for young children. Libraries may also provide childcare providers with books about young children. Children's librarians may, in addition to offering programs for children, offer programs for early education staff on how to use the library, how to share books with young children, new books for young children, and other topics of librarian expertise. Librarians may also be able to offer similar programs to preschool parents at daycare meeting, or use daycares to publicize child and parent programs offered at the library.

Though it may be time consuming and require additional work, serving daycares furthers the library's mission to reach the whole community and provide library service tailored to the needs of the user. Giving young children a good start on their way to becoming readers and learners is satisfying and essential to their education. One study showed that as many as 40 percent of children entering kindergarten are as much as three years behind in their language development (Fielding 2006, 32). Providing language experiences and training teachers and parents to use books with young children is meeting an important educational need. Reading aloud builds language and sharpens thought even for the youngest children (Fox 2001, 17).

WORKING WITH CHILD SERVING AGENCIES

Libraries have often served groups and organizations that are not traditionally educational. Scouts and other youth organizations visit the library, get help with badges and other projects, or simply explore books or websites of interest. Librarians, particularly if they have other affiliations with these programs, may visit meetings, provide leader training, or even develop libraries at scouting headquarters. To build on this tradition, many libraries are seeking out youth serving agencies and providing programs and services. Libraries do this to support youth in the community and to reach a bigger audience. There is even more variety in these agencies than in early education, so finding the organizations and making lasting contact is the first challenge in providing service. Some examples of non-traditional outreach are:

- Many libraries offer services to children in homeless shelters. Multnomah County Library in Oregon opened a small reading room for homeless people and then used donations and withdrawn books to place book collections in 30 homeless shelters in its service area. (Osborne 2004, 12–13)
- Memphis Public Library serves its immigrant community with a bookmobile and a multilingual staff including a children's librarian who works with ESL (English as a Second Language) students. (Osborne 2004, 9–10)
- Many libraries provide outreach to after school programs for students ages 6 to 12. These programs may be run by school districts, churches, boys and girls clubs, libraries themselves, or other service organizations. Services include providing library collections, storytelling, age appropriate programs at the centers, bus trips to the library, and space for tutoring and homework help.

Finding an agency with which to work may happen naturally. Agencies may request services of librarians and find out about a program, but a more systematic approach may be useful. Some communities have a youth commission or children's advocate as part of city or county government. These agencies may keep a current list of youth serving agencies and be willing to share access to it. States may offer similar lists of social service agencies. The local United Way organization should have a list of organizations it funds and the nature of the service offered. Again listening to kids, families, and teachers may help you identify agencies with which to work.

In developing programs, it is important to listen carefully to what each agency is trying to do. One program or service does not fit every agency. Be creative. Be flexible. Try to begin with very focused programs that relate directly to the mission of the organization and expand as possible to include more library-oriented activities. If a local museum or zoo wants the library to provide storytelling for a family day event, start there and then explore other ways the library can do outreach to users of the museum or zoo. Be aware that you may also be able to cooperate to let other organizations present programs at the library. While you might tell stories at the zoo, zoo staff may do animal programs at the library. Or when you provide a list of books about conflict resolution for children to a group of local social workers who counsel children, these social workers may provide library staff training in dealing with troubled children. These outreach partnerships can be very beneficial to both organizations

Outreach is a powerful tool to help children's librarians to reach new or infrequent users and to meet the library's mission of helping children learn and grow. Having a good sense of what will make outreach activities successful, what fits the library's mission, and how to schedule and support outreach activities is essential to providing ongoing, valuable programs. Set goals, ask for honest evolution from outreach partners, and be open to finding new, better, and easier ways to provide service outside the library building.

REFERENCES AND ADDITIONAL READING

Bostwick, Arthur. 1914. *Library and School: The Relationship between the Library and the Public Schools.* New York: H. W. Wilson.

Bromann, Jennifer. 2005. *More Booktalking That Works.* New York: Neal-Schuman.

Fielding, Lynn. 2006. Kindergarten Learning Gap [April]. *American School Board Journal* 193.

Fox, Mem. 2001. *Reading Magic: Why Reading Aloud to Our Children Will Change Their Lives Forever.* New York: Harcourt.

Goldberg, Beverly. 1996. Public Libraries Go Back to School. *American Libraries* 27: 54–55.

Irving, Jan. 2004. *Stories Never Ending: A Program Guide for Schools and Libraries.* Westport, CT: Libraries Unlimited.

Norfolk, Sherry, Stenson, Jane, and Williams, Diane 2006. *The Storytelling Classroom: Applications across the Curriculum.* Westport, CT: Libraries Unlimited.

Osborne, Robin ed. 2004. *From Outreach to Equity: Innovative Models of Library Policy and Practice.* Chicago: American Library Association.

Pfeil, Angela B. 2005. *Going Places with Youth Outreach: Smart Marketing Strategies.* Chicago: American Library Association.

15

Marketing Children's Services

Sometimes library services for children and families, particularly new services or programs, are a very well kept secret. Only children who are already regular visitors to the library know about what goes on there. This kind of secret can leave program attendance low, and it can dim the visibility of the library as a vital youth serving organization in its community. The library may be well known and well regarded as a place for young children because preschool story-time is so popular, but not seen as a place for older children. Or it may be seen as a place only for books, if children are unaware of the availability of online or electronic resources. An effective library tries to ensure that all members of the community know about library resources and services through a carefully designed marketing and public relations program.

OVERVIEW

Marketing generally refers to the overreaching activities that promote the library to the community. Many libraries have a marketing plan that identifies needs of the community, including children and families, and how the library can inform the community about how it meets these needs. *Public relations* usually refer to the specific activities a library uses to inform the community about specific services and activities. Marketing activities, for example, would have a goal of community families regarding the library as a good place for their children, and public relations would help families understand and use specific library services or attend programs at the library.

Many library activities involve a public relations component, but librarians should also give some thought to an overall, ongoing departmental marketing plan. Having a marketing plan will allow library staff "to exercise their creativity as they develop memorable and meaningful messages to communicate...the common core of information that always forms the basis of the library's public relations" (Karp 2002, 3–4).

Larger libraries may have a marketing department or a staff member or part-time consultant to direct marketing and public relations. In this case, the children's librarian would work closely with these professionals to craft the children's department marketing message and to execute public relations activities. Oftentimes marketing professionals have background in promoting activities to adults and will need the help and expertise of children's staff who know about children in general and the community's children specifically.

In smaller libraries the library director or other administrative staff may coordinate marketing and public relations, or the library director and the children's librarian will work together to get the library's message out to the community. In some libraries, there is no formal marketing program and the children's staff can take the lead by informing the public of all that is happening at the library.

Whether working as a group or as the one staff who markets the library, the children's librarian should seek help by attending marketing workshops, working with other government, or non-profit agencies such as the local United Way to learn more about marketing and developing both a basic library message as well as a marketing plan. Some advertising or marketing firms may offer free or low cost help to the library as a donation. It is helpful to seek outside help from time to time to get a fresh perspective and to augment the knowledge and skills of library staff.

Developing a Marketing Plan

The library may have a formal marketing plan or an informal understanding of how it wants to project its image and convey information on specific programs and services to the community. Or the children's department may be expected to market itself independently. In either case, the children's librarian should have a sense of how all the various promotional activities for the department fit together. Having a written marketing plan for the children's department or a children's section in the library's marketing plan will help coordinate all the individual promotional activities, keep them on target, and make promotional activities more efficient and effective.

An effective marketing program will:

- Identify what drives users
- Help build services and programs around user needs
- Enable highly differentiated service, not one size fits all
- Attract non-users and increase use by existing users
- Influence attitudes toward the library as the best service in town (Kendrick 2006, 9)

Marketing plans describe target markets, identify needs and concerns of users and non-users of libraries, and suggest effective ways to convey library information to each target audience. A marketing plan may also identify a theme and catch phrases to use in talking and writing about the library, effective timing of media messages, the expected cost of promoting the library as well as the expected results of library promotion. Having the big picture plan in place will make individual public relations activities easier to manage and evaluate.

No matter how much or how little promotion the library does for adults, their needs to be a marketing plan that addresses marketing to kids. James McNeal, an expert in business marketing to kids, points out that the kids' market is different from the adult market and has three distinct targets. They are:

- Kids are the primary market. They spend their own money [and time] on their own wants and needs.
- Kids influence the market. They determine much of the spending [and use of time] of parents.
- Kids are a future market. Eventually they will be a potential market of all goods and services. (McNeal 1999, 16)

While McNeal uses business language, it is good to understand that kids influence their own library use, they also bring parents and other adults into the library, and they will continue to use and support libraries for a lifetime. Or they can decide not to use the library, they can discourage parents' use of the library, and they may never be library supporters. How kids decide often depends on the library's ability to successfully market itself.

Developing a Public Relations Program

Once the library and the children's department have a marketing plan or strategy, specific public relations techniques can be used to communicate library information to the public. The ongoing public relations program includes all of the contacts librarians make with the community both inside and outside the library and through websites, electronic or print announcements, displays, radio or television spots, and news stories. An effective public relations program provides an honest and persuasive account of what the library offers and its value to the community. Because the children's department is an important and highly visible part of library service, children's librarians should make an effort to publicize the department's services.

The goals, objectives, and role of the department (discussed in chapters 1 and 2) suggest ideas for the types of information given to library users and potential users. Many adults have the idea that a children's collection consists of picture books and literary classics, and services are limited to story programs for young children. Sometimes this image is perpetuated by newspaper or television stories that feature traditional library programs but do not mention parenting books, homework help, and electronic and print-based reference services. In recent years, the availability of computers in children's departments has caught media attention, but they are often presented as an alternative to traditional books, not as an integral part of an overall service program. Children's librarians should encourage the media to present a balanced picture of the department's services.

Just as many adults think of the children's department as primarily a storytelling room, they often think of children's librarians as women who love books and are more at home with *Peter Rabbit* than with science fair projects and databases. While children's librarians are knowledgeable about picture books and children's classics, they also know a great deal about other subjects. The objective of a public relations program is to ensure that librarians determine the message that will be conveyed to the public by consciously choosing factors to be publicized rather than relying on the media or others to decide what to share with the public.

Librarians also have to overcome the belief that libraries are boring and the Marian the Librarian image. This special marketing concern has been described this way:

> The library, tradition says, must be perceived as a center for serious thought and contemplation....The librarians and staff who work in the libraries must be perceived as serious scholars....Herein lies the problem for a marketing person: how to bring customers into an environment that often chooses to present itself as a place where even life insurance salesmen would look like party animals. (McGinn 2006)

The task is to respect our serious side, portray the breadth and depth of children's services, and make the library attractive and fun for young users.

PUBLIC RELATIONS TECHNIQUES

There are a variety of ways to publicize both the library and children's department in general as well as specific programs and services. Few libraries have enough time, staff, and finances to use all the techniques available all the time to inform the community about the library. Not all public relations activities are available to all libraries and not all techniques work equally well in all locations. It is the job of the children's librarian to figure out how to create the best combination of public relations activities that meet the specific needs of the department. Good public relations activities should:

- Attract use of the children's department (attendance or visitation or website hits).
- Promote an accurate, positive, and informed public attitude toward the children's department.
- Be cost effective use of funds and staff time.
- Be lively, attention getting, fun, and fresh.

Quality Library Services

A public relations program is often thought to be aimed at people outside of the library, but encounters within the library—the way patrons are treated by staff and what services are offered—affect the public's perception more than anything else. Every time a librarian helps a child or parent to find a book, explains the way the catalog works, or fails to locate information, he or she is affecting the way the patron thinks about the library. The first step for a department head in planning a public relations program is to make sure that everyone on the staff follows accepted standards for dealing with patrons. No amount of external publicity will make up for the rudeness or neglect of a staff member in the library, an inadequate collection, or unnecessary rules. Publicizing library resources raises expectations, which the library staff must be prepared to meet. Otherwise, publicity will have a negative effect.

A cheerful, knowledgeable, and willing staff is the greatest asset of any children's department. Any publicity efforts to bring more patrons into the library should be made in cooperation with staff members whose work will be affected by the additional traffic. If new services, such as Internet access or a homework hotline, are to be established, the librarians should ensure that staff members can efficiently handle these services. Premature publicity about services can give a bad impression about the ability of the library to help patrons.

Meeting the Public

The library staff is the public's chief source of information about library activities, and talks to community groups about this topic can be effective. Most librarians are not practiced public speakers or entertainers, but almost anyone can learn to give a successful speech about a topic of interest. The keys are planning, enthusiasm, and clarity. Nothing is more discouraging than a rambling talk that attempts to cover the entire field of children's literature or mention all of the good picture books for children. Since most talks to community groups will be limited to about a half an hour, the librarian should try to make only two or three points, but make them effectively.

Visual aids and handouts help focus attention during the talk and act later as a reminder to the listeners of a particular book or author. A blackboard or a Power Point presentation can be used for listing titles during the talk, but a handout that can be taken home is helpful too. The handout can also include information about library hours and service. Anecdotes about children's reactions to books bring life to a talk and emphasize the importance of books in children's lives. Showing books and having them available for browsing demonstrates their attractiveness. Lists of materials developed for a specific program can be mounted on the library website, where they create additional publicity and demonstrate the library's activities.

When giving a talk, the librarian should speak in a clear, enthusiastic, and informal manner; taping a rehearsal before the event can help to achieve these goals. Eye contact is important, but be sure to include the whole group, transferring attention from one person to another. This will help in gauging the listeners' reactions. If listeners appear puzzled, a point can be expanded or explained, and questions may be solicited.

If the audience becomes restless, remarks should be cut short. Even if a talk ends sooner than expected, at least some of the points will have been made. Time should be allowed for questions. Many people are reluctant to ask questions in an open forum, but may approach the speaker after the talk, so try not to rush away from the meeting. Stress that the library staff are available to answer questions in the library by telephone or through the library's website.

In addition to parent or teacher groups, librarians should try to speak to business, civic, or service groups whenever possible. Discussions about the library's efforts to increase literacy or to help persons with disabilities may interest these groups and raise their awareness of the importance of children's services in libraries.

Outreach services as described in chapter 14 also bring good will to the library and will attract nonusers to the library. Finding a way to make sure parents know the library visits their child's preschool or classroom will help encourage family visits to the library. Some libraries ask daycares or school to inform parents of library visits or give out library stickers when they visit, so parents will know their child heard library stories. Teachers, too, may be encouraged to make more use of the library for their class or personally after an outreach visit from the library. Always leave the library newsletter, flyers about upcoming programs, information about how to get a library card, and a business card with the teacher to encourage further use of the library's services.

Handouts: Flyers, Posters, Bookmarks, and Brochures

Almost all children's departments find a way to create print handouts about upcoming events, specific services, and general library information. With the advent of computer programs that include graphic design, clip art, and high resolution printing, creating professional quality handouts is relatively easy. While not every children's librarian has fine tuned graphic design skills, handouts should:

- Be accurate: times and dates correct, books and websites listed up-to-date
- Have attractive, appropriate illustrations
- Not be cluttered
- Include the library's name, address, phone number, web address, and logo
- Have correct spelling and grammar
- Use color if possible

As well as producing print materials, some thought needs to be given to distribution of these materials. Some libraries have mailing lists and send announcements directly to users, teachers, or parents. Many libraries mount print materials on their website and email handouts to web users. Most libraries make print materials available at the library or hand them to children who attend programs. Make sure that each handout is timely and needed and that there is a distribution plan before it is produced. Too many handouts at one time can overwhelm users and not enough can leave users unsure of what events are coming up. Program budgets should include funds for promotion including handouts such as flyers, booklists, or posters.

Electronic Promotion of Children's Services

A website offers a public library the chance to give current information about its location, services, programs, and collections, as well as access to its catalog, community and regional information, and other electronic resources. Because many users of the Internet are young, the youth services department should make sure that it has a highly visible presence on the library's website.

The most basic use of electronic communication to promote the children's department's services is by using the library's own website. The children's department should be listed on the home page of the library, not two or more mouse clicks away, through a public services heading. An attractive graphic next to the spot where children should click, will better entice the audience to go to the children's department page than a text-only entry.

Some types of information included by most children's departments on the web are the following:

- Location
- Contact information
- Library events
- Programs, including registration
- Reading lists and reading activities/games
- Homework help and other services
- Links to the library catalog, data bases, and other sources of information
- Instructions on how to get a library card

In addition to using the library's website, youth librarians may also post library information on other websites that are aimed at children and families. This might include a community bulletin board run by city government, a recreation website run by the park district, or the websites of other nonprofit groups like the local scouting councils, the Y, or a daycare site. Using these sites will get the word out to new audiences about specific programs as well as raise the profile of the library's children's programs to the community in general.

Some libraries have set up email lists for individual children or families. Libraries ask users if they would like to receive announcements sent directly to them at their email address, then the library can send or broadcast messages about programs, new books, or highlight services without the cost of mailing. Some libraries offer the library's newsletter by email. Teachers may also be willing to receive library announcements through their email. Care should be taken not to overuse this form of communication—no user wants library spam—and users should be able to unsubscribe from the list easily.

Some libraries have also used the Internet to communicate information about the library by participating in chat rooms or live discussion groups, offering virtual library tours to school groups, or participating in youth-oriented websites. Younger and younger children are socializing online, using online help sites, and shopping online. If there are ways for the library to be a legitimate presence on these popular sites, they provide another way to attract young users to more conventional library services, including the library's website. Some librarians have their own blogs (personal online journals) or participate in the blogs of other people to promote the use of the library.

News Releases

Many local newspapers, television, and radio stations depend heavily on information sent to them by community groups because they are always looking for interesting local stories. The library should keep a file of contact information for local newspapers (including foreign-language papers) and radio and television stations, as well as the person at each source who is responsible for library coverage. Follow each news outlet's directions for submitting press releases. Most news outlets want releases sent electronically, or program information entered electronically in a specific format at the reporter's address. Electronically transmitted announcements may also include digital photos, but again each news agency will have its own rules for technical quality and content of photos.

News releases should be sent for any special event or change of policy in the library. News releases can also:

- Announce new programs or services at the library
- Report on the progress and success of a program or service offered at the library
- Provide new information about existing programs and services offered at the library
- Announce special events, seasonal programs, or meetings at the library
- Inform the public about positions or policies adopted by the library
- Communicate statements made by officers or directors of the library on topics of interest to the community
- Introduce new library staff to the community
- Describe materials that have been added to the library's collections (Banks 1995, 1)

News releases should be written clearly and concisely in newspaper style—that is, with the most important information presented in the first paragraph. The short paragraphs that follow give additional information that the newspaper may print or cut depending on the amount of space available. Releases for radio and television must be even more concise than those for newspapers; broadcast news releases should use short, easily understood words for broadcasting (see chapter 13).

Often the story will be rewritten for presentation, so the library should concentrate on giving facts that will be useful in preparing the story. The name, telephone, email address, and fax number of a contact person should be included with each release.

Devising news connections for library events requires imagination. A successful summer reading program may warrant a story in the local paper if it can be tied in with a national issue, such as literacy. Media personnel may not think of the library as a source for stories, so it is up to the librarians to provide the connections. A community plan to encourage recycling might suggest a story about the library's books and films on environmental issues. A special exhibit at a local art or historical museum might lead to a story about the library's holdings in these areas.

A library event that warrants coverage by a newspaper photographer or a television station offers a department an opportunity to make a strong impact on the community. More people look at pictures in the newspaper than read the stories, and more people get their news from television than from newspapers. Some thought should be given to the impression of the department presented by pictorial coverage. Pictures that show or imply action generally catch the viewer's attention better than static pictures.

The librarian should provide the photographer with the names of the individuals shown. Names must be spelled correctly. If individual children are to be featured in a picture and their names given to a newspaper, obtain their parents' consent in writing. Just as with a news release, the photographer should be given the name of a contact person in the event that further information should be needed.

Public Service Announcements

Radio and television stations are required to carry public service announcements (PSAs), brief messages about nonprofit organizations. Some websites also carry them. Messages to be broadcast on the radio are the easiest to prepare. They can be read live by the station announcer or prerecorded. Because they are designed to be heard, rather than read, the sentence structure must be simple and the message clear. The pronunciation for difficult words or names should be included.

Check with local radio stations to obtain the length of PSA that they require. Usual lengths are 10, 20, 30, or 60 seconds. If the radio station prefers a specific length, the PSA should not exceed that time. Only about 25 words can be said in 10 seconds. If a telephone number is included, each number counts as a word.

A 10-second message might look like this:
Have any questions?
The Beaverton Public Library can send the answers to your home computer.
Call three-four-two...one-four-six-eight for information.

PSAs are sent to radio stations in much the same format as news releases. The library should be clearly identified and a contact person's name included. Other items that should be included are an indication of the PSA's length and the dates for which the announcement is in effect. Radio PSAs should be triple-spaced and set in all capital letters (Banks 1995, 7).

Local cable television stations or webcast outlets can be contacted for information about how much access they give to community groups. Some stations will give the use of a studio and perhaps some staff assistance to prepare PSA messages for television use. Professional help can make a library's message more effective than an amateur effort. If the television station cannot provide expertise, volunteers may be found at a community college media program or among the Friends of the Library. Remember that if resources are limited, the time and expense of preparing releases for television might not be worth the effort. More people can be reached by brief PSAs on radio at much less cost in time and money. Radio stations are also effective in reaching non-English speakers, so PSAs in several languages can be very useful.

Media Interviews

Interviews with the media can be an important way to publicize the services of a department. Sometimes a journalist seeks an interview because of a sudden news development: a library patron has demanded the removal of a book from the library, or someone has been charged with stealing library materials, or there has been a change in Internet regulations. Most reporters will try to call the chief librarian, but occasionally one may contact someone at the department level. It is usually wise to suggest that questions be directed to the chief executive or to the library board as any information given to reporters may be made public. Such referrals are essential if a legal case is being brought against the library.

Even if the issue is less formal—for example, someone has written to the local newspaper complaining about the availability of supposed immoral, sexually explicit Internet sites in the children's department, and the reporter wants a department head or staff member's point of view—follow your library's guideline for who can speak for the library. Reporters may be friendly and imply that they understand the library's side of the story, but care should be taken in what is said. Casual or joking comments that sound innocuous in conversation may appear foolish or insulting in print. Reporters look for good stories. Drama and conflict are emphasized, and remarks may be quoted out of context, either through error or deliberate distortion. The interview should be handled carefully and nothing unnecessary should be stated.

If you are busy or distracted when a media contact calls, ask the reporter to call you back in a few minutes. To avoid the risk of giving inaccurate information if questions are asked about dates, facts, or specific holdings, the interviewer should be told that time is needed to check these details. Most reporters try to present the news in a clear and unbiased way, but they do not have library backgrounds and often do not understand the problems of running a public institution or the reasons for many library regulations. Give the background of library practice whenever relevant, rather than dealing solely with the immediate conflict.

Most library interviews are not conducted in the rush of a news story but are planned as general-interest items for newspapers or for radio and television talk shows. If the library maintains contact with the media through news releases and publicity, it may be easy to suggest that an interview about children's books or reading might be of interest to readers and listeners. Sometimes the reporter or talk show host will suggest an interview on a library-related topic. Given time to prepare, a librarian should become familiar with the work of the journalist conducting the interview. What kinds of stories does this individual do? Do they prefer a folksy, neighborly tone or a more formal, professional one? The more that can be discovered about the interviewer's expectations, the more likely the interview will be successful.

In preparing for the interview, the librarians should think of one or two points to be made. These points can be worked into the interview and, if repeated several times, will usually be reported in the written story. Questions that the interviewer is likely to ask should be considered, and answers prepared for them. Specific facts and statistics can be written down to be given to the interviewer or consulted when questions are raised. A librarian who is not accustomed to being interviewed may stage a mock interview with a friend or colleague to practice responding to questions.

Paid Advertising

Larger libraries may have funds to pay for advertising, or grants may allow smaller libraries to pay for advertising to support use of the library. This could include paying to put program announcements in the local paper, or on a popular news website. The advantage is that the library controls the message—that is, the librarian writes the ad—and you get the information placed on a page where readers are more likely to see the ad. For example, a local paper might run a special section on things kids can do in the community during the summer. While the library' s summer reading program may be reported as one program among many, placing an ad on the page, may highlight the library's program in an effective way.

Libraries may buy ads in magazines, on websites, or in nonprofit newsletters, or place ads on local movie theater screens. Often the libraries ad can run for a month or more on the screen as the audience settles into their seats. Libraries can also pay to have PSAs played at particular times of day and on particular television or radio stations. Stations are required at part of their licensing regulations to run PSAs, but they often run them at times when they have the fewest listeners. By paying a fee the library can have these messages run at times while commuters are in their cars listening to the radio rather than at 2 A.M. when there are fewer, and possibly less alert, listeners.

Libraries can also place ads on municipal buses and commuter trains. Ads on the inside will be read by passengers and ads on the outside will be viewed by both passengers and people in the community—these become moving billboards. Libraries may also pay for billboards along highways or major streets. These boards can get the library's messages to people who do not go to the library or highlight a new library service.

Libraries may also pay for direct mail to the community. This can be a newsletter mailed to each user household, a postcard to teen cardholders asking them to join a specific program, or a letter to teachers telling them how to get a library card. Some libraries buy or share mailing lists from other community institutions like museums or zoos, and write letters to people on these lists in an effort to reach non-library users. Most states will sell lists of licensed daycare providers by zip code. Then the children's departments could use this list to contact these providers about preschool services.

Marketing and public relations may seem like an extra burden to the children's librarian, adding more work to program planning than necessary, or it may seem hopeless to have the library's message compete with mainstream advertising. But it is vitally important that children, their parents, and teachers know about library services. It gives every child in the community fair access to all library services and it keeps the library in the forefront as a child serving agency. As Angela Pfeil says "marketing is an essential tool for building successful relationships with the community. Marketing services to children may be the most powerful but underused part of a library's marketing plan" (2005, 2). Used correctly and done regularly, marketing is essential to the success of the children's department. It can be fun and once started, should become fully integrated into the work of the children's librarian.

EVALUATING MARKETING AND PUBLIC RELATIONS

The simplest way to evaluate your marketing and public relations program is to see if library use is increased and to count the number of positive mentions the children's department gets in the press. In the children's department marketing plan you have stated the results you expect. When a particular public relations technique is used, there is an expectation of what will happen. Ask the questions "did we succeed?" and "how will we measure success?" When you have the answer, you will have an idea of what is working (and what is not). Part of the marketing plan should be stating goals and how progress toward these goals will be measured.

For example, children's staff may want to increase participation by middle school children in the summer reading program. It is important to state how many more participants are desired and how they will be tracked as well as what marketing will be done to attract this group of children. Or a library many want parents to believe that the library computers are safe for their children to use. In this case, the children's librarian will need to survey parents initially to find out their attitudes, develop marketing to meeting parent concerns, and do another survey after the marketing campaign to see if attitudes have changed.

It is important to find systematic ways to evaluate both the overall marketing program and the individual techniques used. As with any library evaluation, planning ahead, gathering relevant information from users, thinking about the results of evaluation, and adapting the next evaluation to improve library use and reputation, should be an integrated part of marking children's services.

REFERENCES AND ADDITIONAL READING

American Library Association. 2006. *Kid's! Tool Kit*. http://www.ala.org/ala/alsc/project spartners/KidsToolKit.htm (Accessed April 9, 2007).

Banks, Paula. 1995. News Releases, Photo Releases, Public Service Announcements. In *Part-Time Public Relations with Full-Time Results,* ed. Rashelle Karp, 1–9. Chicago: American Library Association.

Holt, Leslie Edmonds, Holt, Glen, and Lloyd, Stratton. 2006. *Library Success: A Celebration of Library Innovation, Adaptation and Problem Solving*. Ipswitch, MA: EBSCO Publishing.

Karp, Rashelle. 2002. *Powerful Public Relations: A How-to Guide for Libraries*. Chicago: American Library Association.

Kendrick, Terry. 2006. *Developing Strategic Marketing Plans That Really Work: A Toolkit for Public Libraries*. London: Facet Publishing.

McGinn, Howard F. 2006. Getting Started: Case Histories. Carlson Library, Clarion University. In *ALA (American Library Association). Public Information Office, Campaign for American Libraries*. http://www.ala.org/ala/pio/campaign/academicresearch/success fulacademic.htm (Accessed April 9, 2007).

McNeal, James U. 1999. *The Kids Market: Myths and Realities*. Ithaca, NY: Paramount Market Publishing.

Pfeil, Angela B. 2005. *Going Places with Youth Outreach: Smart Marketing Strategies*. Chicago: American Library Association.

Section IV

Professional Development

16

Sharing Ideas with Other Youth Librarians

Most librarians spend their working days with colleagues in their library and the patrons they serve. Work patterns can become standardized and the library may continue to offer the same kind of collections and services year after year even though both the patrons and their community have changed. Reaching out to the wider world of youth librarians who share a professional viewpoint and set of problems can keep librarians from falling into a rut. Librarians have always networked, and technology has made it easier and more efficient than ever before to maintain contact with colleagues far beyond the individual library.

ELECTRONIC LINKS

The Internet provides an easy way for individuals with similar interests to communicate. Because libraries were among the first institutions to establish links to the Internet, there are many electronic discussion groups devoted to librarians' concerns. This provides access to a group of experts who can answer questions, suggest solutions to problems, or recommend materials.

The first step in joining an electronic list is to identify one that reflects your interests. The American Library Association's website (http://www.ala.org) lists the Association's various mailing lists and gives directions for subscribing to them. Many state and provincial library associations also host discussion lists. The most direct way of learning about useful discussion lists is to ask for recommendations from other children's librarians.

Many mailing lists handle subscriptions through their website. A request for membership can be sent through the homepage. You will receive a confirmation of your request and information about how to send messages to the list and how to unsubscribe. This message should be saved for future reference.

Some lists are moderated, meaning that an individual checks each message to make sure it is relevant to the list and is not offensive. On other lists, the messages are sent without being read by anyone other than the sender. Most library-related lists are free from the acrimonious messages (flaming) that occurs on some Internet discussion groups.

On any discussion list, the majority of the members (often called lurkers) read the messages but do not post any themselves. Many librarians prefer to lurk when they first subscribe to a list. Later, when they understand the tone and content of the discussion, they join in by answering messages and posting some of their own.

GUIDELINES FOR HAPPY LIST MEMBERSHIP

- Read the directions that come with your subscriber acceptance.
- Be aware of the address line on your message—do not send a message to the whole list when it is meant for an individual.
- For an active list, set your format to digest, so that you receive posts only once each day.
- Do not post off topic (OT) messages that are unrelated to the subject of the list.
- When replying to a message (especially in digest format) delete the original message except for the few lines that relate to your reply.
- Do not express anger or use sarcasm in a message to the group.

NETWORKING WITHIN A SYSTEM OR REGION

In developing face-to-face professional networks, start with librarians working in other branches of your library system. Large library systems often have an association of children's librarians, which meets regularly to select materials, listen to speakers, discuss issues, or attend events. The coordinator of children's services generally plans and chairs these meetings. In smaller systems, children's librarians may maintain contact through periodic meetings at the main library or a branch. The head of the main library's children's department often takes the lead, but sometimes each librarian takes a turn in planning meetings. In some jurisdictions, a number of libraries form a regional system that meets for materials selection and professional development.

Part of the value of meeting colleagues is to enjoy social contacts, but beyond this purpose is the larger professional aim of improving children's services. Each individual has a responsibility to bring to the meetings helpful information and ideas. If one branch has discipline problems, discussing them with other librarians may help resolve them. If particular programs or specific materials have proved notably successful, it is important to share this information. A willing, cooperative spirit generally leads to better service for the entire community or region.

At any meeting, one person should have the responsibility of taking notes and distributing them by email to each participant. Be sure to follow up suggestions and requests. If someone offers to share the outline of a particularly successful program, and it does not arrive, send a reminder. Take time to send a thank-you when the material does come. Similarly, be sure to carry through on promises to send information or materials.

Visiting other local children's departments enables librarians to see how well different room arrangements, decorations, or materials actually work. Some systems and regions hold rotating meetings so librarians eventually see most of the departments, but other jurisdictions hold all meetings at one central location. Making an effort to visit other departments is   worthwhile even on your own time. You can gather many ideas in 20 minutes or so.

Meetings with local librarians need not be limited to professional staff. These meetings can become opportunities to recruit other staff members into the profession. Many people become librarians because they have worked in a library, and librarians have taken an interest in their career plans. Encouraging staff to enter library programs is a good way to increase diversity in the workplace (Adkins 2005). When employees in the library show an aptitude for the work and appear to be capable of undertaking graduate education, it is worth discussing the possibilities. Library assistants who are interested in becoming professionals should be invited to attend conferences and workshops to learn more about the range of options in the field. Recruiting effective new librarians is one of the major obligations of library professionals.

MOVING BEYOND THE SYSTEM

Colleagues within one system or region are a starting point, but many librarians also belong to larger professional groups, such as a state or provincial organization. These groups allow librarians working in different systems to share information and experiences and they can offer workshops or programs that are too expensive for an individual system. For many librarians, especially those in the larger states and provinces, these groups continue to be the major focus of their professional life. Beyond the state level, the wider world of youth librarians includes national and international associations where librarians can meet their counterparts in widely varying locations, receive national journals, and attend national and international conferences.

Choosing a Professional Association

Membership in professional associations is expensive, so new librarians should choose carefully.

Tips for Choosing the Right Association

- If you are in library school, join several associations at the student rate.
- Read association journals to discover which is closest to your interests.
- Check association websites to see which is most useful to you.
- Find out what support you can expect from your library.
- Ask colleagues about associations they belong to and conferences they attend.
- Attend a conference or workshop before deciding to join.

Most library systems regard membership and participation in professional associations as a sign of commitment to librarianship. They may reward this work with commendations on annual reviews and sometimes with merit pay increases. Encouragement from the library is an important factor, but individuals must choose for themselves which associations will be most helpful in their professional development. State and provincial associations offer less expensive conferences and workshops than national groups, but the national associations offer exposure to a more diverse group of librarians who work under a wide variety of conditions. National associations can present specialized programs and publications dealing with particular groups such as deaf children, new immigrants, or native children. The large conferences sponsored by national associations attract many exhibitors and are one of the major benefits of attending a conference. For many librarians, the exhibits are the most important part of conferences because they provide an opportunity to see new materials and equipment, to contact salespeople, and to get on mailing lists from important publishers.

International associations such as the International Federation of Library Associations and Institutions (IFLA) or the International Board on Books for Youth (IBBY) hold conferences throughout the world and publish journals of interest to youth librarians, but few library systems encourage or support participation in their work. The costs of attending international conferences are high. A decision to participate in international organizations is usually made by an individual librarian who has a personal interest in widening the horizons of his or her professional life.

Professional associations outside of librarianship also provide opportunities. The Children's Literature Association has children's literature as its major focus rather than library services for children. Many librarians belong to the association and attend its conferences to hear the scholarly papers given on various aspects of literature for children.

Educational associations such as the International Reading Association and the National Council of Teachers of English publish journals that include articles about children's books. Their conferences have sessions of interest to librarians as well as teachers and often feature talks by noted children's authors.

In some communities, multi-agency groups of people serving youth form associations. These offer valuable networking opportunities for librarians, and the meetings and programs are worth attending. Libraries are not always highly visible and may be overlooked unless the librarians make an effort to find out about, and join these local associations.

While librarians may join non-library professional associations, the major focus of association work is usually on library groups. Professional library associations not only provide professional development opportunities for members, they also lobby to enhance the status of the profession. The groups also work to alert the public to the importance of libraries in the community, the state, and the country. Participation in association work may bring enhanced career performance and professional visibility (which can lead to increased job opportunities) as well as offer professional contacts that often develop into long and rewarding friendships.

Attending Conferences

Attending a professional conference is expensive in time and money, yet many librarians find them worth the cost.

Benefits of Attending a Conference

- Participating in professional workshops
- Learning from well-known speakers
- Meeting professionals from other libraries
- Examining new materials and equipment at exhibits
- Practicing skills in chairing committees and speaking in public
- Making new friends who share professional interests

Unlike conferences in some other professions, most library programs do not offer many presentations of research findings. Programs tend to focus on topics of practical concern and to feature speakers who have had experience in the area. A typical program format is for one speaker to give an overview of the topic—serving homeless children, or selecting graphic novels, for example—followed by a panel of four or five librarians who respond. The value of the program depends on the speakers. Some speakers talk almost exclusively about the policies of their library, while others draw from a wider background. Because the audience is diverse, speakers must balance their talks to be of interest to new librarians as well as experienced administrators. This is not an easy task. Fortunately, organizers have a large pool of speakers, and most panels have at least two or three speakers who give new information or fresh viewpoints. No one program will make the entire conference worthwhile. The librarian should look for a number of sessions on topics of interest and attend at least half a dozen of them.

Talks by authors of children's books are popular features at most professional conferences. Authors are generally fluent and entertaining speakers, and many of them have wide experience in public speaking. Their talks deepen a librarian's appreciation of the author's books, but do not necessarily improve library services. They are cultural rather than professional events, and despite their inherent interest, they should not dominate a librarian's conference schedule. The authors can often be seen at their publisher's booth during book-signing periods.

Contacts made at conferences can help you solve professional problems, gather new information, and enlarge your view of the profession. The most long-lasting contacts are usually made through committee work.

Exhibits are a valuable part of most conferences and one of the major reasons why librarians attend conferences year after year. For librarians in small systems, conferences may be their best opportunity to see new materials and equipment. Children's publishers have booths at many large conferences, and librarians can browse through the new books to decide what to order. Conferences also offer opportunities to examine the newest technology and see demonstrations of new software. Librarians can compare brands and ask questions of the salespeople at each booth. A large conference such as the American Library Association's Annual Conference has thousands of exhibitors offering an overwhelming variety of products. Any conference attendee should allow several sessions of two or three hours each to look at the exhibits. Trying to view them all in one day guarantees exhaustion. An added bonus is that most children's publishers and many other exhibitors give away attractive posters and pre-publication copies of books. Exhibitors also give away catalogs, which are useful to most librarians. Asking to have your name added to the publisher's mailing list is generally more efficient than trying to carry the catalogs home.

Tours of libraries and other sites of interest such as processing centers or media production units can be valuable. Children's librarians can gather ideas about how children's rooms are designed and operated in other communities. Most local librarians are eager to show conference visitors their operations and explain their programs and services. Special collections of children's materials may offer insight into different types of collections.

Libraries support conferences because they increase knowledge about the profession and heighten commitment to it. A good conference lifts an individual out a particular job and offers a glimpse of the wider world of librarianship.

Competition for funds to attend a conference is often strong. Membership in the association, or on a committee, may be required. Applying early for funding is a good idea. If the application is approved, check on the time and money that will be allowed for attendance and the expense records that will be expected. Most institutions reimburse expenses only with a receipt. Another frequent requirement is a written report to be circulated on the staff email list, or an oral report at a staff meeting. If staff members win awards or present programs at conferences, accounts of the event may be posted on the library website.

When more than one person from a library goes to a conference, they should attend different sessions to achieve greater overall coverage. If the library pays expenses, the administration expects each individual to attend meetings useful to the institution, and if necessary, to sacrifice some meetings that might be more interesting to the individual. Writing good reports and demonstrating a professional attitude toward conference attendance is likely to lead to greater support in the future.

Serving on Committees

Most work of a professional association is done by volunteer committees. Serving on a committee is the best way to find out how an organization works and to meet other members of the association. Some libraries will send individuals to conferences only if they are members of a committee. Library associations are often large and seem impersonal to newcomers, who may feel that it would be difficult to be invited to join a committee. In most library associations, however, it is not difficult to become a committee member. All it takes is a little planning. Before jumping in, a new librarian should realize that being a committee member requires regular attendance at meetings. Unless a person can commit to attending conferences for two or three years, it is not wise to seek committee membership.

Tips on Choosing a Committee

- Don't expect to start at the top—ALA's Newbery and Caldecott Committee members have a record of association service.
- Local arrangements committees are important and a good place to start if a conference is nearby.
- Membership committees often welcome newcomers with fresh ideas.

- Try to choose a committee whose work is closely tied to your library work. This will be useful to colleagues and will impress administrators.

A newcomer can get a sense of the committee's work by attending committee meetings as a visitor. Although visitors do not participate, they are given a copy of the agenda. The committee chair usually records the names of visitors and uses the list as a source of nominations. Another way to indicate interest in joining a committee is to write to the person in charge of committee appointments (often the vice-president/president-elect) and offer to serve, either on a specific committee or wherever your services might be helpful. Associations are always looking for active new members for committees.

Working with a Committee

Once on a committee, the time and effort necessary to complete committee work should become a priority. Your job takes precedence over organizational activities, but you must find time to complete the committee tasks you have agreed to do. Most librarians are allowed to spend some time on organizational work during the workday, but many people find they have to do a great deal of their committee work on their own time. Libraries also differ on how much support they will give for committee work, which often involves printing documents, photocopying, faxing, and postage. Associations sometimes have committee budgets for these items, but they also rely on members' libraries to support some expenses. Using electronic communication can keep the costs down, and should be used when possible. Before incurring any expenses, be sure to check on the policy in your institution.

After the excitement of committee meetings and conferences are over, members may return to their jobs and forget about the committee tasks they have promised to complete. People who habitually neglect their committee obligations are not invited to join other committees. The way to move ahead in association work—to be asked to serve as committee chair, to be invited to join the committees of choice, and perhaps to run for office—is to treat association work as though it were part of your job.

While you are at a conference, or immediately after returning, enter committee obligations on your calendar and attend to them carefully. Give yourself ample time to check facts, contact other members, write a report, or do whatever other tasks you have taken on. Keep the committee chair informed by copying on email messages and minutes. Professional associations must run in a businesslike way to accomplish their objectives.

CONTRIBUTING TO THE PROFESSIONAL DIALOGUE

Reviewing

Because children's librarians make decisions about purchasing books and other materials, they rely on evaluations of new books, periodicals, films, and other possible purchases. Professional journals, both print and online, provide reviews for librarians and these are the major source of reviews in most libraries. Some library systems arrange for local reviews to judge materials on their value for the particular community. Librarians who work for systems that do in-house reviewing are expected to do their share. This is excellent professional training because it forces the reviewer to articulate a reaction to the item and to choose specific examples to back up each judgment. Because many in-house reviews are presented orally at staff meetings, differing points of view can be raised and questions about the assessments can be asked. Beginning librarians benefit from listening to the evaluations of more experienced colleagues while those who have been in the field for some time can also learn from the fresh, un-jaded approach of newer staff members. Reviews can be circulated online and that too brings out varied points of view.

Many librarians find it challenging to review for a wider professional au-dience. Some of the reviewing journals, such as *School Library Journal*, rely on a corps of volunteer reviewers. A librarian who wants to become a reviewer is usually asked to write sample reviews. If the work is satisfactory, the new reviewer will be added to the journal's list. Although there is usually no pay except for a copy of the reviewed book (practices vary for materials other than books), reviewing can be a satisfying professional opportunity. It offers a chance to read new books and make independent judgments on them. It also provides the satisfaction of seeing your work published. Most libraries encourage staff members to review in their fields, so a successful record of reviewing is an asset on a resume.

Journals that commission reviews want well-written, competent reviews, and they want them on time. The best way to be successful in reviewing is to take the job seriously and treat it as a professional obligation. Several professional sources offer guidance on writing good reviews (Horning 1997). Most reviewing is done outside of normal working hours, although it draws on the background knowledge and skills developed in the library.

Writing for Journals

Reviewing is one of the most common ways of breaking into publication, but other types of writing are also important. Professional journals exist to maintain communication among people in the field. Children's librarians are very busy with their day-to-day work and often believe do have no time to write about what they are doing, but unless information is exchanged, much work is du-plicated. Many librarians throughout North America are struggling with the same problems and trying different ways of solving them. If the profession is to grow and share a common base of knowledge, successful techniques must be recorded and published.

Library journals are generally receptive to articles dealing with realistic prob-lems and solutions or offering helpful insights. A librarian who reads profes-sional literature becomes aware of the kind of articles published by various journals. Many journals offer guidelines, most of them available online or in the print journal, for the types of articles wanted, as well as the appropriate length and style. An author should follow the guidelines carefully.

In many professional journals, articles are not chosen by one editor but are sent out to a panel of reviewers (often called referees) for assessment. This makes the selection procedure slow, and an author may suspect that the manuscript is lying unnoticed on someone's desk. Eventually, however, the editor and referees will make a decision and the author will be notified whether the article is accepted or rejected. Often revisions are requested and it is sensible to agree to make the revisions unless they drastically change the focus of the article. Revisions are usually designed to make the article clearer and more useful to potential readers. Paying attention to the type of revisions suggested helps a writer learn to write more effective articles. Needless to say, revisions should be made quickly and the article returned to the editor so publication will not be delayed.

Organizing Workshops

Workshops are a popular form of professional development for children's librarians. Many large libraries and regional systems offer workshops and other continuing education programs, as do library associations. Some workshops are organized and staffed by commercial groups, but most are run entirely by volunteers. When planning a workshop, there are a number of questions that should be asked:

1. What is the purpose of the workshop? Was it suggested by an administrator as a way to improve library service? Have staff or association members identified a need for it? Is it primarily a way of bringing professionals together for discussion and networking?
2. Who is the audience? Do you want to reach beginning librarians; experienced people who need updates on technology; or librarians facing challenges from a changing community? Both the style and content of a workshop depends on the expected audience.
3. What will be the topic? If you need to choose one, talk to colleagues with different interests and levels of experience to get a wide range of ideas. Perennial themes such as storytelling, programming, and building multilanguage collections are popular if the approach is new and the speakers lively. Other topics such as selecting graphic novels, starting a readers' blog, or building homepages may appeal to more experienced librarians. The key to mounting a successful workshop is to choose a theme that is relevant to a number of librarians but has not been overdone.
4. Who will be the speaker? Often a workshop has one high profile outside speaker and a few local librarians to serve as a response panel or discussion leaders. The outside speaker presents the issues in general or theoretical terms and the reactor panel relates them to the local library situation and experience. This format works because it encourages interaction between the speaker and participants. The more interactive the workshop experience, the more impact it is likely to have on participants.
5. How will you arrange publicity? The first step is a memorable title tailored to the audience you want to attract. Brainstorm to come up with several possible titles and get feedback from colleagues. The title should be catchy, but also give an honest representation of the content. You may tailor your workshop to a narrow group such as children's librarians in your city. In this case you need to distribute information, but not distribute extensive publicity. Be sure to use the channels people pay attention to, for example, the staff listserv, blog, or newsletter. If you are looking for a wider audience, you can use the distribution methods recommended in chapter 13 "Organizing Special Events and Ongoing Programs."

6. What will participants gain from the workshop? Workshops provide information that should be useful, but it is difficult for participants to remember all of it. Try to have handouts and lists of print and online resource that will help people use the information. At the very least, there should be copies of any Power Point presentation given. Informal interaction with other participants is also valuable. Be sure to allow enough time and space for coffee breaks and lunch.

7. How will the workshop schedule be organized? Careful planning and attention to detail is important. Be realistic about the time allowed for each part of the program. On the day before the event, helpers should be sent an email message reminding them of their duties. Be sure to arrive on time and keep to the schedule as much as possible. A workshop that starts or ends late interferes with people's schedules and may cause problems as well as dissatisfaction. Remember to ask participants for an evaluation. These are an important part of planning for the next workshop. And, finally, publicly thank the speakers and all of those who helped with the event.

IMPORTANCE OF THE PROFESSIONAL DIALOGUE

Although preparing reviews, writing articles, and organizing workshops may not seem to be a central part of the job of a children's librarian, they are all part of what makes librarianship a profession rather than just another job. A librarian makes important decisions almost every day and often has little time to consider the long-term impact of these decisions. Yet unless the decisions are based on a coherent philosophy of service, they may not fulfill the library's mandate. It is through professional associations, literature, and activities that librarians develop their attitude toward and judgment of library services. The thoughtful analysis of ideas and trends is the foundation upon which meaningful library service rests. Every professional librarian should try to become a participant in the professional dialogue through which library service can grow to meet the needs of all children.

REFERENCES AND ADDITIONAL READING

Adkins, Denice, and Hussey, Lisa K. 2005. Unintentional Recruiting for Diversity [July/August 2005]. *Public Libraries* 44: 229–233.

Cerny, Rosanne, Markey, Penny, and Williams, Amanda. 2006. *Outstanding Library Service to Children: Putting the Core Competencies to Work.* Chicago: American Library Association.

Horning, Kathleen T. 1997. *From Cover to Cover: Evaluating and Reviewing Children's Books.* New York: HarperCollins.

Bibliography

Adkins, Denice, and Hussey, Lisa K. 2005. Unintentional Recruiting for Diversity [July/ August 2005]. *Public Libraries* 44: 229–233.

Ali, Moi. 2001. *Marketing Effectively: Essential Managers*. New York: Dorling Kindersley Ltd.

Alire, Camilla ed. 2000. *Library Disaster Planning and Recovery Handbook*. New York: Neal-Schuman.

Allen Country Public Library. 1996. *Allen County Public Library Web site*. Fort Wayne, IN. http://fuji.acpl.lib.in.us:80/About_the_ACPL/unattended_children.html.

American Library Association. 1996. *Access to Electronic Information Services, and Networks: An Interpretation of the* Library Bill of Rights. Chicago: American Library Association.

American Library Association. 1997. *Access for Children and Young People to Videotapes and Other Nonprint Formats: An Interpretation of the* Library Bill of Rights. http://www.ala. org/ICONN/ICONN-website/video.html.

American Library Association. 1999. *Libraries: An American Value*. http://www.ala.org/ala/ oif/statementspols/americanvalue/librariesamerican.htm.

American Library Association. 2006. *Intellectual Freedom Manual: Compiled by the Office for Intellectual Freedom of the American Library Association*. Chicago: American Library Association.

Arterburn, Tom R. 1996. Librarians: Caretakers or Crimefighters? *American Libraries* 27: 32–34.

Association for Library Services to Children, The. 1999. *Competencies for Librarians Serving Children in Public Libraries, Revised Edition, 5*. Chicago: American Library Association.

Bagan, Virginia J. 1994. No Bucks, No Books. *Bottom Line* 7, no. 3/4: 12–16.

Baltimore, County Public Library. 1987. *STEPS: Staff Training for Emergency Procedures at the Baltimore County Public Library*, Second Edition. Baltimore, MD: Baltimore County Public Library.

Banks, Paula. 1995. News Releases, Photo Releases, Public Service Announcements. In *Part-Time Public Relations with Full-Time Results,* ed. Rashelle Karp, 1–9. Chicago: American Library Association.

Bauer, Caroline. 1993. *Caroline Feller Bauer's New Handbook for Storytellers.* Chicago: American Library Association.

Baumbach, Donna J., and Miller, Linda L. 2006. *Less Is More: A Practical Guide to Weeding School Library Collections.* Chicago: American Library Association.

Bell, Arthur H., and Smith, Doyle M. 2004. *Winning with Difficult People:* Barron's Business Success Guides. Hauppauge, NY: Barron's.

Bell, Debra. 1997. *The Ultimate Guide to Homeschooling.* Dallas: Word Publishing.

Benne, Mae. 1991. *Principles of Children's Services in Public Libraries.* Chicago: American Library Association.

Bernard, Michael L. 2003. *Criteria for Optimal Web Design (Designing for Usability), 4.* Wichita, Kansas: Wichita State University.

Bernard, Michael L., and Mills, Melissa. 2001. *Which Fonts Do Children Prefer to Read Online?, 5.* Wichita: Wichita State University.

Bernstein, Joan E., and Schalk-Greene, Kathy. 2006. Extreme Library Makeover: One Year Later [April]. *American Libraries* 37: 66–69.

Bertot, John Carlo, McClure, Charles R., and Zweizig, Douglas L. 1996. *Public Libraries and the Internet: Survey Results and Key Issues.* Washington, DC: National Commission on Libraries and Information Science.

Blowers, Helene, and Bryan, Robin. 2004. *Weaving a Library Web: A Guide to Developing Children's Websites.* Chicago: American Library Association.

Bostwick, Arthur. 1914. *Library and School: The Relationship between the Library and the Public Schools.* New York: H. W. Wilson.

Bromann, Jennifer. 2005. *More Booktalking That Works.* New York: Neal-Schuman.

Brophy, Peter, and Coulling, Kate. 1996. *Quality Management for Information and Library Managers.* Brookfield, VT: Aslib Gower.

Brostrom, David C. 1995. *A Guide to Homeschooling for Librarians.* Highsmith Press Handbook Series. Fort Atkinson, WI: Highsmith Press.

Brown, A. 2004. Reference Services for Children: Information Needs and Wants in the Public Library. *Australian Library Journal* 53: 261–274.

Brown, Carol R. 2002. *Interior Design for Libraries. Drawing on Function and Appeal.* Chicago: American Library Association.

Burlingame, Dwight F. ed. 1995. *Library Fundraising: Models for Success.* Chicago: American Library Association.

Burnett, Ken. 2006. *The Zen of Fundraising: 89 Timeless Ideas to Strengthen and Develop Your Donor Relationships.* San Francisco: Wiley.

Carlson, Mim. 1995. *Winning Grants Step by Step: Support Centers of America's Complete Workbook for Planning, Developing, and Writing Successful Proposals.* Jossey-Bass Nonprofit Sector Series. San Francisco: Jossey-Bass.

Carson, Paula Phillips, Carson, Kerry David, and Phillips, Joyce Schouest. 1995. *The Library Manager's Deskbook: 102 Expert Solutions to 101 Common Dilemmas.* Chicago: American Library Association.

Cerny, Rosanne, Markey, Penny, and Williams, Amanda. 2006. *Outstanding Library Service to Children: Putting the Core Competencies to Work.* Chicago: American Library Association.

Champelli, L. 1996. *Understand Software That Blocks Internet Sites.* http://www.monroe.lib.in.us/~lchampel/netadv4.html.

Chicago Public Library. 1997. *Chicago Public Library Web site.* http://cpl.lib.uic.edu.

Chronicle of Philanthropy, The. *Fund Raising.* www.philanthropy.com/fundraising.

Cirillo, Susan E., and Danford, Robert E. 1996. Library Buildings, Equipment, and the ADA: Compliance Issues and Solutions. Paper presented at *Preconference, June 24–25, 1993,* Chicago.

Cleveland Public Library. 1997. *Cleveland Public Library Web site.* http://www.cpl.org.

Cole, George Watson. 1985. How Teachers Should Co-operate with Librarians. *Library Journal* 20: 115–118.

Cole, Kris. 2002. *The Complete Idiot's Guide to Clear Communication.* New York: Penguin.

Cook, Sherry J., Parker, R. Stephen, and Pettijohn, Charles E. 2005. The Public Library: An Early Teen's Perspective [May/June 2005]. *Public Libraries* 44: 157–161.

Cravey, Patricia. 2001. *Protecting Library Staff, Users, Collections, and Facilities: A How-to-do-It Manual.* vol. 103: How-to-do-it Manuals for Librarians. New York: Neal-Schuman.

Crittendon, Robert. 2002. *The New Manager's Starter Kit: Essential Tools for Doing the Job Right.* New York: American Management Association.

Curry, Ann. 1996. Managing the Problem Patron. *Public Libraries* 35: 181–188.

Curry, Ann, Susanna Flodin, and Matheson, Kelly. 2000. Theft and Mutilation of Library Materials: Coping with Biblio-Bandits. *Library and Archival Security* 15: 9–26.

Curzon, Susan C. 1989. *Managing Change: A How-To-Do-It Manual for Planning, Implementing and Evaluating Change in Libraries.* New York: Neal-Schuman.

Dalrymple, Prudence W. 1997. The State of the Schools. *American Libraries* 27: 31–34.

Deerr, Kathleen. 1995. Budgeting. In *Youth Services Librarians as Managers: A How-to Guide from Budgeting to Personnel,* eds. Kathleen Staerkel, Mary Fellows, and Sue McCleaf Nespeca, 11–21. Chicago: American Library Association.

Des Enfants, Sherry. 1995. Seeking Alternative Funding: Grantsmanship. In *Youth Services Librarians as Managers: A How-to Guide from Budgeting to Personnel,* eds. Kathleen Staerkel, Mary Fellows, and Sue McCleaf Nespeca, 22–40. Chicago: American Library Association.

DeWitt, Sara. 2006. The Secret of Their Success. In *School Library Journal.* http://www.schoollibraryjournal.com/index.asp?layout=articlePrint&articleid=CA6386668.

Dillon, Ken. 1997. Serving the Professional Information Needs of Rural Secondary-School Teachers in New South Wales, Australia. *School Library Media Quarterly* 25, no. 3: 171–176.

Doll, Carol A., and Barron, Pamela Petrick. 2002. *Managing and Analyzing Your Collection: A Practical Guide for Small Libraries and School Media Centers.* Chicago: American Library Association.

Dolnick, Sandy ed. 1996. *Friends of Libraries Sourcebook.* Chicago: American Library Association.

Dowd, Frances Smardo. 1989. Serving Latchkey Children: Recommendations from Librarians. *Public Libraries:* 101–106.

Dowd, Frances Smardo. 1991. *Latchkey Children in the Library and Community: Issues, Strategies, and Programs.* Phoenix, AZ: Oryx Press.

Dowd, Frances Smardo. 1996. Homeless Children in Public Libraries: A National Survey of Large Systems. *Journal of Youth Services in Libraries* 9, no. 2: 155–165.

Doyle, Robert P. 2006. The Current Legislative Challenge: DOPA and the Participation Gap [October 2006]. *The ILA Reporter* XXIV: 16–21.

East, Kathy. 1995. *Inviting Children's Authors and Illustrators: A How-to-Do-It Manual for School and Public Librarians.* How-to-do-it Manuals for Librarians; 49. New York: Neal-Schuman.

Eaton, Gale, and McCarthy, Cheryl. 1995. The Art of the Possible: Integrating Information Skills and Literature into the Curriculum. *Emergency Librarian* 23, no. 1: 24–30.

Ellis, Judith Compton. 1988. Planning and Executing a Major Bookshift/Move Using an Electronic Spreadsheet. *College and Research Libraries News* 49: 282–287.

Emery, John Whitehall. 1917. *The Library, the School and the Child.* Toronto: Macmillan.

Falbel, Aaron. 1997. *Homeschooling FAQ.* http://www.netc.com/gok/faq/html.

Farmer, Lesley. 1993. *When Your Library Budget Is Almost Zero.* Englewood, CO: Libraries Unlimited.

Feehan, Patricia. 1994. Take Me to Your Ladder: The Issue of Plateauing in Children's Services Positions. *Library Administration and Management* 8: 200–203.

Feinberg, Sandra, Kuchner, Joan, and Feldman, Sari. 1998. *Learning Environments for Young Children.* Chicago: American Library Association.

Fielding, Lynn. 2006. Kindergarten Learning Gap [April]. *American School Board Journal* 193.

Flint Public Library. 1997. *Flint Public Library Web site:* http://www.flint.lib.mi.us.

Foundation Center, The. *Knowledge to Build On.* http://foundationcenter.org.

Fourie, Jacqueline A. 1995. Pupils as Curricular Information Seekers and the Role of the Public Library. *South African Journal of Library and Information Science* 63, no. 3: 129–138.

Fox, Mem. 2001. *Reading Magic: Why Reading Aloud to Our Children Will Change Their Lives Forever.* New York: Harcourt.

Garlock, Kristen L., and Piontek, Sherry. 1996. *Building the Service-Based Library Web Site: A Step-by Step Guide to Design and Options.* Chicago: American Library Association.

Geever, Jane C., and McNeill, Patricia. 1993. *The Foundation Center's Guide to Proposal Writing.* New York: Foundation Center.

Giesecke, Joan ed. 1997. *Practical Help for New Supervisors.* Chicago: American Library Association.

Goldberg, Beverly. 1996. Public Libraries Go Back to School. *American Libraries* 27: 54–55.

Grobman, Gary, Grant, Gary, and Roller, Steve. 1999. *The Wilder Nonprofit Field Guide to Fundraising on the Internet.* St. Paul, MN: Amherst H. Wilder Foundation.

Gutterson, David. 1992. *Family Matters: Why Homeschooling Makes Sense.* New York: Harcourt Brace Jovanovich.

Guy, Jennye E. 1995. Establishing a Library Foundation and a Fundraising Campaign. In *Library Fundraising: Models for Success,* ed. Dwight F. Burlingame. Chicago: American Library Association.

Hagloch, Susan B. 1994. *Library Building Projects: Tips for Survival.* Englewood, CO: Libraries Unlimited.

Hamilton, Patricia, and Hindman, Pam. 1987. Moving a Public Library Collection. *Public Libraries* 26: 4–7.

Harrison, Maureen, and Gilbert, Steve eds. 1992. *The Americans with Disabilities Act Handbook. Landmark Laws Series.* Beverly Hills, CA: Excellent Books.

Hartsook, Robert. 2005. *Closing that Gift: How to be Successful 99% of the Time.* Englewood Cliffs, NJ: Prentice-Hall.

Hauptman, Robert. 1988. *Ethical Challenges in Librarianship.* Phoenix, AZ: Oryx.

Heller, Robert. 1998. *Motivating People:* Essential Managers. New York: DK Publishing.

Heller, Robert. 1998. *Making Decisions:* Essential Managers. New York: DK Publishing.

Himmel, Ethel E., Wilson, William James, and ReVision Committee of the Public Library Association. 1998. *Planning for Results: A Public Library Transformation Process.* Chicago: American Library Association.

Holt, Leslie Edmonds, Holt, Glen, and Stratton, Lloyd. 2006. *Library Success: A Celebration of Library Innovation, Adaptation and Problem Solving.* Ipswitch, MA: EBSCO Publishing.

Homeschoolers and the Public Library: A Resource Guide for Libraries Serving Homeschoolers. 1993. Chicago: Public Library Association.

Homeschooling. 1997. *Homeschooling Information and Homeschooling Resource Pages.* http://home-ed-press.com.

Horning, Kathleen T. 1997. *From Cover to Cover: Evaluating and Reviewing Children's Books.* New York: HarperCollins.

Hughes-Hassell, Sandra, and Mancall, Jacqueline. 2005. *Collection Management for Youth: Responding to the Needs of Learners.* Chicago: American Library Association.

Immroth, Barbara Frohling, and Lance, Keith Curry. 1996. Output Measures for Children's Services in Public Libraries: A Status Report. *Public Libraries* 35: 240–245.

Intner, Sheila S., Fountain, Joanna F., and Gilchrist, Jane E. 2006. *Cataloging for Kids: An Introduction to the Tools,* Fourth Edition. Chicago: American Library Association.

Irving, Jan. 2004. *Stories NeverEnding: A Program Guide for Schools and Libraries.* Westport, CT: Libraries Unlimited.

Jaeger, P. T., Bertot, J. C., and McClure, C. R. 2004. The Effects of the Children's Internet Protection Act (CIPA) in Public Libraries and its Implications for Research: A Statistical, Policy, and Legal Analysis. *Journal of the American Society for Information Science* 55: 1131–1139.

Johnson, Peggy. 2004. *Fundamentals of Collection Development and Management.* Chicago: American Library Association.

Jones, Patrick. 1992. *Connecting Young Adults and Libraries: A How-to-Do-It Manual.* New York: Neal-Schuman.

Jurkowski, Odin. 2005. Schools of Thought: What to Include on Your School Library Web Site [Spring 2005]. *Children and Libraries* 3: 24–29.

Kachel, Debra E. 1996. Improving Access to Periodicals: A Cooperative Collection Management Project. *School Library Media Quarterly* 24 no. 2:93–103.

Karp, Rashelle S. ed. 1995. *Part-Time Public Relations with Full-Time Results: A PR Primer for Libraries.* Chicago: American Library Association.

Kay, Alan. 1994. *Observations about Children and Computers.* Cupertino, CA: Advanced Technology Group.

Knuth, Rebecca. 1999. On a Spectrum: International Models of School Librarianship. *Library Quarterly* 69: 33–56.

Kratz, Abby, and Flannery, Melinda. 1997. Communication Skills. In *Practical Help for New Supervisors,* ed. Joan Giesecke, 43–57. Chicago: American Library Association.

Krug, Steve. 2006. *Don't Make Me Think: A Common Sense Approach to Web Usability.* Second Edition. Berkeley, CA: New Riders Publishing.

Leighton, H. Vernon, Jackson, Joe, Sullivan, Kathryn, and Dennison, Russell F. 2003. Web Page Design and Successful Use: A Focus Group Study. *Internet Reference Services Quarterly* 8: 17–27.

Lighthall, Lynne. 1994. Automated Systems in Canada's School Libraries: The Fifth Annual Survey. *Feliciter* 40, no. 11–12: 26–42.

Lincoln, Alan Jay. 1984. *Crime in the Library: A Study of Patterns, Impact, and Security.* New York: Bowker.

Liu, H, Maes, P., and Davenport, G. 2006. Unraveling the Taste Fabric of Social Networks. *International Journal on Semantic Web and Information:* 46–78.

Lockwood, Annette. 1996. Bookmobile Provides Home-Schoolers with Regular Library Period. *American Libraries* 27: 32–33.

Lushington, Nolan, and Kusack, James M. 1991. *The Design and Evaluation of Public Library Buildings.* Hamden, CT: Library Professional Publication.

MacDonald, Gregory. 1996. Building ReUse: Right for the Times. *Public Libraries* 35: 288–291.

MacLachlan, Rachel. 1996. Safety and Security Considerations. In *Library Buildings, Equipment, and the ADA: Compliance Issues and Solutions,* eds. Susan E. Cirillo and Robert E. Danford, 53–58. Chicago: American Library Association.

Magid, Larry, and Collier, Anne. 2007. *MySpace Unraveled: A Parent's Guide to Teen Social Networking from the Directors of BlogSafety.com.* Berkeley, CA: Peachpit Press.

Magid, Lawrence J. 1996. *Child Safety on the Information Highway.* Produced by the National Center for Missing and Exploited Children and Interactive Services Association: http://www.missingkids.org/information_superhighway.html#rules.

Maness, J. 2006. Library 2.0 Theory: Web 2.0 and Its Implications for Libraries. *Webology* 3: Article 25.

Mathews, Virginia H. ed. 1994. *Library Services for Children and Youth: Dollars and Sense.* New York: Neal-Schuman.

Matthew, Kathryn. 1997. A Comparison of the Influence of Interactive CD-ROM Storybooks and Traditional Print Storybooks on Reading Comprehension. *Journal of Research on Computing in Education* 29, no. 3: 263–274.

McCabe, Gerald B. 2000. *Planning for a New Generation of Public Library Buildings.* Westport, CT: Greenwood Press.

McCallister, Myrna J., and Patterson, Thomas H. 1997. Conducting Effective Meetings. In *Practical Help for New Supervisors,* ed. Joan Giesecke, 58–74. Chicago: American Library Association.

McClure, Charles R., Owen, Amy, Zweizig, Douglas L., Lynch, Mary Jo, and Van House, Nancy. 1987. *Planning and Role Setting for Public Libraries: A Manual of Options and Procedures.* Chicago: American Library Association.

Mediavilla, Cindy. 2001. Why Library Homework Centers Extend Society's Safety Net. *American Libraries* 32, no. 12: 40–42.

Michaels, Andrea, and Michaels, David. 1996. People, Assistive Devices, ADAptive Furnishings, and Their Environment in Your Library. In *Library Buildings, Equipment, and the ADA: Compliance Issues and Solutions,* eds. Susan E. Cirillo and Robert E. Danford, 40–47. Chicago: American Library Association.

Michigan Library Association. 1995. *Youth Access to the Internet through Libraries:* http://statelib.ut.us/intacc.txt.

Minow, Mary. 1997. Filters and the Public Library: A Legal and Policy Analysis. *First Monday* 2, no. 12. http://www.firstmonday.org (accessed March 7, 2007).

Minow, Mary, and Lipinski, Tomas. 2003. *The Library's Legal Answer Book.* Chicago: American Library Association.

Mitchell, K. J., Finkelhor, D., and Wolak, J. 2003. The Exposure of Youth to Unwanted Sexual Material on the Internet. *Youth and Society,* 34: 330–358.

Mosher, Paul H. 1982. Collection Development to Collection Management: Toward Stewardship of Library Resources. *Collection Management* 4.

Multnomah County Public Library. 1997. *Cool Spots on the Web.* Multnomah County (Oregon) Public Library Web site: http://www.multnomah.lib.or.us/lib/kids.

Multnomah County Public. 2005. *Acceptable Use of the Internet and Library Public Computers.* Multnomah County Public Library.

Munroe, Mary H., Haar, John M., and Johnson, Peggy eds. 2001. *Guide to Collection Development and Management Administration, Organization and Staffing.* Vol. 10. Collection Management and Development Guides. Lanham, MD: Scarecrow Press.

Murphy, Tish. 2007. *Library Furnishings: A Planning Guide.* Jefferson, NC: McFarland.

Mutz, John M., and Murray, Katherine. 2000. *Fundraising for Dummies.* Foster City, CA: IDG Books Worldwide.

National Guide to Funding for Libraries and Information Services. 1993. New York: Foundation Center.

National Survey of Public Libraries and the Internet: Final Report. 1996. Syracuse NY: Syracuse University.

Nelson, Sandra, Garcia, June, and Association, For the Public Library Association. 2003. *Creating Policies for Results: From Chaos to Clarity.* PLA Results Series. Chicago: American Library Association.

Norfolk, Sherry, Stenson, Jane, and Williams, Diane 2006. *The Storytelling Classroom: Applications across the Curriculum.* Westport, CT: Libraries Unlimited.

O'Keefe, Claudia. 2005. Publicity 101: How to Promote Your Library's Next Event [June/July 2005]. *American Libraries* 36: 52–55.

Orlando, Marie C. 1995. Staff Evaluation. In *Youth Services Librarians as Managers: A How-to Guide from Budgeting to Personnel,* eds. Kathleen Staerkel, Mary Fellows, and Sue McCleaf Nespeca, 115–133. Chicago: American Library Association.

Osborne, Robin ed. 2004. *From Outreach to Equity: Innovative Models of Library Policy and Practice.* Chicago: American Library Association.

Padilla, Irene M., and Patterson, Thomas H. 1997. Rewarding Employees Nonmonetarily. In *Practical Help for New Supervisors,* ed. Joan Giesecke, 35–44. Chicago: American Library Association.

Panszczyk, Linda A. 2004. *HR How-to—Intergenerational Issues: Everything You Need to Know about Dealing with Employees of All Generations in the Workplace.* Chicago: CCH Knowledge Point.

Peck, Penny. 2006. *Crash Course in Children's Services.* Westport, CT: Libraries Unlimited.

Peck, Robert. 2000. *Libraries, the First Amendment and Cyberspace: What You Need to Know.* Chicago: American Library Association.

Pfeil, Angela B. 2005. *Going Places with Youth Outreach: Smart Marketing Strategies.* Chicago: American Library Association.

Philliber, William, et al. 1996. Consequences of Family Literacy for Adults and Children: Some Preliminary Findings. *Journal of Adolescent and Adult Literacy* 39, no. 7: 558–565.

Pistolis, Donna. 1996. *Hit List: Frequently Challenged Books for Children.* Chicago: American Library Association.

Pitman, Mary Anne, and Van Galen, Jane eds. 1991. *Home Schooling: Political, Historical, and Pedagogical Perspectives.* Norwood, NJ: Ablex Pub.

Prentice, Ann. 1996. *Financial Planning for Libraries:* Library Administration Series. Lanham, MD: Scarecrow Press.

Robbins, Jane B., and Zweizig, Douglas eds. 1992. *Keeping Books: Public Library Financial Practice.* Fort Atkinson, WI: Highsmith Press.

Roberts, Anne F., and Blandy, Susan Griswold. 1989. *Public Relations for Librarians.* Englewood, CO: Libraries Unlimited.

Robertson, Chris, Lovatt, Paula, Morris, Debbie, and Nuttall, Carole. 1996. Reading: A Pastime of the Past? *Reading: A Journal about Literacy and Language in Education* 30, no. 3: 26–28.

Robinson, Cynthia A., and Dowd, Frances Smardo. 1997. Public Library Services to Disabled Children: A National Survey of Large Systems. *Journal of Youth Services in Libraries* 10, no. 3: 283–290.

Rollock, Barbara. 1988. *Public Library Services for Children.* Hamden, CT: Library Professional Publications.

Rosenberg, Barry J. 2005. *Spring into Technical Writing for Engineers and Scientists:* Spring into Series. New York: Addison-Wesley.

Rovenger, Judith, and Wigg, Ristiina. 1987. *Libraries Serving Youth: Directions for Service in the 1990s.* New York: Youth Services Section, New York Library Association.

Rubin, Richard. 1992. The Future of Public Library Support Staff. *Public Library Quarterly* 12: 17–29.

Russell, Thyra K. 1997. Interviewing. In *Practical Help for New Supervisors,* ed. Joan Giesecke, 6–14. Chicago: American Library Association.

Sager, Don. 1997. Perspectives: Beating the Homework Blues. *Public Libraries* 36: 19–23.

Salazar, Ramiro. 1994. The Bottom Line: Saving Youth Means Saving Our Future. In *Library Services for Children and Youth: Dollars and Sense,* ed. Virginia H. Mathews. New York: Neal-Schuman.

Salter, Charles A., and Salter, Jeffrey L. 1988. *On the Frontlines: Coping with the Library's Problem Patrons.* Littleton, CO: Libraries Unlimited.

Salvadore, Maria B. 1995. Recruiting and Retaining Youth Services Librarians. In *Youth Services Librarians as Managers: A How-to Guide from Budgeting to Personnel,* eds. Kathleen Staerkel, Mary Fellows, and Sue McCleaf Nespeca, 74–82. Chicago: American Library Association.

Sass, Rivkah K. 2002. Marketing the Worth of Your Library. *Library Journal.* http://www.libraryjournal.com/index.asp?layout=articlePrint&articleid=CA220888

Schexnaydre, Linda, and Burns, Nancy. 1984. *Censorship: A Guide for Successful Workshop Planning.* Phoenix, AZ: Oryx.

Seattle Public Library. 1997. *Seattle Public Library. Friends of the Library.* http://www.spl.lib.wa.us/friends/friends.html.

Shipley, David, and Schwalbe, Will. 2007. *Send: The Essential Guide to Email for Office and Home.* New York: Alfred A. Knopf.

Staerkel, Kathleen, Fellows, Mary, and Nespeca, Sue McCleaf eds. 1995. *Youth Services Librarians as Managers: A How-to Guide from Budgeting to Personnel.* Chicago: American Library Association.

Steele, Anitra. 2001. *Bare Bones Children's Services.* Chicago: American Library Association.

Steele, Victoria, and Elder, Stephen D. 2000. *Becoming a Fundraiser: The Principles and Practice of Library Development.* Chicago: American Library Association.

Stephens, Michael. 2006. *Web 2.0 & Libraries: Best Practices for Social Software, 68.* Chicago: ALA TechSource. Library Technology Reports: Expert Guides to Library Systems and Services, Vol. 40, No. 4.

Sullivan, Michael. 2005. *Fundamentals of Children's Services:* ALA Fundamentals Series. Chicago: American Library Association.

Swan, James. 2002. *Fundraising for Libraries: 25 Proven Ways to Get More Money for Your Library.* New York: Neal-Schuman.

Symons, Ann K, and Harmon, Charles. 1995. *Protecting the Right to Read: A How-to-Do-It Manual for School and Public Librarians.* New York: Neal-Schuman.

Tallman, Julie I. 1995. Curriculum Consultation: Strengthening Activity through Multiple-Content Area Units. *School Library Media Quarterly* 24, no. 1: 27–33.

Taney, Kimberly Bolan. 2003. *Teen Spaces: The Step-by-Step Library Makeover.* Chicago: American Library Association.

Tannen, Deborah. 1994. *Talking from 9 to 5: How Women's and Men's Conversational Styles Affect Who Gets Heard, Who Gets Credit, and What Gets Done at Work.* New York: William Morrow and Company.

Todd, Ross J. 1995. Information Literacy: Philosophy, Principles, and Practice. *School Libraries Worldwide* 1, no. 1: 54–68.

Toronto Public Library. 1913. *Annual Report.* Toronto: Toronto Public Library.

Unattended Children in the Public Library: A Resource Guide. 2000. Chicago: Association for Library Service to Children; Association for Library Trustees and Advocates; Public Library Association.

UNESCO. 1994. *Public Library Manifesto.* The Hague: International Federation of Library Associations and Institutions.

Valauskas, Edward J., and John, Nancy R. eds. 1995. *The Internet Initiative: Libraries Providing Internet Services and How They Plan, Pay, and Manage.* Chicago: American Library Association.

Wagner, Mary M., and Wronka, Gretchen. 1995. Youth Services Policies and Procedures. In *Youth Services Librarians as Managers,* ed. Kathleen Staerkel, et al., 41–50. Chicago: American Library Association.

Walling, Linda Lucas, and Karrenbrock, Marilyn H. 1993. *Disabilities, Children, and Libraries: Mainstreaming Services in Public Libraries and School Library Media Centers.* Englewood, CO: Libraries Unlimited.

Walster, Dian. 1993. *Managing Time: A How-to-Do-It Manual for Librarians.* New York: Neal-Schuman.

Walter, Virginia. 1992. *Output Measures for Public Library Service to Children: A Manual of Standardized Procedures.* Chicago: American Library Association.

———. 1994. Research You Can Use: Marketing to Children. *Journal of Youth Services in Libraries* 7, no. 3: 283–288.

———. 2001. *Children and Libraries: Getting It Right.* Chicago: American Library Association.

Wendover, Robert W. 2002. *Smart Hiring: The Complete Guide to Finding and Hiring the Best Employees.* Naperville, IL: Sourcebooks, Inc.

White, Barb. 1997. Connections: Building Coalitions to Serve Our Youngest Patrons. *Youth Services in Libraries* 10: 215–218.

Wibbels, Andy. 2006. *Blog Wild! A Guide for Small Business Blogging.* New York: Penguin (Portfolio).

Wilkinson, Ian A., and Anderson, Richard C. 1995. Sociocognitive Processes in Guided Silent Reading: A Microanalysis of Small-Group Lessons. *Reading Research Quarterly* 30, no. 4: 710–740.

Willits, Robert L. 1997. When Violence Threatens the Workplace: Personnel Issues. *Library Administration & Management* 11, no. 3: 166–171.

Wirth, Eileen. 1996. The State of Censorship. *American Libraries* 27: 44–48.

Young Adult Library Services Association [YALSA]. 2005. *Teens and Social Networking in School and Public Libraries: A Toolkit for Librarians and Library Workers.* Chicago: American Library Association.

Zeff, Robbin. 1996. *The Nonprofit Guide to the Internet:* Nonprofit Law, Finance, and Management Series. New York: John Wiley & Sons.

Index

About the Authors

ADELE M. FASICK has been active for many years in the area of public library service to children and young adults. She was a faculty member at the University of Toronto for 25 years and served as dean of the Faculty of Information Studies. Currently she is a part-time faculty member at the School of Library and Information Service at San Jose State University, where she teaches courses on services and resources for children. Books she has written include *ChildView: Evaluating and Reviewing Materials for Children* (with Claire England; Libraries Unlimited, 1987) and *Managing Children's Services in Public Libraries, Second Edition* (Libraries Unlimited, 1998). She has contributed many articles to library journals. Her recent research has been a study of children's use of libraries published as *Opening Doors to Children: Reading, Media and Public Library Use by Children in Six Canadian Cities* (Regina Public Library, 2005). She has been active in the American Library Association and served on the ALSC Board, the Canadian Library Association, the Association for Library and Information Science Education, and the International Federation of Library Associations She received a BA in English Literature from Cornell University, an MA in American Literature, and an MLIS from Columbia University, and a PhD in Library and Information Science from Case Western Reserve University.

LESLIE E. HOLT currently consults with libraries, schools, and child serving agencies. She worked in public libraries for 25 years including as director of youth services at the St. Louis Public Library as Director of Youth Services for 14 years. She taught at the Graduate School of Library and Information Science at the University of Illinois at Champaign. Dr. Holt has published several articles in the area of literacy, planning, and evaluation of children's services and information access for youth. She is co-author of *Dynamic Youth Services* (with Eliza

Dresang and Melissa Gross, ALA, 2006) and *Measuring Your Library's Value* (with Glen Holt, Donald Elliott, and Sterling Hayden, ALA, 2007). She is a past president of the Association of Library Service for Children (ALSC) and has been active for many years in ALA, PLA, and ALSC. Dr. Holt received at BA degree from Cornell College (Iowa) in History and Secondary Education, a MA from the University of Chicago in Library Science ,and her PhD from Loyola University of Chicago in Curriculum and Reading (1984).